Virginia & Robert
What great neighbors
you were to mama
and Daddy.
Susonette

C.G. and Ethel

C.G. and Ethel, 2004

C.G. and Ethel

A Family History

Susie H. Baxter

Cover photograph:
C. G. and Ethel Howell
on their wedding day, September 8, 1940

ISBN 978-0-615-21348-4

First printing, June, 2008
Typefaces used: Times New Roman and Bodoni MT
Includes 111 illustrations

Printed on acid-free paper
Renaissance Printing, Gainesville, Florida
United States of America

5 4 3 2 1

To Mama and Daddy

Contents

Preface

Many of the stories in this book have been told so often that my sisters and I know them by heart, but only recently did it occur to us that these tales and our family's history should be recorded. By the time this project got underway, Mama was beginning to lose her short-term memory. Thank God her recollections of earlier times were as vivid as ever, and Daddy's would never fade.

We often reminisced while seated on the rattan furniture (which Mama had recovered twice) on their air-conditioned "porch," formerly a screened porch, the place where everybody always gathered. There, I began asking my parents questions about their early lives. They were happy to oblige. Recording their words on a yellow legal pad, I had to scribble faster and faster to keep up.

After typing up a tale, I often asked them to read the draft to see if I had the story straight. Often, their reading triggered another tale or caused them to add a detail. Other times, they recognized and corrected grammatical errors (*you was* became *you were*; *he don't* became *he doesn't*, etc.) "Correct anything we miss," Daddy said one day as he was reading a story and correcting his misspeaks. Mama agreed. Normally, I did as my parents told me, but their instructions that day gave me pause. I wanted their stories to be in *their* voices. *The stories wouldn't be Mama's and Daddy's if I changed words, would they?* But as time passed, I came to realize—as I usually did—that they were right. I honored their wishes, for the most part, in hopes that the corrections would allow readers to focus, not on verbal agreement, but on the stories themselves. Other times, I thought they said something so *perfectly* in conversation—roosters a-crowin', chickens a-squawkin'—that it was a keeper!

As narrator, I found it a bit awkward to write in the third person—calling them *C.G.* and *Ethel* and myself

Susanette—and did so only after a cousin who read an early draft said, "It was hard for me to keep track of who was who because you call your mother *Mama*, she called her mother *Mama*, and her mother called her mother *Mama;* and the same went for your father." Point made! Third person it is.

In conversations with my parents, their life experiences were recalled randomly. But in finalizing the manuscript, I tried to piece their stories together in chronological order, along with unedited correspondence and historical events, as if I were Ethel piecing various shapes of fabric—bright, busy prints, dark colors, and soft pastels—into patchwork quilts. I have also included ancestry charts, maps showing towns that no longer exist, and endnotes for those interested in the nitty-gritty—like who married whom.

In chapters 1, 3, and 5 where C.G. told the stories, his words are not enclosed in quotation marks; the same goes for Ethel's words in chapters 2 and 4 where she did all of the storytelling.

In chapters where two or more people told the tales, quotation marks set off their words; but PLEASE NOTE, these marks of punctuation do not mean the words are verbatim; rather, the words in quotes represent *my best effort* to capture and retain the person's voice. Despite efforts to get it right, there will be errors in statements, names, dates, spelling, verb tense, and general content. Also, there are gaps in time (e.g., what did Ethel's brother, Harold, do between the time he married until he is mentioned again?). Just know that, with much help, I have recorded this family history as completely and accurately as time and information would allow.

If, in reading the pages that follow, you have a correction, a different version, or another story altogether about our family that you would like to share, please e-mail me at *CGandEthelBook@aol.com.*

Susanette

Acknowledgements

Thank you, Denice, Liza, and Logan, for allowing me to assist your Papa and Grandma in completing the *Grand-parents' Book* you gave them. As you know, that fill-in-the-blank book asked questions about their childhoods and their early lives together. You wanted to know more about them, but they were still too busy living life to fill in the blanks. My helping them complete that book was the spark for this one.

Thank you, Peggie, for writing to your cousin Ethel, asking her to identify relatives in your old photographs and for asking questions about our mutual great-grandparents, Tip and Dosia Lanier: "What were their everyday lives like? What did they eat? What did they do for fun? What was their home like?" Thank you also for reading early drafts of the manuscript and for providing details about Uncle Alonzo and his family.

Thank you, Dr. Hilda Ross, for your guidance in piecing together a life history. Thank you for listening, for reading, and for your encouragement.

Thank you, Bill Boatright, Elaine Boatright, Spessard Boatright, Bette Harrison, Clarence Howell, Oleta Howell, Merine Hunter, Bernice Lanier, Denise Lee, Jaimee Marcia, Beth and Loren Midgett, Theresa Miles, Harold Rye, and Michael Schemer for contributing to this book, be it stories, photographs, or genealogy research.

Thank you to my husband, Gilbert, for putting up with my sitting in front of the computer for hours on end. Thank you for reading and rereading story after story and for catching so many typos. Thanks also for the use of your flatbed scanner that enabled me to import photographs.

Thank you to my friends Maxine Botti, Sharon Geurkink, Carolyn Meyer, Beverly Rogers, and Linda Wesner for reading—when you needed to be out Christmas shopping—an unfinished manuscript that I knew was in need of being trimmed or trashed. Thank you for your questions and suggestions. Thank you, Barbara Dockery, Katy Gunn, and Carolyn Horter, for your expertise, your eagle eyes, and your quick turnaround on such short notice.

Thank you to my daughters, Pamela and Jeanne, for having confidence that I would complete this book—someday—and for asking every once in a while, "How is the book coming?" You seemed ecstatic when I finally finished; and I was overjoyed at how quickly you read the pages. As wonderful as I know you are, you still never cease to amaze me. Thank you also for letting me take advantage of your expert editorial skills.

Thank you to my grandchildren, Curtis and Rachel, for reading, and commenting on, some of the stories I wrote about the farm. Thanks also for asking me, when you were younger, to tell you bedtime stories, which I often embellished or made up as I went; and thanks for helping me to remember how the made-up stories were supposed to go when you asked to hear them again!

Thank you, Patsy and Anetha, for being excited about this project from beginning to end and for remembering dates and details I could not. Your enthusiasm kept me going when I wanted to give up. Considering that we disagreed on a few story details, I was apprehensive when I gave you the first bound pages; I was afraid I might have to revise large sections of the book! My fears were wasted. Editorial collaborators you were; critics you were not. Your stamp of approval meant the world to me.

Thank you to those who influenced me to write (or made me think I could!) and to everyone who helped in some way to make this book possible.

Most of all, thank you, Mama and Daddy, for being the role models you were and for your willingness to sit down and share your lifetime of memories. You will live forever in the hearts of those who loved you.

Ethel Rye's Ancestry

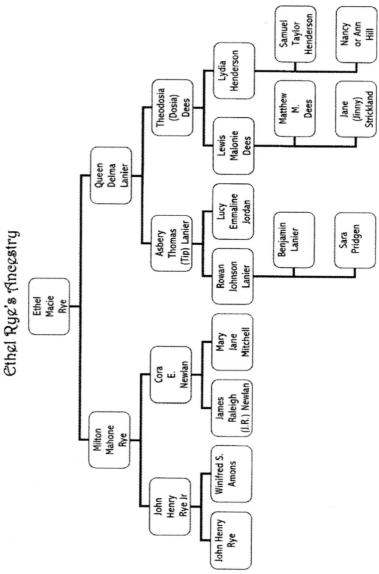

---

* This chart and the chart on the facing page are not typical ancestry charts but will perhaps help to show who was who. For example, Ethel Rye's father and mother were Milton Mahone Rye and Queen Delma Lanier. Her paternal grandparents were John Henry Rye Jr and Cora E. Newlan. For the names of C.G. and Ethel's descendants, see captions next to photographs on pages 352-356.

C. G. Howell's Ancestry

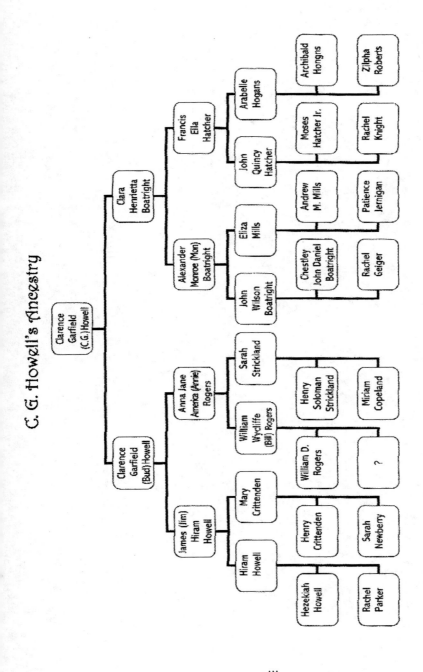

$\backsim$ 1   My Boyhood (by C.G.)

$\mathbf{D}$addy was sick in bed after collapsing in the field while breaking corn. I was seven years old and Mama was expecting her seventh baby. We were living on the Cheshire place after moving there from the Gamble place. It was the end of 1923.

While Daddy was sick, Granddaddy Boatright came by one day. I think he came over to get me to help him. I often rode on his plow; my weight helped hold it in the ground.

Mama happened to have baked some pies that day, so she offered some to her daddy.

"Thanks, Clara. Believe I will," Granddaddy said.

So, Mama served him a slice.

"Any of you kids like crust?" Granddaddy asked as he was eating near his crust.

"I do!" I said, before anybody else could.

Granddaddy Boatright didn't have any teeth and couldn't eat that hard crust, so I ate his crust. He then ate another piece and gave me that crust too. I think my granddaddy went on to eat three or four pieces of pie before he quit. I ate every bit of crust he gave me. Since that day, though, I've never cared much for pie crust.

I Wish

Daddy was still sick in bed, and one afternoon he told Mernest and me to go out and bring in some wood for the fireplace. Well, we drug around and it was about dark and we still hadn't done it. I don't remember what we were up to that day, but we liked to do things like roll a metal band (one that came off an old bucket) around the yard—pushing it with a wire. We pretended it was our car, and the wire hitting our "wheel" always made a big racket.

That day we had been playing around and hadn't done what Daddy had told us to do, so he called us to his bedside and told us to go out on the porch and get the braided calf whip he kept hanging out there and bring it to him.

"It's too dark out there, Daddy. We can't see to get it," I said.

"You feel around out there till you do find it and don't you come back in here without it."

That day, he really got on our dog hide [gave us a whipping].

"The son of a bitch! I wish he was dead!" I said to my brother Mernest after I got out far enough away that I knew Daddy couldn't hear me.

C.G.'s father, Clarence Garfield (Bud) Howell

105 Days

Daddy lay in bed for 105 days, a little more than three months. Every time he got worse, even if it was late in the night, we'd call old Doctor Anderson, and he would always come. We kids would walk way over to Dora Mills's house to a telephone—there were just a few telephones scattered around Suwannee County back then. To make a call, you took the receiver off and turned a crank and got the operator and gave her the number you wanted.

Dr. Anderson had to put a hole in Daddy's stomach or intestinal area and a tube from there to a bucket under the bed for drainage. He said Daddy had heart dropsy and his kidneys weren't working, so fluid wasn't draining from his body like it was supposed to. We had no money to pay Dr. Anderson. Yet, he came every time we called, even during the middle of the night, and even though we couldn't pay him a dime and he knew it.

Then, Daddy died.

I Still Remember Well

Daddy was buried at Philadelphia Baptist Church in Suwannee County, Florida. The marker on his grave reads:

Clarence Garfield Howell
Born October 1, 1882
Died February 28, 1924[1]

I was upset that Daddy was dead. Yet I could not shed a tear. What I had said to Mernest, when I was mad at Daddy—about wanting Daddy dead—it kept coming back to me. I still remember well what I said that day, and to this day I would give anything to take my words back.

Daddy and His Family

Daddy was forty-one years old when he died, yet he had actually lived longer than many people had ever expected.

He was what they called then "a blue baby," so nobody thought he would live to be a grown man.

At birth, he was given the name Clarence Garfield (he was born less than a month after President James A. Garfield was assassinated); but his sisters, Flora and Laura, started calling him Bud, and pretty soon, Bud was what everybody called him.

His parents were James (Jim) Hiram Howell—one of the first deacons to be ordained at the Philadelphia Baptist Church—and Anna Jane America (Annie) Rogers. But she, Daddy's mother, died when Daddy was just a baby.

C.G.'s paternal grandfather, James (Jim) Hiram Howell

His father then married another woman whose name was also Annie (Mary Annie Williams Madison Howell).[2]

Daddy was still just a little boy when his father died; so his sisters, Flora and Laura, had their father's grave dug just far enough from their mother's that it left a child-sized plot between them for their baby brother (my Daddy) because, like I said, nobody expected him to live to be a grown man.

Daddy's stepmother was still living when I was born, and she is the one I knew as Grandma Howell. I remember visiting her a few times at her home near Dowling Park. Most of all, I remember the well where she got her drinking water. It had sulfur in it and that water tasted awful. I purely hated that water.

Mama and Her Family

My mother, Clara Henrietta Boatright, was born on May 1, 1895, in the Pine Mount community of Suwannee County, just south of CR252 and Hughes Road, near McAlpin.

Her parents were Alexander Monroe (Mon) Boatright[3] and Francis Ella Hatcher Boatright.[4] I never knew Grandmama Ella Boatright; but I know she had two sets of twins (Mama was a twin) plus the other children. First, there were: Ethel,[5] John Q.,[6] Joe,[7] twins Clarence[8] and Clara (my mama). Then, Ella Mae was born (in 1897), but she died when she was just three years old.

C.G.'s maternal grandmother, **Frances Ella Hatcher Boatright (She had two sets of twins!)**

Soon after losing her youngest child, Ella became pregnant again; and on April 14, 1902, she gave birth to her second set of twins: Andrew and Oliver.[9] That same day, at the age of thirty-one, Ella died. So did baby Andrew. Twin Oliver lived without his mother and twin brother for just five months.

Granddaddy Boatright eventually married again, but in 1902, the year he lost his wife Ella and his twin boys, his future wife, Della Ross Jones,[10] was—by all accounts—a happily married woman.

How Della Ross Jones Became Available

Della Ross Jones and her husband Tom Jones were neighbors of the Boatrights. They also went to the same church (Philadelphia Baptist), and their children often played together, especially the Boatright twins, Clarence and Clara, and the Jones girls, Alma and Mary, since the four of them were about the same age.

Then one day, Tom Jones was murdered.

Who-did-it rumors started flying around the community. Some said J.G.[11] had reason to kill Tom Jones because, they said, Tom Jones had propositioned J.G.'s wife.

On the day Tom Jones was murdered, it was reported that both he and J.G. ate lunch at Ward's Café in Live Oak, though at different times. Sources said that J.G. mentioned, while in the restaurant, that he had just bought himself some buckshot shells, and somebody commented—

"Sounds like you're planning to kill yourself a buck."

"Yeah, a two-legged one," J.G. allegedly replied.

Later that same day, Tom Jones was found slumped in his own wagon, dead from a buckshot blast.

J.G. was the one who reported the death to the sheriff, saying he had come upon Tom Jones, already dead, in his own wagon.

Some thought J.G. was guilty of murder, but he never served any time for it, and both he and his family and the Jones family continued attending Philadelphia Baptist Church. After the tragedy, however, the two families would pass one another in the church and never utter one word to one another.

Combined Families

Not long after Della Ross Jones became a widow, she and Granddaddy Mon Boatright married. Their combined family included Ethel, John Q., Joe, Clarence, Clara (my mother), Alma, and Mary. Then, Mon and Della had two children together: Ross and Lillie Mae.[12]

Years later, Mama confessed that the combined family had their ups and downs. For one thing, the older children didn't accept their stepmother; and for another, she (Clara) didn't always get on well with her stepsisters, Alma and Mary.[13] They were close to her age, so the three of them would play together, but they were always bickering and somebody would always end up crying. One of the girls—I think it was Alma—had a health problem, and she would occasionally, for some reason or for no apparent reason, be unable to catch her breath.

One day when the girls were playing in the yard, they started fussing at one another, and it escalated until Mama said she got so mad with Alma that she just wanted to smack her. She caught herself just in time, knowing her stepmother would see it. Then, Alma suddenly got short of breath—then couldn't get her breath at all. Alma's mother, watching from a window, saw what was happening and realized she couldn't get out of the house and across the yard fast enough, so she yelled—

"Clara, hit her! Hit your sister! Hit her across the back! Hit her hard!"

"I was more than happy to obey my stepmama," Mama told me. "I hauled off and hit Alma across the back just as hard as I could. Wham! It felt real good."

But Mama said, as time went by, she eventually accepted her stepfamily and enjoyed being with them.

Mama said she always got along real well with her father. She often bragged that she would help him when he robbed the beehives by holding the flambeau—the torch that gave off lots of smoke—to help protect them from bee stings. She said she was never stung, but the bees always managed to get her daddy.

Uncle Joe, Mama's brother, who went on to become a Suwannee County Commissioner in the late 1950s, described their childhood, in an article published in the *Suwannee Democrat* [June 17, 1969]:

> *The boys helped their father in the fields with the plowing; the girls helped in the house with the*

scrubbing, cooking, washing, ironing, and sewing; and they all helped with other chores like picking cotton and pulling fodder.

The boys and girls attended school when they could, walking nearly three miles to get to classes at Middleton School, a log building with wooden doors and shutters.

I think Mama and Daddy met when they were attending Middleton School. Mama completed just seven grades, but with that she had more education than Daddy.

They married on July 31, 1913; she was eighteen and he was thirty-one. After getting married, they headed down to south Florida to work in fruit—picking it—but didn't stay there long before coming back to Suwannee County where they planted a crop on the Jim Howell place.[14]

My Brothers, Ernest and Mernest

Two years after they married, Mama had twin boys. She said it was on a cold day in early 1915. She named the babies Ernest Arnold and Mernest Donald. But before the twins were two months old, Mama discovered Ernest one morning, dead in bed. The cause of death was unknown.

Ernest was buried behind Philadelphia Baptist Church with a small marker. Many years later, it was replaced with a granite one that was engraved:

Ernest Arnold Howell
Born January 13, 1915
Died March 10, 1915

Soon after Ernest died, Mama and Daddy got on as sharecroppers for the Land family in Lafayette County and moved into one of Mr. Land's tenant houses. They didn't have to pay rent, and in return for their help on the farm, Mr. Land gave them a share of the profits after he sold the crops. The Land place was northeast of Mayo, about four miles across the Suwannee River from Wilmarth. That's where I was born, on Mernest's first birthday: January 13, 1916. Dr. Haig from Mayo delivered me.

Cecil Monroe

We lived in the tenant house on the Land place until I was about two. Then Daddy got a job at a nearby sawmill in the town of Alton. Not long after we moved there, Dr. Haig

C.G.'s parents, Clarence (Bud) and Clara Howell. Bud is holding C.G.'s brother, Mernest; and Clara is holding C.G.

came to our house and delivered my brother, Cecil Monroe (Monroe after Granddaddy Boatright). It was on March 29, 1918. But I can hardly remember Cecil. He got sick during the 1919 flu epidemic and died on the ninth of June. Mama was pregnant when he died, but I didn't know it yet.

Mama and Daddy wanted to bury Cecil next to Ernest, but they didn't have any transportation to Suwannee County. So Jasper Johnson, a friend, came over to Lafayette County where we were living and took all of our family to the funeral at Philadelphia Church in his Model-T Ford touring car. That was my very first car ride.

My baby brother's grave marker reads:

Cecil M. Howell
Born March 29, 1918
Died June 9, 1919

Ira James

When I was almost four, Dr. Haig came to the house again to deliver my brother Ira James. It was December 16, 1919.

That house in the town of Alton where Cecil and Ira were born is the first house that I remember living in. It had a well and hand pump but no running water.

One day, Mernest and I (Ira was still too little to play with us) went across the road where the Grandhand boys were cleaning a rifle—and they made out like they were going to shoot us! It scared me and Mernest nearly to death. I remember going back across the street and Mernest was crying and talking with me about it.

"That's all right, buddy," I said to Mernest, "We cussed 'em, didn't we?"—not knowing Daddy had come home, and he had heard me.

When we got in the house, Daddy took off his belt and wore out both our butts for cussing. I remember that, too.

That night, we were telling Mama all about nearly being shot by the Grandhand boys.

"Mama, if they'd a killed me," Mernest said, "I never would of got to eat no more. Would I?"

Times were hard for us, but at Christmas we would hang our stockings by the fireplace and get something like an apple, an orange, and marbles—or socks and some little ten- or fifteen-cent toy. One Christmas, I got a cap pistol. Another year I got a pocketknife with a chain on it.

When any of us got a new knife, Mama or Daddy would break the point off before we could play with it. We played a game we called *stick frog* where we would throw the knife in the dirt. If you flipped the knife off your fingers a certain way, it was called *break the chicken's neck.* The knife had to land with the blade sticking in the dirt. When you missed, and the knife ended up lying sideways on the ground, it was somebody else's turn.

Sometimes, we played marbles. Other times, we played a game of *leap frog* where one person would jump over the other, or *hail over* where we'd throw a ball back and forth over the house.

To Suwannee County in an Oxcart

When Daddy lost his job at the sawmill in Alton, we moved into the back of a store, owned by old man Toole. Daddy operated the store, a mercantile store that sold all kinds of dry goods and food.

I got sick while we lived at that store, and I hated to take medicine, so Mama and Daddy got so they would give me a penny to take it. By the time I got to feeling better, I had a little matchbox *full* of pennies.

We were still living in the back of Mr. Toole's store in Alton when Mama got pregnant again. Then Daddy lost his job at the store, so we had to move out. It was in January or February of 1921—and really cold. We put all our belongings in an oxcart and moved over the river from Lafayette to Suwannee County and into an old frame house that belonged to Grover Mills. Soon after we settled there, Daddy got a job working for Mr. Aught, who lived down the road and owned a sawmill, run by a steam engine. Uncle Clarence Boatright, Mama's twin brother, also worked at Mr. Aught's sawmill.

Sister Clara Mae

While Daddy was working for Mr. Aught, Mama went over to Uncle Clarence's house one day to visit Aunt Daisy and to help her cook dinner for the menfolks. At noon, when dinner was ready, they all sat down to eat—including old man Aught, the boss at the sawmill.

I don't know what the deal was, whether Mr. Aught was furnishing Uncle Clarence and Aunt Daisy with groceries or just paying them so much to eat with them, but he ate there a lot; and that day he really embarrassed my mama, who was still expecting a baby.

Mama said everybody was sitting around the table eating dinner, and the plate of biscuits got passed around the table, and everybody took one. A while later, Mama's brother Clarence asked for another biscuit, and Mama did too, so the biscuit plate was being passed back and forth. That's when Mr. Aught said, "Well, Daisy, I guess you'd just better bring the sack of flour in here and set it down over there by Clara!"

Mama said she didn't know old man Aught that well, and it embarrassed her so much that when the biscuits were passed her way again, she wouldn't take another one.

It wasn't too long after that episode with the biscuits that Mama sent Mernest and me off to spend the night with Mrs. Dora Mills. Ira didn't get to go; he was still too little. The next day, when we got home, Mama showed us a new baby. It was our baby sister, Clara Mae. She was born on July 26, 1921.

Daddy Wouldn't Squeal

Daddy's jobs kept changing, so we moved several more times. From Grover Mills's place, we moved to Frank Hingson's old log house and then to Curtis Gamble's place.

There was always a reason Daddy lost each job. When he lost it at the Mayo sawmill, it was because he wouldn't squeal on his buddies, Jake Futch, and I don't know who all else. Several of the men got high on moonshine, and the superintendent found out about it and asked for somebody to tell who was involved. If somebody would tell, he said, that person would get to stay on. Daddy wouldn't squeal, and none of the others would squeal either, so the boss just fired everybody—the whole business.

Riding the Plow

Sometimes Daddy would do plowing for other people, using their mules, and he would let us young'uns ride, sitting on the beam just above the plow and next to the

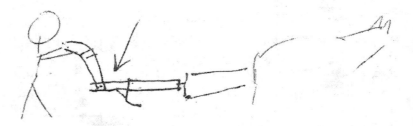

handles. I'm not very good at drawing, but maybe that gives you an idea. Riding up there was fun, and I think our weight helped Daddy hold the plow down in the ground.

Back then, people made their own plow stocks out of a hard wood, like hickory. But the plows themselves were made of steel. They were different shapes, depending on what the plow was used for.

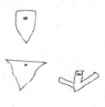

Daddy Would Drink

Of course, Daddy would drink. I've heard a lot of people say that drinking was the only failing he had. If he ever got around to where he could get hold of a drink, he wouldn't quit until he could hardly walk. Then he would go home drunk, and if one of us kids did something wrong, he would put in that he was going to wear us out.

"No, Clarence, you ain't gonna hit 'em a lick," Mama would say—and he wouldn't.

Bud was what everybody called Daddy—everybody, that is, except us kids and Mama. She insisted on calling him *Clarence* because she had always called her twin brother—whose name was also Clarence—*Bud*. That confused everybody, except Mama.

Late one day, when we were up at Aunt Ethel and Uncle Lawson's house, Daddy really scared Mama. He came in the house and asked Uncle Lawson for his shotgun. Uncle Lawson didn't know why Daddy wanted it but let him have it anyway. Daddy went out with the gun and sat down on a pile of Jap cane that was stacked up for grinding (I think Jap cane came over from Japan; it's not as sweet as regular cane—probably not worth having.) Anyway, Daddy sat on the cane pile and pulled off one of his shoes. About that time, Mama saw what Daddy was up to. He had pointed the shotgun at his head and was trying to get his toe on the trigger.

"Lawson, stop him!" Mama yelled, and Uncle Lawson ran out and pushed the gun away just as the gun discharged—"Bam!"—into the air.

Daddy was just out of his head, drunker than a coot. Mama might have fussed at him or something. But they say as long as Daddy wasn't drinking, he was well-liked and you could depend on him. He never tried something like that again. I wasn't but about five years old at the time.

That's one of the reasons I vowed later on not to drink. I didn't want to follow in Daddy's footsteps where drinking was concerned. He couldn't handle it, and I was afraid if I kept on drinking, I might not be able to handle it either.

Trying Tobacco

I did try using tobacco though—chewin' and smokin' it— when I was six or seven. One day, Mama and Daddy and all of us kids were going to town in the horse and wagon. Uncle Joe Boatright, Mama's brother, was headed for town too, and we came up behind him. He pulled on the reins of his horse and eased his wagon to a stop and asked if one of us wanted to ride with him. I sailed out of our wagon and climbed up there with Uncle Joe—got right beside him in the jump seat where he sat to guide the horse, and we headed on for town. After a while, Uncle Joe took a plug of chewin' tobacco out of his pocket, cut off a piece with his pocketknife, and stuck it in his mouth. He glanced over at me and saw me staring.

"Son, you care for a chew?"

"Yes, Sir!"

So Uncle Joe cut off a piece for me. I leaned over toward him when I took it so my mama and daddy, in the wagon behind, couldn't see, and then I eased the piece up to my mouth. Right soon, the juice began to accumulate in my mouth. I was afraid to spit, because I knew Mama and Daddy could see if I spit and would know I was chewin' tobacco. So, I just kept swallowing that juice. By the time we got to Live Oak, I had swallowed a right smart amount of juice and was so sick I could hardly sit up. We stopped in town under some oak trees, and everybody else got out of both wagons and went around town doing their business. I just lay there in Uncle Joe's wagon all day long, under the shade of the trees, too sick to move. I remember seeing the birds flying all around in the trees overhead and around the buildings, and I couldn't have cared less. I stayed in that wagon all day long, sick as a dog.

Not long after that, I tried smoking. Daddy asked Mernest and me one day if we wanted to smoke. We did! So he put some tobacco in his pipe and let us smoke it. That made me sick all over again—and my brother too.

Sister Laura Belle

Mama was expecting another baby at the time Daddy fell in the field and took to the bed. He was still in the bed when our baby sister, Laura Belle, was born on February 12, 1924. I think Dr. Anderson came out and delivered her, but I'm not sure, because all of us kids were shooed out of the house as soon as labor got underway.

Seventeen days later, Daddy died. I was eight years old.

Daddy's adult-sized coffin couldn't be squeezed into the child-sized plot, between his parents, that had been set aside for him by his sisters. Besides, by then he had a wife and us kids, so Mama had Daddy buried right next to the graves of my brothers, Ernest and Cecil.

People were nice to us; after the funeral, Lillian and Wayne Ross[15] invited Mama and all of us kids to their house for dinner.

With Daddy Gone

Daddy died with us owing Dr. Anderson for his many trips to our house, and Mama was twenty-eight years old with no money, not much education, and five kids to feed. Laura was only sixteen days old, and Mernest, the oldest, was about nine.

With Daddy gone, we had to move again. This time we moved into Uncle John Q. Boatright's house.[16] At the time, he and Aunt Mamie were living down the state in Arcadia, where Uncle John Q. was picking fruit.

After we got settled, I started going to the Philadelphia School (where the Philadelphia Baptist Church parsonage would eventually sit), and one day in class, the teacher asked a boy to spell *turpentine.*

"I can't spell it," he said, "but I can tell you what it's good for. Mixed with sugar, it's good for a sore throat. But I know an even better use. We rubbed a cat's tail with a corn cob and turpentine, and that cat ran so fast it could of outrun two race horses."

All of us kids snickered, but the teacher just stood there looking at that boy without cracking a smile. I saw that she didn't have a funny bone in her body.

Mama tried to make ends meet by farming. Uncle Joe's place was right next to where we were living, so he plowed up some land for us, and Mama and Aunt Lizzie planted a crop of corn there—by hand—and covered up the kernels with their bare feet. Mama also borrowed some money from Mr. Tom Moore and bought a gilt. Later on, that sow had eight or nine pigs, and Mama was able to sell the pigs and pay Mr. Moore back and still have a little money left.

We were still living on Uncle John Q.'s place when I got malaria. I was about ten then, and I got real sick. Mama gave me Six-Sixty-Six[17] for it. Oh, Man! That stuff was bitter. Some people took Calamel for malaria, but if you took that and then ate something sweet, they said it would salivate you and make your teeth loose.

One day, a tan-and-white cow came up to Uncle John Q.'s house with her calf, and Mama saw a way to get us some milk. She put the calf in a pen—but not the cow. She let the cow wander off in the woods during the day to eat grass and stuff, knowing the cow would come back every so often to let her baby calf suck. When she did, Mama could milk her to get milk for us kids to drink.

After Mama milked the cow, she would draw cool water from the well and set the sweet milk in the water so it would stay sweet until noon, and we could drink it. By supper, of course, it was sour, and by morning it was clabber. But she could still skim the cream off it and make butter with the cream.

That cow's hide was branded *HL*. Mama figured the heifer belonged to old man Lamb, but she didn't think he minded her milking his cow.

One day a fellow by the name of Patrick (Pat) Sullivan came by and asked Mama if he could buy the cow. She told him the cow was not hers to sell—that she thought it belonged to Mr. Lamb. So, Mr. Sullivan left. But, later on, he came back, told Mama he had bought the cow from Mr. Lamb, and loaded up the cow and took her off. He then butchered the cow and brought us some of the meat. I thought it was a lot better than the milk. I hated milk.

Pat Sullivan even put new bottoms in three or four of our chairs using that tan-and-white pied cowhide—and he gave Mernest and me a shotgun to share. We liked to hunt.

Besides hunting, all of us kids would find other ways to amuse ourselves. Sometimes we took turns jumping out of the barn loft using an umbrella to slow the fall. One day Ira went in the house and got Mama's umbrella—or parasol—and jumped first. When he did, Mama's parasol went inside out and he hit the ground hard.

Trying to Catch a "Wild Turkey"

Sometimes we would design things to play with—like that car we made with a metal bucket band and a wire when Daddy was sick. We pushed it all around that yard—called ourselves "driving a car."

Other times, we'd find a bottle and use that for a car. We found one up at Uncle Joe's one day, and we made roads with that bottle all up under Uncle Joe's house, which sat high off the ground. Back then, most houses did.

Uncle Joe had a mule he called Babe that he used for plowing, and he could get that mule to do just about anything he wanted. But the mule was scared of gopher holes and would stop every time she came to one. (What we called a gopher, some people now call a *land tortoise*.)

Anyway, one day Uncle Joe was plowing with Babe, and she came to a complete stop at a gopher hole. I just knew that mule wouldn't go any further. But Uncle Joe started gee-hawing and clucking to her, edging her on.

"Gee! Haw! Haw! Babe . . . Gee! Gee! Babe!"

He just kept on, edging Babe forward, until he made that ole mule stumble and fall right in that gopher hole.

Mama sent me over before daylight one morning to Uncle Joe's with a message of some kind. When I started walking back home, it was still not good daylight. I was about halfway home when I thought I saw a wild turkey in the road in front of me. I took off to try and catch him—not recognizing what it really was. A skunk! That thing sprayed his musk and it burned my eyes so bad.

When I got home, nobody could get near me. Mama made me take off all my clothes. Then she buried them to try to get the scent out. After about three weeks, she dug them up and washed them, but when I wore them and it rained, I smelled like a polecat. Mama finally decided to burn the stinking clothes.

Old Man Aught

From Uncle John Q.'s place, we moved in with Aunt Daisy and Uncle Clarence, Mama's twin. At the time, around 1926, they were living on Mr. Hughes's place, about four miles east of Tip Lanier's homestead. While living with them, Mernest, Ira, and I went to McAlpin to school. Our sisters weren't old enough yet.

We lived there with Uncle Clarence and Aunt Daisy just a little while before we moved to the Pennington Place. Then, they let Mr. Aught, the man who had been Daddy's boss, move in with them. Aunt Daisy said that Mr. Aught woke up early one Saturday morning, took a bath, and got cleaned up like he was going out.

"What you fixing to do?" Aunt Daisy asked, "You getting all dolled up and spruced up first thing!"

"Well," he said, "I had a dream last night—'bout me and Clara—if we could just get our watches to ticking together, *we* could get together."

That was Mr. Aught's way of saying he wanted to go out with my mama. That old man Aught was a sport. But as far as I know, they never got their watches synchronized.

The Pennington Place

At the time Mr. Aught was interested in Mama, she had plans of her own, and that was to farm the John L. Pennington place. We moved there in 1927, and the first thing she did was buy a mule. Then, Mernest and I dropped out of school to help her with the farming, while Ira stayed in school at McAlpin.

Mr. Pennington raised cows, and he would get Mernest and me to help him move the cows from here to there. For our help, he'd pay us with a liver or some other cut of meat when he butchered a cow. One day Mernest was on the mule trying to round up cattle for Mr. Pennington when the mule ran up under a tree, and a limb dragged Mernest right off that mule. He fell hard on the ground and broke his arm. After that, Mernest hated that mule's guts.

Later on, the mule got sick—got so she just trotted around twenty-four hours a day. Then she died, and Mernest, Ira, and I got up on top of her, on top of that old dead mule, and danced 'cause we were glad she was gone. Of course, with no mule to ride after that, we could only ride the cows. But we had a Texas saddle, a regular roping saddle that had a horn on it, so we could use it and throw a rope and lasso a yearling.

We also had a little dog we were crazy about, but he fell out of the wagon one day, and the wagon rolled over him and killed him. We all cried about that.

One time we made ourselves a fancy wheelbarrow using two-by-fours and attached a steel wheel to it. To that we added a kerosene lantern parking light that we took off an old junked car—a Model-T Ford. We must have pushed that wheelbarrow a thousand miles.

On the Pennington property there was a pond where the cows got their water and we swam. The shore on one side was real boggy, but the other side was sandy. We got so we started taking our clothes off and going in, and Mernest and I learned to swim there. One day, Mernest found a bottle and threw it at me. I ducked under the water just in time. If it hadn't missed, it would have hurt bad.

Ira couldn't swim but said he could, and he would get in the real shallow water and pretend. What he was doing was pulling himself along with his hands, which were touching the bottom.

One day Mernest and I said we would find out if Ira could *really* swim. There was also a sinkhole on the property that would sometimes fill up with water, so we took Ira there. We took off our clothes and Ira's too. Then we took his hands and led him in—all of us naked as jay birds. The sink had more water in it than usual, and before we knew what had happened, we had stepped in a gully and lost our grip on Ira. That confirmed right shortly that Ira couldn't swim a lick.

Mernest and I both grabbed hold of Ira and started pulling him—but we were getting nowhere. I finally realized we were working against one another: I was trying to pull Ira to shore and Mernest was trying to get him to a *tree* out in the middle of the sinkhole. When we finally got Ira to shore, he was choking and coughing up water.

"What were you going to do?" I asked Mernest after Ira was safe. "Let him sit there on the *tree* three or four days till the water went down?" Then we threatened Ira if he ever told Mama.

In 1928, the Suwannee River came up real high. It rained a lot, so water even filled low places in the roads. One day we were out wading in the water and took Laura in with us. She was about four years old, and the water was about two-feet deep. Old man McClellan saw us leading Laura in and yelled at us.

"Yaw bettah get dat baby outta dere, 'fore she jown!"

Mr. McClellan couldn't talk plain, but that old man was smarter than people thought. By cleaning outdoor privies in Mayo and Alton—for which he was paid a dollar a day—he managed to save enough to buy forty acres of land.

There was a lot a work to do from 1927 to 1928 when Mernest and I stayed home to help Mr. Pennington and Mama with the farm. But we had our share of good times.

One day when Mama went to town, we decided to have some fun on the roof. The roof on the back side of the house had tin on it, but the front side was covered with tar paper. We climbed up a ladder, got on the tar paper, walked up to the peak, and started taking turns sliding off the tin roof. When it came Mernest's turn, he started to go down—but then stopped.

"I want to go down fast!" he said, grabbing a handful of pine straw from a tree overhanging the roof. He sat down on that straw and—well, he went fast all right! He soon realized he was going too fast and looked around cockeyed as he got to the edge of the roof. He tried to grab hold of the edge of the roof to slow his fall, but that just caused him to do a somersault as he fell. When he hit the ground, it about knocked the breath out of him.

There was another thing kids liked to do back then—though I never did it. They would fill a paper sack with rice or peas or something that would rattle and tie the sack on a cat's tail. The cat would run like crazy. One time Marvin Warren[18] and his friend did it and then decided to set the bag on fire. But, they got a surprise. The cat took off and headed straight for the barn. They knew they had to catch that cat before it got to that barn, so they took off after it. Marvin stripped that blazing bag off that cat's tail just as it was headed up a post for the hayloft.

One night while we were still on the Pennington Place, I asked Mama to let me spend the night with Roy and Arthur Smith, boys that lived nearby. They told me I might not want to, because they had the itch. But I went anyway. That night when we went to bed, they put me in the middle, and—teasing me—they started scratching themselves and then scratching me. Well, I caught the itch that night and took it home and the whole family got it. It's what they now call scabies. You itch so bad you can hardly stand it. I remember this little girl Lora[19] that also had the itch. She was so cute.

"Tie my hands behind my back," she told her mama, "so I cain't scratch no more!"

To get rid of our case of the itch, Mama made soap with beef tallow and sulfur and made us wash with it in our old zinc tub.

Sometimes we sat on the back steps and Mama sang songs to us—"The Great Speckled Bird," "When They Ring Those Golden Bells," and one I really liked, "Why Bob Your Hair Girls?"

It's an awful shame
To rob the head God gave you
And bear the flapper's name.
You're taking off your covering,
It is an awful sin;
Don't never bob your hair, girls,
Short hair belongs to men.

That winter it got really cold. And snowed! We had never seen snow before and had never had any ice cream either. So, we got a big bucket and went out and scooped up as much snow as we could in the bucket and took it in to Mama. She put sugar in it and made us some ice cream.

C.G.'s mother, Clara, on the Pennington place after she bobbed her hair

Mama's New Man

We were still living on the Pennington place, when one day we saw a buzzard with a Prince Albert can tied to his neck. He looked sick, and we were able to catch him and take the can off his neck. Mama opened it, and there was a note with a man's name on it and an address in Alabama. In the note, the man was asking anyone who found the bird either dead or alive to please write and tell him where they found it. Mama sat down and wrote the man a letter and mailed it, but I don't think she ever heard back from him.

Not long after Mama mailed that letter off to the man in Alabama, Pat Sullivan started hanging around. He's the one that had helped us out when we were living in Uncle John Q.'s house. He had given us some of his cow meat and made us chair bottoms from its hide. He had even given Mernest and me a twenty-gauge shotgun, bought us shells, and taken us hunting, so of course we kids thought Pat was the greatest.

Pat wanted to marry Mama, and to our surprise Mama finally said she would marry him. On June 14, 1927, all of us kids went with them to Mayo. Pat parked in front of the courthouse, and we kids sat in the car while Pat and Mama went inside the courthouse and got married. He signed his name Patrick J. Sullivan. The *J* stood for *John.*

Pat was a steeplejack—painted smoke stacks for industrial plants. After they married, he wanted Mama to move to Texas with him, but she wouldn't. Even though Mama had known Pat for about two years—ever since he had come up to the house wanting to buy that cow that belonged to Mr. Lamb—I don't think Mama ever completely trusted Pat. I don't think she was sure he had actually paid Mr. Lamb for the cow, even though she accepted the meat he brought for us to eat (it was good!) and let him cover our chair bottoms with that cow's hide.

After they married, Pat gave us kids a twenty-two rifle, and Mama bought us a box of cartridges to share—twenty-two shorts, rim fire. We used that rifle to hunt rabbits and squirrels that we could eat. We killed possums and coons, too, but didn't eat them.

Pat was a character. He would brag about shooting hats off Mexicans, just for the fun of it. He was a cracker shot, so I think he could have done just that. And he was from everywhere! If he hadn't already been there, to hear him tell it, he was "soon a-going."

Pat would go off on jobs, and one time he took me with him on what was supposed to be a six-month trip. We camped in his Model-T panel truck—slept in it. He had an old dog, Jack, that guarded his truck.

While we were in Valdosta where he was doing some work, I saw my first picture show—Bud Abbott and Lou Costello—at an indoor movie theater. The movie had lots of action but no sound.

At the end of the day, Pat would go to the post office to see if there was any mail sent to him, general delivery. One day he came back from the post office with a letter.

"Got a letter from your mama," he said as he handed it to me to read.

"What do you think?" he asked, after I finished reading the letter.

"Mama wants me to go home, so I ought to go."

Early the next morning, we went home. When we got there, Mama was sick. She told Mernest to go get some pans from Pat's truck to cook breakfast. Then, after breakfast, Pat was ready to roll.

"Rinse them pans," he said to Mernest, "I'm gonna blow out in a few minutes."

A while later, Pat left—without me—and we never heard from him again. Not ever.

I don't know when Mama got a divorce from Pat. I ended up with the twenty-gauge shotgun he'd given us. I'm not sure what happened to the twenty-two rifle. Maybe Ira got it. I'm sure Mernest didn't mind, because when our daddy had died, Mernest had gotten Daddy's twelve gauge.[20]

Live Oak and Jacksonville

Late in 1928, Mama decided we should quit trying to farm the Pennington place. She was a good seamstress and decided she might be able to make a living by taking in sewing, so she went to Live Oak one winter day when it was freezing cold and found a house to rent on North Hamilton Street near City Hall and the waterworks.

Mernest had been making a little money plowing, and once we got to Live Oak, I worked some in the Pennington Meat Market on West Howard Street. But I guess our Live Oak living—having to pay rent and buy all our food instead of growing it—didn't pan out too well, because when Mama saw a classified ad in *The Florida Times Union* for a live-in woman to do the cleaning and cooking for a man in Jacksonville, she answered the ad. And she got the job.

Mama was to keep house for the old man in exchange for room and board for the five of us—Mama, Ira, Clara Mae, Laura, and me. Mernest wouldn't be going; Aunt Laura Garrett,[21] my daddy's only living sister, had written Mama soon after we moved to Live Oak and said if Mama would send Mernest to live with her in Loughman (south of Orlando), she would send him to school. So, Mernest had left in March for Loughman.

We had no transportation or any way to get to Jacksonville, so the man who was hiring Mama drove his car over to Live Oak and got us. It was April 5, 1929. The road from Live Oak to Jacksonville was a brick road then. We moved into the old man's house in the St. Johns Park vicinity—on the other side of the railroad.

While we were living there, I got so mad with Clara Mae one day that I popped her good, and then Mama got real mad with me.

Clara Mae loved to aggravate me. She'd get right in front of me and make all kinds of ugly faces—right in front of my face!

That day, like many others, Mama was reading one of those old romance magazines, like *True Story*. Any time Mama got her nose stuck in a book and started reading it, hell would freeze over before she would quit.

Well, Clara Mae just kept on and kept on, and I couldn't take it anymore.

"Mama, make her go and let me alone."

Mama was lost in her story. She kept on reading and didn't pay me a bit of a mind. Clara Mae kept on doing all kind of things in front of me. Oh, man! She could make me so mad I could just about die.

"Mama, make her quit, now," I said, but Mama didn't say a word.

"Mama, if you don't stop her, I'm gonna slap her face."

Mama still didn't say anything—didn't stop or scold Clara Mae or anything—didn't even look up. So when she got right up at my face again, I popped her good! Boy, I meant business.

Mama jumped up!

"I'm gonna wear you out for that, C. G. Howell. You go get me a switch!"

"Mama, there ain't no use to get you a switch 'cause I ain't taking no whipping for that."

"You go get me a switch!"

We argued back and forth a while.

"All right, Mama," I finally agreed, "I'll go out and get you a switch!"

I went out and got one and brought it to the house. Mama came to the kitchen door. I pulled the screen door to the kitchen open just a bit and handed the switch in to her, but then, right quick, closed the door and put my foot up against it so she couldn't get out and get to me. That's when Mama got *real* mad.

"You open that door, C. G. Howell! I'm gonna wear you out."

"Mama, if you'd of got your nose out of that magazine—but you get to reading and you hear nothing! I asked you three or four times to stop her but you— "

"Open that door!" Mama yelled.

"Are you gone try to hit me with that switch?"

"I'm gonna wear you out!"

"Then you ain't coming out."

"Well, you'll have to come *in* after while."

I was nearly thirteen then—big enough that I was stronger than Mama, and I didn't budge my foot from that door. She walked back through the house and out the front door and started around the house after me. So, I opened the back door, stepped in, and latched it so she couldn't get back inside. That's when she got mad as a wet hen.

"You open this door! I *mean*, open this door!"

"Mama, I'll open the door, but I ain't gonna take no whipping for that. And if Clara Mae does it again, I'll pop her again."

"You ain't gone do no such thing! You open this door!"

"No Ma'am," I said.

This was the first time I had ever before put up any resistance to Mama. I had always taken her whippings. But I didn't intend to that day. After awhile, though, I decided to let Mama in—but before I did, I warned her.

"Mama, I'm gonna unlatch the door now, but I ain't gonna take no whipping."

I waited a minute. Then I unlatched it. She opened it and started inside, and I backed up to let her in.

"Mama, I don't want to hurt you. But I ain't gonna take no whipping."

She stepped inside. I reached my hand out. She put the switch in my hand. I broke it into a half dozen pieces and threw it out in the yard.

I guess by the time I opened the door, Mama had cooled down some, and I had too. That wound up the episode, and we never did speak cross to one another from then on.

That's the only time I reckon I would have hurt Mama. I know if she had put in to whip me that day, I would have fought back.

Clara Mae used to aggravate Ira, too—until one day he picked up one of Mama's high heel shoes and hit Clara Mae in the back. It about knocked her out. After that, she didn't mess with Ira either.

Food Was Running Low

Mama's new job in Jacksonville seemed to be working out, until one night in July when the old man came in drunk and Mama told him to "get out." Yep. She ordered him out of his own house. Well, actually, he didn't own the house, but he was paying the rent. And Mama ran him off.

There was just one problem with that. With him gone, Mama didn't have any way to pay the rent, and food was running low. Word of our predicament got around though, and Mr. Sellers, a man she knew at Euclid Baptist where we went to church, came over and told her that he had a house we could move into, and she wouldn't have to pay rent. So we moved into Mr. Sellers's house just across the road, and the church brought us some groceries. Then, I— the oldest now that Mernest wasn't with us—found a job to earn some money. It was at a plant nursery at Lake Shore, west of Jacksonville. I was proud to be helping out.

The second day on the job, I finished hoeing alongside all the rose bushes, like I was told to do. Then, I stopped to rest for just a minute. Just a minute! But that's when the boss saw me—that minute I was resting. He let me go that night. Fired me.

The Baptist Children's Home

Mama had never been a physically strong woman, and after we moved to Jacksonville, she started having female problems; what she needed was surgery, but there was no money. Then, times got really hard for us.

Aunt Laura Garrett sent us a little money, and the church offered some support. But in September of 1929, Mama accepted that she had to have surgery and wasn't able to take care of us kids. So, Ira, Clara Mae, Laura, and I were placed in the Baptist Children's Home there in Jacksonville. I was thirteen, Ira was ten, Clara Mae was eight, and Laura was five.

The Children's Home was at 17 Cottage Avenue, right off Main Street[22] in downtown Jacksonville. It was different there—different from being with Mama. But it wasn't a bad place to live. In fact, Laura seemed to love it.

"That's because little Laura Bell was so cute!" Clara Mae said later, "Everybody there doted on Laura."

Mama had surgery at St. Luke's Hospital, and after the surgery, she went and stayed for a while with Aunt Laura Garret, where Mernest was living.

When Mama thought she had recovered, she went back up to Jacksonville and started working as a matron at the orphanage—the Children's Home—where we were, but that lasted only a few days. She really didn't have her strength back yet, so she had to quit and find something else. She found another job there in Jacksonville, one that just required light housekeeping, at the home of the Henderson family. It was close enough that I could ride a bike from the Children's Home to the Henderson's house, so, for a while I got to see Mama nearly every week.

I remember there was an old man named *Fox* that lived on Cottage Avenue just west of the Children's Home, and he put together a rocking chair using Pet milk cans. First, he took the labels off. Next, he soldered the cans together. Then, he put the labels back on. I think he thought the Pet Milk Company might pay him some money for his can rocker, but I don't think they ever did.

The Children's Home was a two-story brick building with a basement. That's where we gathered at Christmas and where Santa Claus came. We also ate our meals in the basement, except when the weather was nice and we had picnics on top of the building, which was flat.

The girls lived on the first floor and the boys on the second, the top floor. I think the building would hold about fifty kids. Our cots were all lined up, one after the other. A man by the name of McDaniel, The Reverend E. D. McDaniel, was in charge of our area.

I learned to roller-skate there. Having seen other people do it plenty of times, I knew how it was done. So, one day I put on some roller skates and took off from one end of the top floor, headed to the other end. When I got to the end of that long stretch, a cot got in my path, and my shins slammed against its steel edge. I *did* know how to skate. I just didn't know how to *stop*. But that steel cot stopped me in my tracks. My leg hurt something awful. But I couldn't complain to Mr. McDaniel or tell any adult that my leg was hurt, because I knew I had been doing something I wasn't supposed to do.

Baptist Children's Home in Jacksonville

‹» 2 My Childhood (by Ethel)

When my brother Harold was little, he loved to bite. I think he did most of his teething on my arm. About the only way I could make him stop biting was to slap him right in the face. If Mama caught me, of course, I got spanked; but Mama's spankings didn't hurt that much (she spanked with her hand). Harold's bite hurt a lot worse than Mama's hand.

I finally got Harold back good by yanking one of his teeth out. It was after he had started shedding his baby teeth and we were playing. I had something he wanted, and when I wouldn't give it to him, he really sunk his teeth into my arm. I jerked back—as you naturally do when somebody bites you—not knowing his tooth was caught in the sleeve of my sweater. When I jerked, I pulled his tooth right out! I didn't get a spanking that day, though. I told Mama it was an accident, and she believed me.

Now, when Daddy whipped us, we knew it. He'd get the razor strap—a leather strap he used for sharpening his straight razor—and he'd put it on us good. He was firm with us—stubborn to a point in some ways. In other ways, he was soft as a marshmallow.

I'd be willing to bet he cried after he whipped us because afterward he would always get away from us right away—go out to the barn or something. Then a little while later, he would figure out something to do for us. Once, he let me and Harold ride on the plow stock—the Big Dixie, we called it. The Big Dixie was used to break the ground before you planted a crop, and a sweep was used later for plowing the crop.

The Day Daddy Ignored Me

I never will forget the day Daddy totally ignored me. That broke my heart.

We were staying with my grandparents, Tip and Dosia Lanier. I called them Granddaddy Tip and Granny. Their place always seemed like home because we lived with them more than we lived anywhere else. Daddy's jobs were often temporary; but he did a little bit of everything, so when one job ended, he could usually find another.

At the time, Daddy was working with the State Road Department, helping build secondary bridges. He was home on weekends, but during the week he lived at the construction site. The state furnished tents for the work crew, and the boss and his wife lived in a nearby house. The boss's wife ran the mess tent, and Daddy said she cooked things the men liked—things like lima beans, sow belly, and hot bread.

We didn't have a car, so Daddy caught a ride with other people to go to work on Mondays and to come home on weekends. One Friday after working away all week, he caught a ride with the Williamsons who lived near us and had a big truck. Daddy had run up with them in town after work and rode out with them.

After Daddy had been gone for a week, we were always glad to see him.

By the time Daddy got home that day, though, he had already had too much to drink.

Harold and I were playing in the front yard when the truck drove up. Daddy got out and came through the gate, but he didn't speak to me or pay any attention to me at all.

"Hey, Spug," Daddy said to Harold as he picked him up.

Ethel's father, Milton Rye, with her baby brother, Harold—with a teething pipe?

Spug was what he had nicknamed Harold. (Daddy nicknamed everybody.) He headed to the house with Harold in his arms, still not paying me any attention whatsoever. When he got to the doorstep, he stumbled, and it looked like he just threw Harold. He flew in the air through the front door—which was open—and landed on the floor in the fireroom (our living area that was heated by a fireplace). Harold, of course, started crying, so Granny went over and looked after him, while Mama got hold of Daddy and led him straight to their bedroom, off the back porch.

"Get in that bed," I heard her tell Daddy.

Then, Mama came out and started fixing something hot for him to drink. It was black coffee and vinegar, a standard remedy for sobering him up. After Mama got the concoction ready, she went to the door of the bedroom, intending to make Daddy drink it, but she couldn't open the door. The bedroom was so little that Daddy could lie on the bed and prop his feet up against the door, and that's what he was doing.

Ethel's mother, Delma Rye, with Ethel and Harold

With his feet against that door, he kept Mama out of that room for I don't know how long. But I guess his knees finally got weak and Mama got in and started pouring the black coffee and vinegar in him. But you know, Mama didn't fuss at Daddy that day. Not then, not ever, that I remember.

Lord, Harold cried for I don't know how long. I guess he thought Daddy had just thrown him away.

Living on Palm Island

When Daddy decided to try his hand at commercial fishing—what his father was doing at the time—we moved down the state and in with his parents, Grandmama and Granddaddy Rye. They lived on Palm Island, a little island just off the west coast of Florida, near Punta Gorda.

At night, the sea turtles would come up on the island to lay their eggs in the sand. If you were quiet and listened, you could hear them packing the sand on their eggs to bury them. During the night, Daddy and several other men would go out and turn the turtles over on their backs. The turtles were not able to turn themselves back over, so the next morning, they would still be there on their backs. The men would then butcher them and get several good-sized turtle steaks that we could eat.

Ethel and Harold visiting George Knight Island. "I was mad," Ethel said. "I wanted my shoes off. They were too tight and killing me."

Some people would break up the nests and eat the turtle eggs, but we didn't do that. We left them so they could hatch.

Harold said he could remember coons knocking on our windows at night when we lived on Palm Island. He said they woke him up. I don't remember

- 36 -

that at all, but I can well remember the 1926 hurricane.

We didn't have much advance warning of the storm. I was about five years old then, not yet in school. The house we lived in was just a hundred yards or so from the water. A bay was in front of us, and the Gulf was in back. When we woke up that morning, the wind was just a-roaring. Mama and Daddy knew we had to work fast to save our chickens.

Our chickens liked to roost in the low branches of the trees around the place, and the wind was blowing the chickens out of the trees and into the water. Everybody got up and moved all the furniture out of one of the bedrooms. And then we went out and caught the chickens and brought them in the house and shut them up in that bedroom.

If you can imagine, we had roosters a-crowin' and chickens a-squawkin' all day and night. But they were our food! Because of the weather, there was no way of knowing when we would get out of there—to the mainland—to get more food. (Grandmama Rye also raised Indian Runner ducks, but they couldn't fly up and roost in the trees. To keep them from getting away, all she had to do was put up a fence about a foot high and they couldn't fly over that.)

Daddy, his father, and his brothers Ovieda and Aubrey, stayed up that night, all night long, to keep the boat afloat so we could get out if we needed to when the storm passed. The water came up so high that the water was lapping at the front step, but luckily it never did flood the house.

I think there were some prayers said that night. We didn't go to church then—or I don't remember going—but Grandmama Rye was very religious. I think she attached "the good Lord willing" to just about anything she said.

On the island, we had a well where we got water. It never was salty like the bay water, until after that storm; then it was so salty we couldn't drink it. So, the men would buy ice by the hundred pounds, and each day Mama or Grandmama Rye would chip off a piece of the ice and put it in the water bucket and let it melt so we would have water to drink and cook with. We used the salty water to wash dishes—and bathe; it was like we were pickled in brine.

Daddy's Family

Daddy always claimed to be one-sixteenth American Indian. I think it was Seminole, but my brother Harold thinks it was Cherokee.

Daddy's father was John Henry Rye. He was born in Madison, Florida, during the Civil War. The date was December 2, 1864. His mother was born Cora E. Newlan on September 26, 1878, in the Rocky Sink area of Suwannee County. Rocky Sink is probably where they met, because it's one of the places where he guarded convicts. He guarded them in different areas in north Florida. When they married, on December 22, 1892, he was twenty-eight years old and she was a girl of fourteen.

They had eleven children, but only seven lived to adulthood. Nobody had screens on their windows back then and mosquitoes were terrible, especially where they lived: in the Rocky Sink area of Suwannee County, around Alton in Lafayette County, and in Taylor County—all places that were swampy. I think most of their children died of malaria. They called it black malaria back then. Daddy caught it too but somehow survived.

Grandmama Rye wrote all her children's names in the Family Record: Milton (my daddy), Ruby May, Raleigh, Thelma, J.L. (Jessie), Ellis, Cora, Erma, Oviedo, Aubrey, and Edward.[23]

Daddy was born in Rocky Sink on March 18, 1894 (his mother was just fifteen). He was named Milton Mahone Rye after his mother's brother, Mahone Newlan. He was two when his sister Ruby May was born, but then she died when he was six.

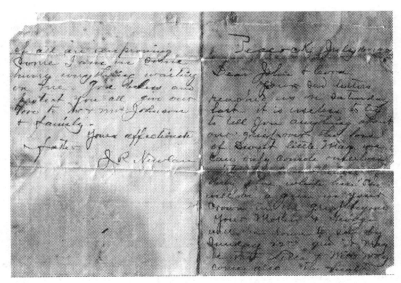

Above: Letter that Cora's father, J. R. Newlan, wrote to her, sharing his grief over the loss of little Ruby May. The letter reads as follows:

Peacock, July 16, 1900

Dear John and Cora,

    Your sad letters reached us on Saturday last. It is useless to try to tell you anything about our grief over the loss of sweet little May. We can only console ourselves with the consolation, duty done while here. She will be a jewel in your crown in the great beyond. Your Mother and George will be down to see [you] by Sunday 22nd and it may be that Lilla and Will may come also. The health of all are improving.

    Corrie, I am in some hurry, everything waiting on me. God bless and protect you all. Give our love to Mr. and Mrs. Johnson and family.

Your affectionate father,
J. R. Newlan[24]

- 39 -

Daddy's sister Thelma, born the year after Ruby May died, lived just five months; and J.L., the one they called Jessie, was born the year after Thelma died, and he also lived just five months.

Daddy was a teenager when his sister Erma was born—with a cleft palate. She lived to the age of eight.

Daddy's brothers and sisters that I knew were Uncle Raleigh, Uncle Ellis, Aunt Cora, Uncle Oviedo, Uncle Aubrey, and Edward who was about my age.

Uncle Raleigh, Uncle Aubrey, and Daddy all went into the army during World War I. Daddy enlisted in 1918, but he never fought. He was sent to Virginia where he expected to get his marching orders; instead, he got pneumonia and was shipped off to a hospital.[25] Uncle Aubrey and Uncle Raleigh were sent overseas. Aubrey was involved in an Asian beachhead invasion and then contracted tuberculosis.

Uncle Raleigh came back from the war with no injuries at all. But then, while he was working on a car—he had it jacked up—the car fell on him and put him in a wheelchair for the rest of his life. He married Bertie Tyler.

Uncle Aubrey married a woman from up north, Thelma Roberts, who had a daughter named Patty. After the war, he became a jeweler, and he's the one who split Granddaddy Tip's gold wedding band.

Granddaddy Tip had lost that gold ring three times and Daddy found it every time. The last time, he plowed it up in the field! That's when Granddaddy Tip told him, "Milton, I've lost that ring too many times, so you just keep it."

Daddy was afraid to wear the ring, though. He had almost lost a finger once because of a ring; it got caught on a piece of equipment. So, Daddy put the ring away until about twenty-five years later when he got the idea of getting his brother Aubrey to split it in half to make two wedding rings.[26]

Uncle Ellis married a woman named Daisy. The story that got told and retold about Daisy was of what she said when members of the family were divvying up some of the family possessions.

"I think that I ought to have the *tay*pot," Aunt Daisy said, "because I drink *tay*."

She was referring to the silver teapot. She did like nice things! Later on, though, when she and Uncle Ellis separated and their son Buddie went to live with Mama and Daddy, she gave her fancy rolled-arm living room sofa and two matching chairs to Mama.

Daddy's brother Oviedo—everybody thought he was so cute when he was little. Mama often told the story of burning his dog.

"When Milton and I were first married," she said, "we lived close to his parents. Oviedo was just a little boy then, and I kept him a lot. If the oven was cool when we got ready to eat a meal, I'd open the oven door and let Oviedo use that for his table, since it was about the right height for him. He had a cute little plate with a picture of a dog on it that he liked to eat off of. One day when he finished eating, his plate somehow got pushed back in the oven and I forgot about it. At the next meal, I heated the oven and *ruined* his plate. It turned black! 'Delma...what'd ya burn my dawg for?' Oviedo drawled, when he saw his burnt plate. I felt real bad about it."

Edward was Daddy's youngest brother. Since he was about my age, I never called him uncle. When he got older, he wanted to go to the Bahamas with Uncle Ellis, but I think he got drafted instead. After that, he became a shoe cobbler and married a woman named Marie.

Daddy's only sister, Aunt Cora, was my favorite aunt. She married Will Taylor, a man much older than she was. They lived in Punta Gorda and had two children, Dorothy (Dot) and Robert. I never will forget the day Aunt Cora brought Dot over on a boat to Palm Island, when we lived there. Dot was just a tiny baby then and she sucked on a pacifier—or a nipple off a baby bottle that served as one.

(Robert wasn't born yet.) The weather was bad that day. Even when it wasn't storming around the island, the water could be rough. Well, little Dot got seasick on the boat that day, and she evidently thought the pacifier was what was making her sick. She would take that thing out and look at it, and then stick it back in and suck some more. Then she would take it out again and look at it again. It was so funny the way she looked at that thing—like she didn't like the way it was making her feel—but didn't hate it so much that she was willing to give it up.

A Day in Bartow

We saw quite a bit of Uncle Billy Rye's family. Uncle Billy was my great-uncle (Granddaddy John Rye's brother); he owned or operated a store in Bartow. One day we went to their house for a visit, and my aunt told her girls to go to the store to get a few groceries. I asked Mama if I could go too. Mama was hesitant, saying it was probably too long of a walk for me; but I begged, so she gave in.

It turned out that Mama was right. It was a pretty long walk, and I soon got tired and wanted to go back. The girls told me I could, but they proceeded to the store. Well, I turned and headed back and thought I was going the right way, but pretty soon I got scared because nothing looked right. I started crying, and an old lady on a porch saw me and called to me and invited me in. She gave me some cookies and asked me questions; then she said she knew the Rye family. Somehow she got hold of them and Mama, and they came to get me. I sure was glad when they drove up.

Moss-Teasing Day

When Daddy quit commercial fishing, we moved back to Suwannee County and in with Granddaddy Tip and Granny. I liked living with them, even though it was crowded. In addition to us, they often had a boarder staying with them.

Every morning Granny and Mama would cook breakfast, and that always included grinding coffee beans and making coffee.

The beans were roasted ahead of time. Granny poured green coffee beans in a pan and put them in her woodstove for roasting. While they roasted, she stirred them every so often with a wooden paddle. She kept roasting them until they turned a deep brown. (If Granny ever ran out of coffee beans—and sometimes she did—she would roast grits until they got brown and use them in place of coffee.)

Granddaddy Tip would *not* drink coffee, and if anybody ever asked why, he had the answer ready.

"I wouldn't kiss a pretty girl that drinks coffee! It'll turn you black!"

I had heard Granddaddy say that more times than I could count; and one moss-teasing day, I thought that information needed to be shared.

Back then, people made mattresses out of moss. A moss mattress was superior to a corn-shuck mattress, which was all that some people had to sleep on.

To make a moss mattress, Granny first made the cover, using a dark, heavy fabric; she cut it to size and stitched it up on her Singer treadle sewing machine.[27] Meanwhile, the men folks pulled the Spanish moss down from the oak trees and draped it over the rail fence that surrounded the house. Then Granny poured scalding water over the moss—water that she had heated in the washpot or sugar kettle. The scalding water served two purposes. First, it killed the red bugs [chiggers] that lived in the moss—you don't ever want to sleep on a moss mattress with red bugs—they will eat you up! Also, the boiling water would cause the gray outer covering of the moss to slough off, leaving black hair-like fibers that, when dried and stuffed into the cloth ticking, made a spongy-feeling mattress. When the mattress was fully stuffed, Granny would beat it into shape. Then it was fit for sleeping.

Naturally, of course, after some period of use, the weight of a person's body would pack down the moss fibers, and the mattress would become flat and bumpy. Then, it was time to "tease" it.

Teasing was a chore Granny seldom had to do by herself because there was a group of colored women in the community that would go around offering to tease your beds. Granny never had to pay them cash; the women would do the job for whatever she could give them in return—lard, cracklins, a piece of meat, greens, sweet potatoes, cane syrup—anything.

To tease the moss, the colored women would yank the moss stuffing out of the tick while they sat around in a circle in the shade of the live oak trees around the house, talking and laughing. Then they would fluff the moss by pulling it apart with their fingers—teasing it.

One of the colored women working that day was Mandy Caldwell. She helped Granny a lot, and I had been taught to call her *Aunt Mandy.*

That afternoon, Granny went to the kitchen to make the moss teasers some coffee. I was too little to be out teasing moss—I hadn't started to school yet—so I went with Granny and watched as she poured roasted beans in her coffee grinder. (I wish I knew what went with [happened to] her old coffee grinder; she probably gave it away after it got so you could buy coffee already ground.)

When the coffee was ready, Granny told the colored women they could come to the kitchen and get themselves a cup. Aunt Mandy was the first to come, and I was waiting. The minute she stepped inside—

"Aunt Mandy," I said, "that coffee is what turns you black!"

"Do, Jesus! Miss Dosia! Listen at that chile!" Aunt Mandy said, laughing as she slapped her thighs and doubled over. Then, to my surprise, she went right ahead and poured herself a full cup of that black coffee.

Aunt Minnie

Aunt Minnie was Granny's youngest sister, and she got married three times!

At first, she married a Brown, and they had two children, Bertie and Nellie.[28] Then one day, Mr. Brown went to work as usual but didn't return. Aunt Minnie got to looking and discovered her husband had taken *all* of his clothes.

After a while, Aunt Minnie decided Mr. Brown was gone for good, so she married Levi Rankin.

Granny couldn't stand Mr. Rankin. He owned a gas station out in the country and would let people buy gas on credit; but then if they didn't pay him soon enough, he would post their names, along with the amount they owed him, on a big board outside his store, for anybody passing by to see.

One day we went to check on Aunt Minnie, who was expecting a baby and having some problems. When we got there, Granny saw that Mr. Rankin had killed a yellowhammer—to make soup for them to eat! That made Granny so mad. We didn't eat yellowhammer; Granny considered it a scavenger bird. So, Granny took Aunt Minnie home with us. Aunt Minnie's baby, a girl, was born a few days later at Granny's house. She was named O.D., but I don't know what the initials stood for.

Aunt Minnie and Mr. Rankin finally separated, and then she changed her name back to Brown. (She also changed O.D.'s, so that it matched hers, Bertie's, and Nellie's).

But then Aunt Minnie's name changed *again* when she married Mr. Peak, who was much older than she was. His place, known as the Peak place, was east of Ladyland (the school Mama and her brother, Alonzo, had attended when they were children and the school I would go to when I was old enough).

As it turned out, Aunt Minnie and her kids hardly got settled on the Peak place before old man Peak died. Aunt

Minnie then moved her family to Branford, and *we* moved to the Peak place.

Dipping Cows

On the Peak place, Daddy farmed and raised livestock. Back then, it was open range, so farmers and ranchers didn't have to keep their animals fenced in as they do today. The cows and hogs were allowed to roam the woods at will. But the woods were full of ticks which naturally got on the animals; so every few weeks, the cattle would need to be run through a dipping vat to rid them of ticks.

The vat was a long runway of concrete that sloped down and then back up so cows could be driven through it and through the water and tick killer it held (I think the water contained creosote).

The vat was close to the Drew Bridge on the Suwannee River. On dipping day, Daddy would get on his horse and round up the cows hanging around the Peak place and drive them over and pick up the ones around Granddaddy's house. Then he'd head through the hammock (the wooded area where he liked to hunt quail and squirrels) picking up the cattle grazing in the woods. He would then drive all of the cattle to and through the dipping vat.

Daddy was good at rounding up and driving cattle. Daddy *knew* how to handle a cow whip!

Blackberries for Granny

Blackberry vines were growing in the edge of the woods around the Peak place and around the Ladyland School, which had let out for the summer. After noticing that the berries were getting ripe, Harold and I asked Mama if we could go out and pick some. Mama gave us a bucket to put them in and we set out. Pretty quick, we had picked a pint or maybe even a quart.

"We should take these over to Granny!" I told Harold. "Go back to the house and ask Mama if we can take the blackberries to Granny."

We could see Granny and Granddaddy Tip's log house across the field from Ladyland School. We could either follow the road to their house or cut across Granddaddy's field and get there quicker.

Harold ran back to the Peak house to ask Mama and then came running back to where I was waiting.

"Yeah, we can take 'em," he said.

So we started out and walked a little ways across the field toward Granny's house. But we were not even halfway there, when Harold changed his mind.

"I don't want to go." he said, "I want to go back home."

I turned around and went part of the way back with him because he was real little—about three years old. I watched him go into the house, and then I turned and headed back towards Granny's with the blackberries.

As I got close to Granny's yard, I saw Daddy. He was on his horse, popping his cow whip in the air, driving the cows. He was also headed toward Granny and Granddaddy's house. It was cow-dipping day.

Daddy made it to Granny's with his cows about the same time that I got there with the blackberries. But instead of going ahead and rounding up Granddaddy's cows, like he usually did, he started getting down off his horse.

"Come here, Mutt!" Daddy yelled at me. Mutt was what he always called me. I could tell Daddy was mad.

"Your mama done told you and Harold that y'all couldn't come over here to your Granny's by yourself— and you did it anyway!"

"But, Daddy, Mama said we *could* come! I sent Harold to the house to ask if we could come and he said Mama said we *could*. Then Harold up and changed his mind—said he didn't want to go to Granny's, so I walked nearly all the way back to the house with him. Then I come on to bring Granny the—"

"No, Mutt." Daddy butted in. "Your mama said you couldn't come, and you came anyway, and I'm gonna wear you out!"

Daddy started pulling the cow whip off the saddle and was fixin' to climb over the fence to where I was when Granny came out of the house—

"Milton, you ain't gonna whip that child!"

"Yes, I am, Dosia! She's my young'un! She didn't mind her mama, and she's gonna get a whipping."

Granny hurried across the yard and stood between Daddy and me.

"Milton, you are *not* gonna whip this child! She has never told me a lie—not once!—and if she said her mama said she could come, that's the way she understood it. Ethel didn't tell you a lie! You ain't gone beat that young'un unless you beat me first."

Daddy stared at Granny, stared at me, then he turned around, climbed back up in the saddle, and headed off on his horse to gather up the rest of the cows in the woods.

Uncle Sammy and Aunt Lou

Uncle Sammy was Granny's only brother. Sometimes our family would visit him and his wife, but when we did, Mama made sure we always left their house well before mealtime. Mama didn't want to be invited to stay and eat, because Sammy's wife's kitchen simply didn't meet Mama's standards of sanitation (Mama washed everything, including rice, before she cooked it and taught me to do it too). But Mama was crazy about Sammy's daughter Katy, and Daddy got along well with the man she married, Raz Lawson. The four of them ended up becoming good friends, visiting often.

Granny's sister, Louise—I called her Aunt Lou—was married to Granddaddy Tip's brother, Uncle Lee. They lived down the road from Ladyland School. At first we saw a lot of them, but as they had more and more children—they had eight—we saw them less and less.

Aunt Mary Ann

Granny often went to visit her sister, Mary Ann Renfroe, in Lafayette County, and I loved to go with her. Daddy would walk with us to the river, where he kept his boat near the Drew Bridge, a railroad bridge.[29] He would put the boat in the river and take us to the other side. On the way there, Granny and Daddy would figure out a plan about when and where he would pick us up.

On that side of the river, Granny and I would walk as far as the Morgan place and visit with them a while, giving us time to rest before walking on to Aunt Mary Ann's. The Morgans had several young'uns (their son, John, taught at Ladyland, but not until after I started to school there).

After resting and visiting with the Morgans, we'd continue on to Aunt Mary Ann's. She had a daughter named Maude, a son Johnny, and another son (I can't remember his name) that I didn't like—not because he ever mistreated me, but because he ignored me. Maude and Johnny were several years older than I was—they were probably old enough to be married, but weren't—and they treated me like a queen, giving me candy and stuff. Occasionally, they would even have a pencil and pad for me so I could write and draw.

Sometimes, we spent just the day at Aunt Mary Ann's. Other times, we stayed two or three days. After our visits, Granny and I would walk back to the river where Daddy was supposed to pick us up, and Daddy never forgot. If he wasn't already at the river bank waiting, we wouldn't have to wait long before we would see him paddling his boat across the Suwannee toward us.

I didn't get to go visiting with Granny as much after I started to school, and it wasn't long before Aunt Mary Ann died. She was, I think, much older than her husband. After she died, we lost track of her husband and the Renfroe children. I don't think any of the children ever married.[30]

My Teacher's Missing Leg

We were still living on the Peak place when I started to school at Ladyland. A girl named Merine Warren was in my class, and she became my best friend.[ii]

My first schoolteacher was Mrs. Etta Carver. She was an older lady, and she had lost part of her leg. I don't know what had happened, but her leg had been cut off just above her knee. She wore an artificial leg, but back then, an artificial leg was a terrible piece of equipment.

She was boarding with Granny and Granddaddy Tip, and one night when we were over at their house, Mrs. Carver was complaining about her wooden leg. It was old and worn down and it had a little nail or something sticking out of it that was hurting her, where it attached to her stump. We were all sitting in front of the fireplace—it was wintertime—and she asked Daddy if he would see if he could fix her leg. He said he would try. Well, Mrs. Carver pulled her dress up right then and there, yanked that wooden leg off in front of everybody, and reached it out to Daddy. I can still see the look on Daddy's face when he took her leg. Without saying a word, he got up, got a pair of pliers, pulled the nail out, and handed the leg back.

Daddy's Bail

Daddy would do just about anything to make a few dollars. Besides farming and raising livestock, at one time or another, he drove a truck for the State Road Department, worked in a garage, fished, cleared land, hauled fruit,

---

[ii] "I thought Ethel Rye was a little rich girl," Merine Warren Hunter said, when she and Ethel were reminiscing in their eighties, "because Ethel came to class on the first day of school with a brand new box of unbroken crayons!"

worked in a sawmill, guarded convicts—and bootlegged—though I didn't know about the bootlegging at the time he was doing it. I didn't find out until after he was out of jail and Granny told me. Oh, she didn't just come right out with it. She *had* to tell me to help my feelings.

It was when I found her looking through some things she had pulled out of her trunk. She had laid a bunch of papers out on her bed and was looking through some little books. I happened to walk over by the bed where she was—and Granny wasn't one to keep secrets. I asked about the papers, and she explained that they were bank receipts. Then I wanted to know about the little books, and she said they were savings passbooks for us grandchildren.

"The passbooks show how much money I've put in the bank for all three of y'all," she said, meaning Harold and me and our cousin, Buck.

"How much money do I have?" I wanted to know.

Granny hesitated, but then said that Harold and I didn't have any money in the bank anymore, that only Buck still had money. I guess I looked confused. What I was hearing was that Harold and I *once* had money, but now we didn't. Yet our cousin Buck, who lived way up in Baltimore, *still* had money! *What happened to ours?* Trying to explain it to me, Granny all of a sudden got tears in her eyes.

"Honey," she said, "I had to take your money out to pay to keep your daddy out of jail."

"Why was Daddy in jail?" I wanted to know.

"Oh, he didn't do anything real bad," she explained. "He just got caught bootlegging, that's all."

Granny knew how to smooth things over and make me feel better.

Times were hard back then, and it wasn't until later that I recognized how hard it must have been for Granny and Granddaddy to come up with money to put in our savings accounts. Granddaddy had, I learned later, designated a pig for each grandchild when one of his hogs had a litter, and when the pigs were fattened up and sold, the money was put into that child's account.[31]

Living in Punta Gorda

By the time I entered the second grade, we were living down the state again, in Punta Gorda. I remember I had my eighth birthday there.

Granddaddy and Grandmama Rye and Aunt Cora and Uncle Will Taylor lived in Punta Gorda, and we moved there so Daddy could work with his daddy and Uncle Will on Uncle Will's boat in the Gulf.

The catch of the day: two large tarpon. Ethel's grandfather, John Henry Rye, is in the center. He is wearing a wide-brimmed hat and holding a pole. "I don't recognize the others," Ethel said. "They probably just wanted to be in the picture."

This time, we didn't move in with Grandmama and Granddaddy Rye, as we had done before when we moved down the state. Instead, Daddy rented a room for us from Mrs. Singletery, a woman that Aunt Cora knew.

After Mrs. Singletery got to know us, she started inviting us kids to play in her living quarters, and she even gave us some old clothes to play with. After we lived there a while, she opened up the whole house to us. We had the run of the place.

It was the beginning of the Great Depression, and times were hard. People coming by on the train would hop off and want a place to stay; and people walking along the road would want food. Mrs. Singletery would give them a room when she had one, and Mama would always feed them.

Most of them didn't have money to pay, though, so they would work in the yard doing whatever Mrs. Singletery or Mama needed done.

While living in Punta Gorda, we sometimes got packages from Granny and Granddaddy Tip. They'd pack up cured meat and stuff and send it to us.

After a while of trying to make a living fishing, Daddy decided we should move back to Suwannee County. Mrs. Singletery cried when we left.

After that, we didn't get to see much of Daddy's family, and Granddaddy Rye died (he was much older than Grandmama Rye) before I ever got to see him again.

When we got back to Suwannee County, we moved in with Granddaddy Tip and Granny.

A Summer in Callahan
Before long, Daddy got another job with the State Road Department. This time, he didn't have to live at the construction site like he had done when he was helping build bridges. This time, Mama and Harold and I got to move with him to the town of Callahan, near Jacksonville.

I remember a man in Callahan, a barber, who couldn't walk, but he could cut hair, sitting on a stool with his legs folded under his bottom; and there was a woman in Callahan that gave me and Harold a little dog that we named Fanny. Fanny was honey colored and not very big. The woman said she was a Belgian police dog. Fanny never barked, but if a stranger came up to the house, she'd get between us and the stranger and start growling.

"Will that dog bite?" the people would ask, and they wouldn't take another step until we told Fanny it was okay.

That dog would have died for me and Harold, but I don't remember what ever happened to her.

I don't remember, either, how old I was then; but we lived in Callahan during the summer months so Harold and I never went to school there. With moving around a lot, we got behind in school. Back then, the school term went for just six months of the year. Sometimes we'd be in school at one place, but by the time we moved and got settled somewhere else, school would be out. So when a school term started, we were often way behind, and we would have to work hard to catch up. One year, I made up one grade, and another year I think I changed grades three times.

When we first got to Callahan that summer, we found out that jumping board was all the rage. If you couldn't jump board, you couldn't do anything! One day Harold and I started stacking bricks and rocks and things up so we could raise the board up to jump higher, but the things kept falling down. Daddy saw our problem and said he would make us a good jump board.

When Daddy made us something, he always made the best. I remember when he, later on, fixed us a swing on a tree limb; he used a good rope and a good board for a seat.

For our jump board, Daddy got a big board; it must have been a 2"x14" board, about ten-feet long. He put it up on a big block and got it balanced just right before leaving Harold and me to play.

"Now, Mutt," Harold said to me—he called me Mutt like Daddy did—"jump me up real high! I think I can fly like a bird!"

So, I jumped just as high as I could and landed hard on that board. It sent Harold flying like a bird—until he hit the ground.

Granny and Granddaddy Tip's Place

After Daddy's job in Callahan ended, we moved back to Granny and Granddaddy's for good, and Daddy started helping Granddaddy farm. Sometimes Daddy still went off to work somewhere for a few days or weeks to make a little extra money, but Mama, Harold, and I always stayed put.

I was crazy about Granny and Granddaddy Tip and fell asleep in Granddaddy's lap many a night—until I was nearly grown. But he and Harold never got along very well.

Tip and Dosia Lanier; Harold, Delma, and Ethel Rye; and Cary Neely

When Harold was little, Granddaddy would tease him—probably too much—and as Harold got older, Granddaddy was always getting on to him about something. In Mama's eyes, though, Harold could do no wrong.

Granny and Granddaddy's log house had a porch all the way across the front and the back. Between the porches was the fireroom—our living and sleeping area. Entering from the front porch, the fireplace was on the right (south wall); Granny and Granddaddy's bed was to the left of the front door; and the bed that Harold and I slept in was to the left of the back door. Harold and I shared a bed until I was a teenager.

The back porch was, like the front, as wide as the house. Daddy had, some time back, closed in one side of the back porch to make that little bedroom for him and Mama where he could lie on the bed and keep the door closed with his feet if he wanted to.

Mama had grown up in that house. When she was a little girl, the house had no kitchen. Her mama, my Granny, had cooked all their meals in the fireplace. At some point, though, they had built a kitchen, which was connected to the main house by a long boardwalk, and the new kitchen had its own fireplace for cooking.

By the time we started staying with them, Granny had a wood-burning stove with four eyes; it sat next to the kitchen's brick fireplace, and Granddaddy had nailed a piece of tin over that fireplace to seal it up. The stovepipe of the woodstove went through a hole he cut in the tin, so smoke could escape up the brick chimney.

Granny and Mama were both good cooks. They worked together in the kitchen, except when the weather was real cold and they just needed to heat a few things up. At times like that, Granny preferred the open fireplace in the main living area. She thought that reheating food there was much simpler than having to heat up the woodstove. She would bunch the red-hot coals up under a four-legged trivet and set the pots on the trivet.

We didn't eat much fresh meat. Granddaddy always had cows; but with no refrigeration, they couldn't kill a cow and keep it for any length of time unless they boiled it and preserved it in canning jars.

They butchered hogs, though, every fall, and smoked the meat. They dug a hole in the ground, put fat-lightered splinters [kindling] in it to get a fire going, and then added green oak, pecan, or hickory wood for smoke. After the meat smoked, it hung in the smokehouse and we could cut off pieces to eat as we needed them. They also made sausage. After the ground pork was stuffed in casings, it was fried up and stored in five-gallon cans of lard. When you were ready to eat some, you just pulled out a link or two, let the excess fat drip back into the can, and it was ready—precooked—but they always heated it up.

Eventually, Daddy built a refrigerator where we could keep a few things cold. First, he dug a hole in the ground under the edge of the house. In the hole, he put a metal box that he surrounded with sawdust for insulation. That's where he put the ice that he bought by the fifty-pound block. With ice in the hole, milk from the cow would stay cool and sweet for a long time—sometimes for more than a day. Having sweet milk was never really a problem, though, because Granny milked her cows twice a day. Granny always had cows for milking.

Gardening
Granddaddy Tip always planted a garden, so we could eat greens, peas, and beans almost any time of year.

To get the garden soil ready, they'd put up a rail fence to create a cow lot. After a few weeks, when manure was piling up, they would move the cows and turn the manure

Tip and Dosia Lanier's house is in the background. Left to right: Delma, before she married; a school-teacher, who boarded with them; and Dosia.

under with a plow. Then, they'd put the cows back in for a few more weeks to build up more manure and then turn the ground over again. After about three times of that, they'd move the cows and turn it one last time. Then, the next spring or fall, they could plant a garden there.

After a year or two of having a vegetable garden in that fertile spot, they'd plant sweet potatoes there. The year after that, they would plant cane. If they planted cane in soil that was too fertile, the syrup from it would be real dark. We liked the looks of light syrup better than dark, and thought it tasted just as good.

Granddaddy Tip planted corn every spring. For good creamed corn, we'd break the ears off when it was to the milk stage, when it was soft enough you could scrape it off the cob. The next stage is the starchy stage, just before it starts to dry. When dry, it was time to pull the fodder, the blades or leaves, from the corn stalks.

When we pulled fodder, other families would come help us, and then we'd go help them. As we pulled the leaves, we draped them over one of the ears still on the stalk to let them dry. Later, the men would bind the leaves into bundles, about ten inches in diameter, and store them in the loft of the horse barn. During the winter, Granddaddy fed the fodder to his horses and to his mule, Roadie.

Granddaddy had a nice barn, and each of his horses had a stall. The number of animals varied, but he always had at least one horse plus his mule for plowing. At one time he also had a carriage that would seat four people. It had an umbrella or parasol for shielding us from the rain and sun.

Fowl

Granny raised chickens, geese, and turkeys for us to eat and for their eggs. She also had ducks and guineas. Ducks don't like to sit on their nests, so Granny would put the duck eggs under a sitting chicken to get the eggs to hatch. After they hatched, the hen would think the baby ducks were her little chicks. But when they headed for water—which ducks naturally do but chicks don't—the hen would have a fit.

Guineas don't like sitting on nests either, so Granny would put the guinea eggs under a sitting turkey. After the eggs hatched, the turkey hen would take care of the little guineas. But the little guineas would do things that surprised the mama turkey. For instance, when a hawk came around, a turkey never made much noise—just a little yelp or gobble sound that wasn't very loud, perhaps because they were larger and didn't feel threatened. But the little guineas would make the biggest racket you ever heard when a hawk came anywhere near. When they started making a racket, the mama turkey would pace back and forth like she was perplexed and embarrassed that her offspring could be so noisy.

Granddaddy Tip purely hated Granny's Blue Runner ducks because they would eat the corn he planted. He would hardly get the kernels in the ground before they went after them—running their bills down the row and scooping the kernels out—leaving a little trench in the soil. And if they happened to miss a few kernels, they would eat the tender plants as soon as they broke through.

After a while, Granddaddy got Granny to start wringing the Blue Runners' necks, so we had several good duck dinners before they were all gone.

Our Pet Squirrel
Sometimes baby squirrels would fall out of their nests and we'd pick them up, put them in a cage, and give them names. Sometimes they would bite, too, especially if you had the smell of food on your hands. We named one Stormy, and he was our favorite. We found him during a rainstorm when he fell out of the nest and nearly drowned. He was the friendliest one we ever had. Mama would let Stormy out of the cage, and he'd sit on her arm and let her comb his fur. Finally, we got so we didn't make him stay in

the cage. He'd come in the open window and sit on the end of the ironing board for Mama and Granny to brush him. But then he got so he thought he owned the place and would act like a guard dog, trying to bite strangers when they walked up on the porch. I don't remember what happened to him.

Cane Grindings

Granddaddy always had a crop of sugar cane, and every fall before the first frost we had cane grindings to make syrup. A cane grinding always drew lots of people from the community, and it lasted all day long.

In the cane patch, the stalks were cut off pretty close to the ground. (The stubbles were left in the ground so they would make a crop the next year.) Then the stalks were hauled from the cane patch to the backyard where they would be run through the grinder. The grinder was turned with the help of a pole and a mule: one end of the pole was connected to the grinder and the other end to the mule, Roadie; she walked around and around the grinder to turn the gears to grind the cane. Granddaddy or somebody would feed the cane through the grinder, a few stalks at a time. The juice ran down into a barrel where we could ladle out some to drink, but most of it would be transferred to the sugar kettle to be cooked down to syrup.

The sugar kettle was a big iron vat about five feet across that sat on a brick foundation, the furnace. Inside that, the fire was built using wood and spent cane stalks. At the back was a brick chimney for the smoke to go up.

One cane grinding day, Harold and the Herring boys started messing around the furnace, throwing cane knots at one another, and one of them threw a charred knot that had been near the fire. It was covered with ashes, and somehow both Dan Herring and Harold ended up with their eyes hurt. They were not taken to the doctor when it happened, but later, when Uncle Raleigh came to visit and saw Harold's red, swollen eyes, he took him straight to the doctor in Jacksonville. The doctor said Mama should put hot compresses on his eyes and put special drops in them, and they eventually got well. I don't know about Dan's eyes—how long it took for his to get well. I know he eventually went nearly blind, but I don't think it was the cane knot that caused it.

Harold's school photo (The spots developed on the photo while it was stored away.)

As far as I remember, that was the only accident that ever happened on cane grinding day. It was normally nothing but fun.

After the cane juice was in the sugar kettle, it had to be cooked a long time—for several hours—and, as it cooked, foam would rise to the top. This foam was skimmed off and put in a drum (these skimmings were saved for later). While the men folks hung around the sugar kettle, stirrin' and skimmin' and jawin', the women would often go in the house and sit and quilt or shell pecans or something.

Late one cane grinding day, the women were in the house, and Uncle Lee was the one doing the stirring and skimming as the other men looked on and milled about.

The syrup was nearly ready because the polecat—the candy that collected around the rim—was beginning to form. Everybody liked to scrape the polecat off the hot kettle, using a strip cut from the outside of a cane stalk. We would stand around the kettle and eat it, warm and stringy.

As the polecat was beginning to form that day, Dave Tomlinson, a neighbor, walked up. He and Granddaddy were about the same size, and Granddaddy looked him up and down, admiring what he was wearing.

"Aye God, buddy, I shore do like them britches you got on!"

"Shore 'nough, Uncle Tip? Want to swap?"

Granddaddy said that he did, so the two men proceeded to take off their britches right there in the middle of the yard. That's when Uncle Lee—knowing the men had their britches off—hollered toward the house.

"Polecat, girls! Come get the polecat!"

The women started pouring out of the doors and open windows heading for the candy, and Mr. Tomlinson and Granddaddy had to run for cover.

When the juice finally turned into caramel-colored syrup, it was put in bottles, jars, cans, and buckets. There was always enough syrup for us to have all year and for Granddaddy to share. Everybody that was there that day, helping or watching, got to take some home.

Sometimes, Granddaddy also made brown sugar, by continuing to cook some of the syrup until it got a little darker and started to form sugar crystals. Then it was poured into wooden barrels that had holes drilled in them. The holes were partially plugged with pieces of cane stalk—but loose enough to let a little of the dark syrup trickle out as the sugar continued to form. The sugar crystals stayed in the barrel and what drained out the holes was molasses. Granddaddy fed that to his animals; we didn't like molasses.

The Skimmings

The day after the cane grinding, Granddaddy and some of his men friends would put the skimmings to use—but not right there in the open yard by the sugar kettle where it would have been convenient. No, they hauled the drum of skimmings across the yard and way out to a clay hole in the middle of the field. The clay hole was where they had dug clay out of the ground for putting on the dirt roads, but more importantly, it was surrounded by trees. What they were up to was secret because it was against the law.

Water collected in the very bottom of the clay hole when it rained, but there was still room in the hole for the barrel of skimmings and the necessary equipment. This was where Granddaddy and his friends made what he called *spirits for medicine*. It was white lightning—clear as water. Straight from the jug, it would knock your hat off.

Granddaddy's still could not be seen from the house or the road, so the men thought they were keeping it a secret. But Harold and I knew what they were up to, and we would slip down there, hide behind a tree, and watch them work.

Granddaddy didn't drink the stuff from the jug—at least I never saw him do it—but he used his *spirits* regularly in the toddy he made for himself every morning without fail:

> 1 cup hot water
> 1 teaspoon sugar
> 1 tablespoon of spirits

Granny's and Mama's Remedies
They had all kinds of remedies and medicines to make you well. If you sprained an ankle or pulled a muscle, you got rubbed with white lightning or camphor. If you stuck a nail in your foot, you soaked it in kerosene. For cuts or bruises, they used turpentine. And Granny thought sulfur water would cure about anything that ailed you. She loved to drink it, and so did Granddaddy Rye. Granddaddy Tip, on the other hand, didn't care for it one bit, and I agreed with him. It stunk something awful.

Worse than sulfur water was asafetida. Oh, it really stunk! And it was one of Granny's favorite remedies. She pronounced it ass-a-*fid*-uh-tee. She would take a block of it and break it up in water and then soak a ball of string in that; we had to wear that stinking thing around our necks to ward off disease. I think it protected you from disease because it smelled so bad that other people and germs couldn't stand to get near you! Granny and Mama would also fill up a bottle with that stuff to use if we got a stomachache.

"Go get a drink of ass-a-*fid*-uh-tee," they would say, and sometimes just hearing that would cure the bellyache. The stuff was grey—it looked like mud!

When people got malaria, they made them wear a camphor gum—a block of camphor they wrapped up and made you wear around your neck on a string. They also made you take Grove's Chill Tonic.

Lots of people got malaria when the river came up high and the mosquitoes were bad. Some people died from malaria, but many a person lived. They finally came out with medicine that would break a person's fever.

I had malaria when I was about nine. First I got the cold shakes and shivers—all kinds of quilts wouldn't keep me warm. Then I had a high fever that lasted for days. The medicine they gave me to break the fever was yellow, and when I finished taking it, I was yellow too.[32]

Harold's Remedy

When Mama blistered her heel one time, Harold told her that he knew what to do for that. He went in the house and came back with something he had mixed up. He asked Mama if he could put that on her blisters and she let him, not knowing it was a concoction of liniment and alcohol.

He didn't put much on Mama's blisters before she started dancing and then running. I think she ran around the house twice before she quit. Seeing Mama run like that was surprising because Mama didn't often get in a hurry.[33]

Roadie

I think Granddaddy's mule was as old as my mama. She's the one that walked around in a circle to pull the gears to grind the cane. Boy, she did like that cane juice! When she got tired, she would stop in her tracks and wouldn't take another step until she got a bucket of juice.

One morning, Granddaddy got up and made an announcement about Roadie.

"I'm gonna set Roadie free today. She's earned it."

He opened the gate and off Roadie went—though not for good. She would roam the woods for a few hours each day, but she would always come back home for food and water. Sometimes, she'd come up in the yard and stick her head in the open window of the house, and we'd give her a piece of corn bread.

Harold and I loved to ride her. We'd nudge her up by an old stump or log and climb up on her back—no saddle, no bridle, just bareback. She would ride off in a trot. But later, when she got tired of us, she'd run fast—then suddenly put on the brakes with her front feet and lower her head and we'd go flying off over her head![34]

Tip Lanier, plowing with Roadie, before he set her free

Corn Shuck Scrubbers and Newspaper Fans

Granny taught me so many things—like how to make a button buzz and how to make corn cob dolls, broom sage brooms, corn shuck scrubbers, and newspaper fans.

She made her indoor brooms out of broom sage, a grass (sedge) that grows tall—up to three or four feet. The lower stems of the grass are stiff and their tops resemble fine straw. Granny would cut the grass off right at the ground, strip off the rough leaves, and gather enough that she could just reach around the bundle with her fingers and thumb. Then, holding it tight, she would start wrapping the bundle at the cut ends of the grass with twine or some cloth string torn off some old clothes. She would work her way down the stems to form the broom handle, then turn back, wrapping it a second time until she reached the cut end where she would tie the string off. The unwrapped, softer ends of the grass would be the part that swept the floor. We had to bend over just a little bit when sweeping since a broom-sage broom wasn't as long as the brooms you can buy today.

Granny preferred not to use her broom-sage broom for sweeping the yard. For that she liked to use dog fennels.

The yard had to be kept clean as a safety measure. In case of a fire in the woods, the house would be less likely to catch and burn. In addition, a clean swept sand yard would record tracks of animals. If you saw snake tracks, you needed to see where exactly they led. They might lead to the house. A snake could get in an open window or door or slide though a crack in the floor.

Granny made her own corn-shuck scrub brushes too, and taught me how. First, she found a board and got Granddaddy to cut off a ten- or twelve-inch piece and bore half-inch diameter holes in it every inch or so with his auger hand drill. The holes were to hold the shucks. She also had him make a slanted hole in the middle; that was to hold the long wooden handle. She would then shuck some dry corn and cut the hard stem off the shuck. Next, she would stick a few shucks through each hole—all except the handle hole—going up through each hole with the loose ends of the shuck until she pulled it so tight that only one to two inches of the shuck showed on the other side. When she finished filling the holes with shucks and put the thing in a tub of soapy water, the corn shucks would swell up so tight they would never fall out. It made a pretty good scrub brush for cleaning the old floors in the log house. (I made and used scrub brushes to scrub my floors too, after I married. But when I could afford to buy a good bristle brush, I tried that and found it lasted a lot longer than the shuck scrubber, which wore down pretty quick on rough wood floors.)

Granny also knew how to make a paper fan that she used to keep flies off the food. She took two sections of newspaper and draped them, side by side, over a straight stick, laying each fold line along the stick. She tacked the newspaper, along the fold line, to the wood. Then, with scissors, she trimmed the newspaper shorter, so it extended down just ten or twelve inches from the stick, before she cut into the paper's edge every inch or so to make fringe.

If the gnats and flies were bad when it was time to eat—and they always were in warm weather—Granny would stand over the table fanning the fringed newspaper back and forth just above the bowls of food on the table while everybody helped their plates. Then she would hurry and help her plate before covering the bowls of food with clean muslin dishtowels.

Earning a Little Cash
Granddaddy made a little money playing his fiddle at square dances, but I don't remember—as Harold said he did—that Granddaddy came home with "his top hat full of money." Granddaddy didn't need *much* money. He grew about everything we put in our stomachs. But he did need cash if he wanted tobacco (he chewed, and Granny dipped snuff). So he would sell a pig every now and then, and Granny would sell eggs. He would also take people from out of town fox hunting and get paid a little for that.

Granddaddy also knew how to train dogs to hunt. Daddy was even better at that than Granddaddy. People would buy dogs and drop them off for Daddy to train. If a dog didn't do what it was supposed to, Daddy would stomp on its neck until it did do it. I thought Daddy was too hard and rough with the dogs—it's a wonder he didn't break some dog's neck—but his customers were happy with how well the dogs could hunt, point, and retrieve when they took their dogs hunting.

The Fox Hunter
After we lived with Granddaddy and Granny a few years, Daddy closed in the other side of the back porch to make a bedroom for Harold. After it was finished, Harold slept in there most of the time.

I still slept in the fireroom with Granny and Granddaddy. Sometimes when the weather got real cold, Harold would still come and get in the bed with me—even after I thought I was much too old to be sleeping with my brother.

One night, I had gone to sleep in my bed, and Harold had gone to bed in his own room. I was sound asleep and didn't know when Granddaddy came in real late from fox hunting with old man Sullivan. I didn't hear Granddaddy say to old man Sullivan—"Aye God, buddy, you might as well just spend the night."

The next morning I was up and dressed when it was time to get Harold up, so Mama told me to go wake him. I went to the door of his room on the porch and called him several times. "Harold, it's time to get up!" He didn't answer. "Harold, Mama said to 'get up!' "

He still didn't answer, so I pushed the door open and went in his room. The wooden shutter that served as a window was fastened shut so it was totally dark in there.

"You gone be late for school," I told him in the dark. He still didn't answer, so I went over to his bed and grabbed a shoulder and gave it a good hard shake. Then the quilt slid, and I saw that it wasn't Harold I was shaking. It was old man Sullivan!

Harold was on the *other* side of the bed, and he came out of bed and out of that room laughing his head off.

After my wake-up call, I don't think old man Sullivan ever spent the night there again.

Mama Didn't Care

When I was in the fourth grade, our school classes were being held in different places in the Ladyland community. The old Ladyland School house had been torn down, so a new one could be built in the same spot.

First through third grades met in a one-room house just off the road south of Granddaddy Tip's place. Fourth through eighth grades met in a two-room house on Sheriff Lyle's place.[35] (See map on p. 135.) My fourth grade class was in the same room with fifth and sixth graders; seventh and eighth graders met in the other room.

By the fourth grade, I had started to hate my hair. It was real long because I had never been allowed to get it cut. At night, Mama would roll it up using strings and rags, and I had to sleep on that mess. When she took it down in the morning, she was real careful—didn't comb or brush it—because that would spoil the ringlets. I hated them. As far as I was concerned, they were good for nothing but attracting the attention of boys and bees. In school, the boys would stick pencils up my ringlets—C. G. Howell, for one; and outside, bees would crawl in them. A lot of folks kept bee hives on their property back then, and Mama had been stung trying to get bees out of my hair.

One day at recess, somebody told me that Miss Hillhouse—she taught the lower grades—knew how to cut hair; so that day on my walk home, I stopped by where she taught and asked if she would cut mine. She said she would if it was okay with my mother. I went straight home and asked Mama.

"I don't really care," she said, "but your daddy would have a fit."

The next day after school I went and told Miss Hillhouse that Mama didn't care. I didn't bother to mention Daddy. So, Miss Hillhouse sat me down and cut my hair real short.

"Your daddy is gonna have a fit," Mama said, when I got home.

It seemed like a long, long time before Daddy finally came home that day. I knew I would be getting a whipping, and I sure knew what Daddy's whippings were like. But I didn't care. I was glad that I finally had short hair.

The minute Daddy walked in, he took one look at me, and I could tell he didn't like what he was seeing.

"How come you did that?" Daddy asked.

I didn't answer him because I knew what was coming no matter what I said. I just stood there waiting for him to take off his belt or get the razor strap. I still didn't care. My hair was short and I liked it. Daddy just kept on staring at me. He

Ethel, after Miss Hillhouse, a Ladyland teacher, cut her hair

stared for the longest time before he finally turned around and walked off and never said another word about my hair.

Granny's Tactical Solution
As I mentioned, Granny dipped snuff, and she liked the kind she called "railroad" snuff. She bought it by the

bladder—something that looked like a sausage. It was about two-inches thick and three- to six-inches long. When she got home from the store, she always transferred a little of the snuff from the bladder to her little snuff box that she kept in her dress or apron pocket.

Some folks were messy with their dipping and spitting, but Granny was always careful with hers. She never let it drool down her chin like some did, and she carried a coffee can around to spit in.

Granddaddy Tip, on the other hand, wasn't so careful with his tobacco juice. If there was a fire in the fireplace, he would spit the juice in the flames—you could hear it sizzle—but when he missed, it made a real mess. To remedy the situation, Granny started sprinkling white sand all over the brick hearth to absorb that nasty spit. When dry, the sand could be swept into the fireplace.

Later on, Granddaddy got so he would try to spit all the way from the bed to the fire, and his spit would sometimes end up on the floor beside the bed! That made Granny real mad. But she remedied that too. She started sprinkling sand on the floor on his side of the bed, and that took care of that.

Sharing with Others
The train track ran right in front of Granny and Granddaddy's house. Folks would hop off the train right at their house as the train slowed for the stop at Wilmarth, and some were hungry.

Granddaddy and Granny didn't have much, but they always had a big garden and were always willing to share their vegetables.[36] Plus, there was meat in the smokehouse. If Granddaddy found out somebody needed food, he would fix that in a hurry.

"Dosia, go out there and cut 'em down a side or shoulder of meat."

Then he'd turn back to them. "Ya got syrup? . . . sweet taters? . . . meal? . . . grits?"

If not, Granddaddy would give them whatever they were lacking. He always grew sweet potatoes and always had syrup; and he had dry corn that could be ground into grits and meal at the mill over by Luraville.

Over the years, a number of school teachers from Ladyland boarded with Granddaddy and Granny, and as I said before, we lived with them more than anywhere else. We were living there (but no boarders were) when, one day, Granddaddy went out and brought back a family that needed a place to stay.

He said he was out on his horse riding around in the hammock, checking on his livestock (it was still open range then) and decided to stop by and say hello to Mrs. Renah Robins and her two boys, Ernest and Jack. At the time, Mr. Robins was in prison for bootlegging (just as Daddy had been). When Granddaddy got to the Robinses' house that day, he discovered that the family was just about on starvation; so he came back home, hitched his horse to the wagon, and went back over there and got them and their clothes and stuff, and brought them home with him. They stayed there with us quite a while—until Mr. Robins got out of prison.

While the Robinses were living with us, Harold and I built a little wood-burning stove under the oak trees, and I would cook out there for all the boys—Harold, the Robins boys, and the George boys that lived nearby.

We all went to the same school and knew each other well. Jack Robins was about my age so we were in the same class. One year, Jack and I were in a school play together—and got married!

In real life Jack was more like a brother to me than anything else, but that didn't stop people from speculating.

"Ethel might go with some other boys," people would say, "but she and Jack Robins will get married some day."

A Band of Gypsies

One time, a group of gypsies came to our area. Their last name was Kelly. They were driving a stripped-down Model T that pulled a wagon. Granddaddy was neighborly with them, like he was with everybody, and shared sugar cane and sweet potatoes with them. They set up camp in the woods near Granddaddy Tip's place. One of the girls was real pretty and slept in the wagon; the others slept in tents. They cooked on a campfire.

During the day, the women would go out and sell lace and material to people in the community. But they carried bugs with them, and they would turn the bugs loose in people's houses. Then they would ask for money to get rid of the bugs. They would also tell your fortune.

Granny soon decided these were not the kind of people we needed to be too friendly with.[37] We didn't have many people like the gypsies coming in from out of town, though. Most of the folks around there had lived there for as long as I could remember.

At the Stroke of Midnight

Nearly every Saturday night, especially during peanut-shelling time, we would go to a frolic—a square dance at somebody's house. First, we would shell peanuts and make candy, and then we'd sweep the peanut shells out of the way and dance.

Granddaddy Tip would play his fiddle, and his brother Lee or somebody else would call the steps. Sometimes, Uncle Lee would tap the strings on the neck of Granddaddy's violin with a small stick, like a broom sage, to get the beat, and sometimes Granny did that. She was good at it. She was a good dancer too.

Granddaddy Tip kept a close eye on his pocket watch as the hour hand and then the minute hand moved closer to midnight. Granddaddy wasn't a churchgoing man at the time, but he had certain beliefs about what was right and what was wrong. He would play the fiddle right up to the stroke of midnight. Then he wouldn't play another note. He believed dancing on Sunday was a sin. In fact, doing anything on Sunday was wrong. It was a "day of rest," he said, so he wouldn't lift a finger, except to feed all of his livestock.

As for Granny, she attended the Freewill Baptist church in the Touchton community, so Mama, Harold, and I started going with her. Later on we all switched to the Philadelphia Baptist Church. Harold Link was the preacher when I joined, and he baptized me in the Running Springs on the Suwannee River.

Later on, Granddaddy joined the Primitive Baptist Church (Patmos) because, he said, "that was what my mama was, and that's what I want to be."

If there wasn't a dance on Saturday night, people would come over to Granny and Granddaddy's house to listen to the radio—after we got one. Granddaddy bought one of the first radios in the community, and Daddy built a little table for it to sit on.[38] The radio required three batteries that were about the size of a car battery, except longer. One went into the back of the radio, one sat behind the radio, and the other, on a lower shelf.

At first the radio nights were fun, but they got old real fast. Nobody ever wanted to leave, and because my bed was in the fireroom, I couldn't go to bed until everybody left. The radio nights got later and later, and I really got tired of them. Granddaddy evidently didn't think that playing the radio in the wee hours of Sunday morning offended God like dancing did.

Christmastime
On Christmas Eve, neighbors like the Robinses and the Georges would go over to Granny and Granddaddy's house,

and we would eat cakes and pies and drink eggnog spiked with Granddaddy's white lightning.

At night we kids would hang our stockings by the fireplace, and the next morning they would be filled with different things like fruit, firecrackers, and a small piece of clothing like socks, panties, or maybe a blouse or shirt.

For Christmas dinner, we usually had chicken, but sometimes we had duck or ham. Although we raised turkeys, we didn't eat them; back then, they were sold. For dessert, we always had tater pie; there were always plenty of sweet potatoes for baking and making pies.

The Ward Family

Edward and Daisy Ward and their family lived just down the road from us. They seemed well off, as farmers go. One of their girls—Oleta—was about my age, so we walked to school together and soon became good friends.[39] Before I knew Oleta, she had an older sister, Edna; but Edna had died, so Oleta was now the oldest.[40] She also had a younger sister, Mae, and a little brother, Ellis.

One day, Mama, along with Harold, me, Granny, and Granddaddy Tip, went down to see the Wards. They happened to be grinding cane that day, so their whole family was out helping with the operation. They seemed glad to see us, and we all stood around talking and drinking cane juice and visiting for a long time. We didn't know then that it would be the last time we saw Mr. Ward.

A few days after our visit, Mr. Ward was butchering hogs and got hog blood and germs in a shaving cut on his face. It caused him to get blood poisoning, and he died on November 30, 1930. When he died, his wife Daisy was pregnant with their fifth child but didn't yet know it.

Everybody thought that Mr. Ward left Daisy pretty well off. She had a car, a truck, some hogs, several Jersey cows, two mules in the lot—and the place paid for.[41] The following year, she had a baby boy and named him Clyde.[42]

Not long after Mr. Ward died, Daisy asked Cary Neely, Granddaddy Tip and Granny's foster son (photo on p. 55), to stay with her and help with the farming. He moved there, but didn't stay long before Will Ward, Daisy's dead husband's brother, went to Granddaddy Tip and told him, "You better get Cary away from there or there's gonna be trouble." Granddaddy told Granny about it and she went and told Cary.

After Cary left, Ozie Hurst started staying there at Daisy's, helping her out. He pronounced his name Oh-zee (he had a twin, Ozzie, pronounced Ahh-zee[43]).

Like Cary, Ozie was a few years younger than Daisy; she was probably in her thirties, and he was in his early twenties. But before long, Daisy Ward became Daisy Hurst, and the couple went on to have two daughters, Evelyn and Geraldine.[44]

Black Stocking Tale
After the new Ladyland School was built and the two-room house on the Lyle place was no longer needed for school, the Williamson family moved there and started sharecropping with Sheriff Lyle; they grew the first crop of tobacco that was grown in our area.

That same year, our family moved into the smaller house on Sheriff Lyle's place.[45] To get to the new Ladyland School from there, Harold and I took a shortcut across the back of Granddaddy Tip's field.

Back then, girls didn't wear britches, but when it was cold, Mama would insist that I wear black cotton stockings to keep my legs warm. I hated stockings because none of the other girls wore them. So, I got to taking the stockings off on my way to school and stuffing them in a hollow stump in the back of Granddaddy's field. At the end of the school day, when Harold and I walked back across the field, I got the stockings out of my hiding place and put them back on.

Well, one day, when I got home from school, Daddy called me over and whispered in my ear.

"I found your hiding place for your stockings, Mutt."

I just knew I was in big trouble.

"But I put them back in the stump," Daddy continued, "and didn't tell your Mama."

Daddy never did tell Mama, even though I kept up that routine for a long time and Daddy knew it.

A Roller-Board Slide

When I started to seventh grade, my class was held in the Raiseback house, right next to the new two-room Ladyland School. Mr. Blume was my teacher that year.

Before Mr. Blume came to teach there, we had played a lot of string ball, using a ball about the size of a baseball. I liked string ball; and I loved to jump board—that was my favorite. But Mr. Blume thought we needed more to play with, so he got the boys to bring tractors and equipment to school, and they constructed a clay tennis court. That's when I learned to play tennis.

Mr. Blume also built us a roller board, a slide made of wood and tin. When Daddy saw it, he thought it was dangerous and told me to "stay off that thing." But I didn't listen. One day, Merine Warren and I decided to slide down together, and as we were coming down I swung a leg out over one of the boards. That's when a four- or five-inch splinter stuck in the back of my leg and went through my thigh to the front above my knee. I was in *some* kind of pain.

Mr. Blume drove me home, and when Daddy saw the big splinter sticking all the way through my leg, he got out his pocket knife to try to get it out. Mama started crying for him to *please* take me to the doctor. So, they took me to Dr. Green in Mayo. He made an inch-long cut on the back of my leg and got the bigger part of the splinter out. Then he made a small slit on the front of my leg to get the point out.

The front healed up pretty good, but I ended up with a bad scar on the back of my leg.

Although Mr. Blume did help us get some playground equipment, he would do other things that would make us so mad. He would sit up close to the potbellied wood heater that sat in the middle of the room where *he* would be warm, but the rest of us would be freezing cold, and he wouldn't let us add any more wood to the heater. We got so mad with him that when he left the school one day to go home (he boarded with Mr. and Mrs. Warren, Merine's parents), we stayed behind and gathered up every piece of chalk and every eraser we could find and threw them up into the overhead ceiling.

The next day he looked and looked for the chalk and erasers. When he finally figured it out, he made us write again and again—like a hundred times—

I promise to never again hide school supplies.

I promise to never again hide school supplies.

I promise . . . .

The Sharecropper's Wife

While we were living on the Lyle place, Ozie Hurst got a black couple to move into one of the tenant houses on the Ward place to help him with the farming. They were share-croppers, so they were to get a share of the profits at the end of the year.

As it turned out, nobody's crops did well that year, and there was no money for Ozie and the black man to split. The black man did the only thing he could do, I guess. He left to find work, but his wife and little girl stayed put in the tenant house.

One day, Daddy and Harold and I were at our cow pen on the Lyle place, not far from the tenant house, minding our own business, when we heard somebody yell. We looked out and saw Ozie walking up to the tenant house with a shotgun.

"Looks like Ozie plans to run that woman off," Daddy said to Harold and me.

About that time, the black woman came out of that house and grabbed the gun right out of Ozie's hands.

They exchanged a few words that we couldn't make out, and then she threw the gun back at him along with words that were loud and clear. "Don't you come back here, Ozie Hurst, or I'll kill you! I ain't gwine nowhere till I be ready to go."

There really wasn't anywhere for that woman to go. She and her husband had worked for Ozie all year with nothing to show for it.

Eighth Grade

When I started to the eighth grade, my class was held in the new two-room Ladyland School. Perry Holmes was my teacher that year, and he boarded at Granddaddy and Granny's house.

Every day after lunch, kids would throw their leftover scraps of food in the woods at the edge of the school yard. The scraps started attracting stray hogs that roamed the woods, and pretty soon, that got to be a problem; the hogs started coming up closer, trying to steal our lunches before we finished eating. So, Mr. Holmes started taking a box to school for us kids to throw our scraps into; then he would take the box to Granny and Granddaddy's and feed the scraps to the animals.

Somehow, word got around to the sharecropper's wife, and she went over to see Granny.

"Lord, a mercy, Miss Dosia, don't y'all throw that food to dem animals. Me and that girl a mine can use dat food."

Granny told Mr. Holmes about it.

"*Any*thing you have left over from your lunch that you don't want," Mr. Holmes told us the next day, "add it in that box. There's a woman and her child nearby that's about to starve."

So every day after that, the woman went down to Granny's house and picked up the box of scraps that Perry collected, and Granny would give her some other things. Then, that summer when Granny found out the woman was real sick, Granny cooked breakfast for her, and we took it to her and her little girl.[46]

Tobacco

After the Williamsons started growing tobacco on the Lyle place, Granddaddy Tip and Daddy started growing it too. Then, they no longer had to buy all their tobacco products.

For making chewin' tobacco, Granddaddy picked out some of the nice mature leaves that had been cooked and cured in the tobacco barn. He rinsed them in water to get all the sand off, pulled the stems and veins out, and soaked the leaves in a mixture of water and cane syrup (some people used honey or molasses for theirs.) Then, Granddaddy took a clean brick and stacked several leaves on the brick, one on top of the other. He topped the stack of leaves off with another brick and left it like that, weighted down, until it formed a half-inch thick plug of chewin' tobacco. Then he could cut off a piece to store in his pocket until he was ready to chew.

Granddaddy also started making his own pipe tobacco. After choosing some nice cured leaves, he removed the stems and veins and put the leaves in a pan in the oven that was still hot, but not too hot. He usually did it after supper or after Granny had finished baking bread and the oven was still good and warm. He needed to dry the leaves without burning them. Once the leaves were dry, he cooled them, crumbled them up, and then added a little dab of syrup. He mixed that up good before storing it in a can.

Nearly everybody back then used tobacco. Daddy didn't chew it, but he smoked cigarettes. To make his own cigarettes (Daddy called them *pooch-eyes*), he would tear a brown paper bag into squares. Then, when he wanted to smoke one, he took one of the little brown paper squares and topped it with a dab of Granddaddy's sweet homemade pipe tobacco, rolled it up, and licked the edge of the paper to seal it shut. Later on, when Daddy had the money, he would buy those ready-made, tissue-thin, white cigarette papers and Prince Albert in the red can.

Pumping Water

Like most of the people we knew and visited, we got our water for drinking, for cooking, and for bathing (and for all the farm animals to drink) by pumping it out of the ground with a hand pump. Then, we toted it into the house in a wooden, enamel, or zinc bucket.

The picture shown here was taken at Aunt Minnie's house in Branford. Aunt Minnie was Granny's sister, and the children shown are her grandchildren (children of her daughter, Nellie).

Lamar, R.A., and Elsie Brown

3 Ups and Downs (by C.G.)

While living at the Baptist Children's Home, I started working at the Pig Whistle eating joint as a curb hop. It was kind of like a McDonald's, or like the A&W root beer stand that later came to Live Oak. When people drove up, I'd go take their orders and then go get their food and take it to their cars. I worked for tips, and back then we got—maybe—a nickel as a tip. If you got a dime, you were in high cotton. But I was earning two or three dollars a day!

Then, somebody at the Children's Home complained about me working when all the kids living there couldn't work to earn money. The people in charge told me they would have to stop me from working.

It bothered me that they made me quit work—but most of the people working at the Children's Home were nice people. When the stock market crashed in 1929, they had to go without being paid for four or five months. I think their pay was about fifteen dollars a week, plus room and board.

On Sundays, we went to the Main Street Baptist Church, just south of Cottage Avenue. That's where I joined the church and was baptized when I was thirteen.

Soon after I was baptized, I had my tonsils and adenoids out. They probably wanted to take my tongue out too. I think I bled pretty bad, because after they finished, they told me I was a "free bleeder."

Ira had his tonsils taken out at the same time; and a little later, they took Clara Mae's and Laura's out. It was all done free, through the St. Luke's Hospital.

In the fall of 1930, when I was almost fifteen, I found out that I would have to leave the Children's Home because they didn't keep kids after they turned fifteen. They wrote to several of my relatives and asked if any of them could take me in. Uncle Clarence—Mama's twin brother— wrote back and said that he could and would.

I left the Children's Home in October of 1930, before I was to turn fifteen the following January. I spent the night at the house where Mama was living with a nice lady, keeping house—cleaning. The next

C.G.'s 1930 school photo

morning, I hitched a ride over to Suwannee County with Fletcher Boatright.[47] He was headed home after hauling meat to Jacksonville. I spent Halloween night at his house—slept with his son, Doc. The next morning, I walked from there to Uncle Clarence's house, carrying my few clothes in a suitcase.

Uncle Clarence and Aunt Daisy's Place

As soon as I got to Uncle Clarence and Aunt Daisy's place, I was handed a shovel, and Aunt Daisy and I went to work, filling up stump holes. Uncle Clarence was in the midst of clearing more land for farming.

Uncle Clarence and Aunt Daisy had four kids: Lucretia, Willie Mae, Monroe, and Lamera. Not long after I went to live with them, they had another baby. It was a girl, and they named her Clara Inez, but she died when she was still just a baby. Then Lucretia died too. That was a strange day—sad—but icicles were glittering on the limbs of the trees, something that rarely happened in Florida. I had seen snow once, but never icicles like that.

Uncle Clarence and Aunt Daisy built a new house while I was living with them, and one day a dog came up to the

new house and started hanging around. Uncle Clarence and all of us kids liked playing with him, but Aunt Daisy didn't want him there. She kept on at Uncle Clarence to get rid of that dog; and one day as the two of them started to Live Oak, Aunt Daisy asked Uncle Clarence to take the dog and leave him in town.

Uncle Clarence took the dog all right; but while Aunt Daisy was busy buying groceries, Uncle Clarence met up with a neighbor and asked the neighbor if he would drop the dog off back at home.

C.G.'s Uncle Clarence and Aunt Daisy Boatright

When Uncle Clarence and Aunt Daisy got home, the dog was already there. Aunt Daisy was surprised to see the dog; she thought he had run all the way back home, on his own.

"If he wants to stay that bad," she said, "I guess we'll keep him."

Uncle Clarence and Aunt Daisy's farm butted up to Uncle Joe and Aunt Lizzie's place. Uncle Joe and Uncle Clarence were brothers, and Aunt Lizzie and Aunt Daisy were sisters, so they saw a lot of one another.

I don't know if Uncle Joe and Aunt Lizzie considered taking me in. They probably knew they wouldn't have room. They had a bunch of kids. J.T. and Susan Myra died when they were small, but they still had five other children: Honorine, Thomas Lee, Winifred, Carra, and Margaret. And then they went on to have six more before they quit: Alfred, Pete, Billy Ray, Sherwood, Ronald, and Spessard.

Uncle Clarence's family and Uncle Joe's went to the Patmus Primitive Baptist Church. I visited there, but I ended up joining Philadelphia Church, the church where Granddaddy Howell had been a deacon, and the church Mama had joined when she was a girl (she had never moved her membership so she was still a member there).

When I joined, I asked to be baptized again because I felt like I hadn't really known what I was doing when I joined in Jacksonville. This time, I was baptized at Telford Springs on the Suwannee River, near Luraville.

The Joe and Lizzie Boatright family

From about 1931 to 1933, I went to school at Ladyland and rode the school bus. At that time, Ladyland classes were being held in a two-room house on the Lyle place. I sat behind Ethel Rye in class. She had lots of curls, and I would take my pencil and run it up through her ringlets. She didn't like that a bit.[48]

At recess, we would sometimes play catch ball. We batted the ball that looked something like a softball, and whoever caught it got to bat next.

I remember the strange reaction my fifth grade teacher, Mr. John Morgan, had over the word *nary*. He asked me to work a math problem on the board and explain how I got my answer. In my explanation, I referred to the zero as *nary*. He looked at me with a puzzled expression, and I had to teach him—my teacher—that *nary* meant *none*. When the year was up, he promoted me to sixth grade.

The next year I went through seventh grade and part of the eighth and was promoted to the ninth grade—but it was conditional.

When I started to Suwannee High in Live Oak the next year, I was making *F, F, F.* The principal called me in to his office one day and talked to me. He suggested that I go back and repeat the eighth grade, so I did that, at a school in Live Oak.

A boy named Clarence Brown rode my bus to Live Oak, and we started talking about spending the night with one another sometime. One day he told me he was going home with me *that day.* I knew it wasn't a good idea—not *that day*—because Aunt Daisy was in the hospital and Uncle Clarence was probably up at the hospital visiting her, but I didn't know what to do.

When the driver got to our stop, Clarence Brown hopped off the bus with me. Uncle Joe and Aunt Lizzie's kids were still on the bus and saw Clarence get off. When they got home, Honorine must have told her mama about it, and Aunt Lizzie evidently got word to Uncle Clarence.

When he came home that night, he got me told! I tried to explain that I hadn't invited Clarence that day—that, in fact, I had found out after Clarence got off the bus with us that Willie Mae put him up to it—she had *asked* him to go home with me. But Willie Mae wouldn't own up to it, and Uncle Clarence wouldn't listen to me.

"From now on, you keep your damn boy friends away from here!" he yelled at me.

After that, Uncle Clarence and I didn't get along quite as well.

Uncle Joe and I got along better. He let me have a gilt so I could raise some pigs (I don't remember if I traded him work or what), and Uncle Clarence did let me keep the hog at his place. My sow ended up having several pigs, several times; and each time Uncle Clarence killed hogs, he would kill some of my hogs, too, for us to eat.

High School and National Guard

I was never on an official school team for any sport, but I played a little softball.

As for music, I never played an instrument of any kind—never could make the notes come out right. I think my brother Ira was the only one of us that learned to play anything; he could play the harp—the harmonica.

I made quite a few friends in high school—Osmond Palmer, Jack Nance, Billy Allen, and Woodrow Crews.[49] Sometimes, some of us fellows would get together and pull pranks. One Halloween, we took the wheels off an old man's wagon, took the wagon apart, and hoisted the pieces up on the roof of a building—where we put the wagon back together. Then, we hightailed it! We didn't think we should wait around to see that man find his wagon. He must have been surprised when he came out and saw his wagon settin' there on that roof.

When I turned eighteen, I decided to join the National Guard. I could do that and still go to high school, since the drills were held at night and during the summer. I still had two years of high school yet to go.

When I applied to the National Guard, they said they needed my birth certificate, a piece of paper I didn't own. So, I went back over to Jacksonville and got Mama to go with me to try to get one.

Mama had worked for several different families, keeping house, after I had left the Children's Home; but she had finally landed a good job, working as a maid for a consul from a foreign country. It was there that she met Charles E. Midgett, the man she would later marry.

When the official behind the desk asked for my full name, I said it was Clarence Garfield Howell. Nobody had ever told me that I was named after my daddy, but I had always assumed it, and Mama didn't dispute it that day.

I enlisted in the National Guard in May of 1934. I got paid forty-five cents an hour to drill, and we drilled for two hours every Wednesday night, so I earned ninety cents. After paying twenty-five cents for transportation up to Live Oak, I was left with only sixty-five cents a week. But, during the summer, I went to National Guard camp for two weeks and got paid for that. After camp, I was thirty dollars richer (I got paid fifteen dollars a week). Once a quarter, I got an additional check for about nine dollars.

I enjoyed camp, except the one time I got so mad with a fellow. He didn't have a bathing suit, and he asked if he could borrow mine, so I let him. Later, he told somebody he got the crabs and he guessed he "got 'em from C.G.'s bathing suit." That thing made me so mad. He might have crabs, but he dad-blamed sure didn't get 'em from me.

Drinks for Friends
The bank charged a dime to cash checks, so instead of going there to get my National Guard checks cashed, I went to the post office where they didn't charge a penny. One day after getting one of the checks cashed, I walked up to

Harvard's Drugstore to pay a little on my bill (I had charged some ink and pencils to use in school).

While I was there that day, I got a Coca-Cola at the soda fountain. As I was leaving, I met up with a bunch of classmates—about nine of them. Osmond Palmer was one. They asked if I would get them a drink. I said I would. So, we walked back to the soda fountain and I asked what they wanted to drink.

"Don't make much difference," they all said.

I turned around to the counter. Sherwood Harvard was working there.

"Pour these boys a drink of water," I said to Sherwood, and headed for the door.

"Well, C.G. said that he would get us a *drink*—and he did!" Osmond said, as the door closed behind me.

Trips to South Florida
In 1934, when Ira was about to turn fifteen and would have to leave the Children's Home like I did, Aunt Laura Garrett said Ira could go live with her and her husband. She was married to Will Garrett, a man so tall he had to stoop to go through doorways. My brother Mernest was also still living there with them, and so was Grandma Howell.

I hadn't seen them for a long time, so one weekend I decided to go down to Loughman and visit them. The trip didn't cost me much because I hitchhiked. On the way down, I caught a ride from Live Oak to Tarpon Springs to Clearwater to Tampa and on to Loughman. One of the rides was with three men who were hauling chickens and pigs to south Florida. There wasn't room in the cab of the truck for me, so I rode in their two-wheel trailer with the chickens and pigs.

That weekend I got to see my brothers and my Grandma Howell—and didn't know then that it would be the last time I saw her. She died just a few months later.

On the trip back to Suwannee County, I hitchhiked

from Loughman to Jacksonville and then to Live Oak, so I had only spent five or ten dollars that weekend out of my National Guard pay. But when I got home, Uncle Clarence was mad that I had spent *any* money on a trip, telling me, "You should have spent that money for clothes!"

Uncle Clarence and I kept having our problems. We just didn't look at things the same way. After he joined the Primitive Baptist Church, he got real interested in studying the Bible, and he would read it all day while I busted wood. One day he was reading and stopped just long enough to tell me to go to the field and get the cows.

"Won't your feet touch the ground?" I mumbled to myself as I was walking out, but he heard me and it made him mad as fire.

I decided to talk to my first cousin, Joe Hingson,[50] about how things were going with Uncle Clarence and me; Joe lived just down the road. He said if things got bad, I could go stay with him. His sister Ella and her husband Luther Williams were living with him at the time, but they were about to move.

It didn't look like my family was ever going to get back together under one roof. Not long after I had gone down to Loughman, Mernest had moved to Miami where he had found a job at the Armour meat packing plant. But, finally, Ira moved up to Suwannee County to stay with Aunt Ethel Houck, so at least I then got to see him once in a while.

About that same time, in 1934, Mama married Charles Midgett, and that enabled her to take Clara Mae and Laura out of the Children's Home. The three of them moved in with Charles and his children, Clarence and Bob. He had four children in all, but his older ones, Kathleen and Charles Jr., were already grown and out on their own.

The new Midgett-Howell family stayed put in Jacksonville for a couple of years,[51] but by the fall of 1936, they had moved to Miami—first to NW 1st Street, and then to NW 14th Street. Their house there was pretty full with

Charles and his two kids, Clarence and Bob—and Mama and her two, Clara Mae, and Laura. But, not long after they moved to 14th Street, they somehow found room for George Frederick, a kid from Suwannee County that moved in with them.

In late October, I went down for a visit; and on Halloween night, Mernest, George Frederick, and I went out to a party. I got paired up with Lois Williams that night.

Mernest Howell

There was another girl at the party that really liked Mernest. Her name was Eloise. Toward the end of the party, she asked Mernest if he would take her home, and he said he would. We all got in the car with Mernest, and he headed for her house. But, when we got to Eloise's house, she refused to get out. She wanted Mernest to take the rest of us home before taking *her* home. He told her he had to work the next day and she'd better get out of the car because he wasn't bringing her back. She refused, so he drove home, got out, went inside, and went to bed.

Eloise then started in on George Frederick to take her home. When he wouldn't, she started on me. She was making a big fuss when my stepfather, Charles Midgett, came out to see what all the noise was about. We told him we

Eloise Avera

had it under control. After Eloise finally saw we weren't going to take her back home, she finally left and walked home. She was my future sister-in-law, but I didn't know it yet.

✐ 4 Trying New Things (by Ethel)

I was never one to do things behind Mama's and Daddy's backs. I had learned better. When Daddy turned you loose, you knew you'd had a whipping.

Daddy didn't whip me when I got older, but he had his own way of disciplining. He could make me so disgusted with myself that I would quit doing what I shouldn't have done. He sure weaned me from smoking.

I had started taking draws off different people's cigarettes, thinking it was a grown up thing to do. Daddy had seen me do it and hadn't said anything—maybe because he smoked.

One day I was home from school, sick with a bad cold, and Daddy came in where I was.

"Daddy," I said to him, "didn't you say that you like to smoke Kool cigarettes when you have a cold?"

"Yeah. I do."

"Well I sure wish I had one, 'cause I've coughed and coughed and—"

"Well, honey, I don't have any Kool cigarettes on hand, but I can fix you up one, just like a menthol."

"You can?"

"I can."

Daddy reached in his pocket and took out his Prince Albert, put a little tobacco in his hand, and then took a little Mentholatum salve from the tin on the mantel (we were still living with Granny and Granddaddy). He mixed the salve and tobacco around good with his fingers, fished a cigarette paper out of his pocket, and rolled up a cigarette. Before handing it to me, he put it in his mouth, struck a match, and lit it.

I put it to my lips, took a draw off it, and puffed the smoke right back out of my mouth.

"Now, Mutt, honey," Daddy said, "it won't do you one bit of good if you don't inhale it."

God! Man! When I inhaled! The top of my head just about came off! I like never to have got through choking on that thing.

"You can have it, Daddy," I said, handing it back.

There was another time Daddy got away with me too. He used to drink a little bit. He didn't drink a lot, but I knew he drank some—and had drunk more.

"Daddy, you know what I'd like to have?" I said to him one day.

"What, honey?"

"I'd like to have some of that—uhm-m-m—what do you call it? . . . Rockin' Rye! I've heard you say it's really good stuff."

"Yeah. It is good. So, you think you want a bottle?"

"Yessir, I do."

A few days later Daddy brought home a bottle of Rockin' Rye and handed it to me.

"Now this is yours, Mutt. Go put it up. And don't drink too much at one time."

Well, I just *had* to tell, you know, that Daddy had bought me a bottle of Rockin' Rye!

I was probably about thirteen. At the time, we were growing tobacco and swapping work with Ozie Hurst and the Ward family; so, one day when we were working in tobacco, I told Ozie about my Rockin' Rye.

"Boy, I really like that stuff," he said.

"Well, I'll give you a drink," I told him.

So, at noon when we went to the house to eat dinner, I got a little glass and poured Ozie some, and he took it. Daddy saw me give him the drink but didn't say a word, until that night.

"Mutt," Daddy said, after nobody was around.

Ethel Rye, as a teenager

"Yessir?"

"I saw you givin' Ozie a drink of your liquor today.

"Yessir?"

"I don't want to see that again. I bought that Rockin' Rye for *you*. It's for *you*! And nobody else!"

Well, Rockin' Rye lost its taste to me after that. I never did drink any more liquor. Just that easy, Daddy could turn you against something.

When I went to sleep that night, I didn't have a clue that Ozie Hurst, the man I had shared a drink with that day, would be dead in a month. Murdered. Shot to death in front of his wife and all the kids.

She Buried All His Clothes

Granny could make anything. She made everything she wore—her sunbonnets, Granddaddy Tip's underwear—anything. And she taught me how to quilt.

The first quilt I made was a Dutch doll quilt.[52] The background blocks were made from five-pound sugar sacks—unbleached muslin. We took the brand name off the sacks with lye soap.

When I was about fourteen, she helped me make some baby clothes for the Allen twins. Susie and Newt Allen were neighbors; they had one little boy, and then they had twins boys. So for each of the twins, I made two outfits: a batiste dress and a kimono, a little sack-like gown that tied at the bottom. I embroidered them, and I was so proud of the outfits. But when the twins were just a few weeks or months old, one of them died. I don't know where they buried him, but Susie told us later that she buried him in the dress I had made for him. I thought that was so nice, until she added, "and we put *all* of his clothes in with him when we buried him 'cause they wuz all *his*."

I could understand burying him in a nice outfit, but I could not understand her burying *all* his clothes. She could have used them for the other twin. It wasn't like she had lots of money. The remaining twin had few clothes.

Granny was a midwife and probably delivered more babies in the Ladyland Community than any doctor did. Somebody was always coming to get her when a woman went into labor.[53] But she didn't deliver the Allen twins, and I never got to go with Granny to deliver a baby. I wasn't allowed to ask about such things, much less to watch a baby being born.

Avoiding an Alligator
Whereas I liked to spend time inside, learning to sew and cook, Harold liked to go hunting and fishing with Daddy and Granddaddy Tip.

"Yep!" I did like to hunt and fish," Harold said, "but I didn't always go with Daddy and Granddaddy. Sometimes my friends and I went fishing in the Suwannee River, at night. We went armed—not with a cane pole like Granddaddy Tip and Daddy used in the daytime—but armed with a gun and a big flashlight.

"We would put a cork in the barrel of our gun to keep water out. After getting ourselves in position, prepared to shoot, with the gun pointed down in the water, we would shine the light down by the rocks where we knew the fish would be sleeping—and fire.

Ethel's brother, Harold Rye, as a teenager

"One night, my buddy and I went out in the river in a boat, and he said he saw a gator under the boat—and was going to shoot it! I didn't want any part of that. I had seen a gator killed once, after the gator got himself caught—entangled in Granddaddy Rye's fishing nets. Killing that gator that was already caught in a net was a struggle. Several men hit him hard over the head a number of times, but it wasn't until Granddaddy Rye sunk an ax in that gator's head that the thing finally quit moving.

"That night on the river—when my buddy said he saw a gator—I told him he was crazy to try to shoot that thing in the water, and I started paddling—easy but fast—and got us out of there in a hurry before that gator could turn our boat over."

Ozie's Murder

Supposedly, Ozie's death was an accident—wasn't meant to happen—and the black tenant woman, who had threatened to kill Ozie, had nothing to do with it. It was a bunch of men that did it. They said later that they were "just trying to teach Ozie a lesson." The rumor was that Ozie was doing things he shouldn't, like sleeping around.

Oh, his murder was terrible. It happened right in front of his family one Saturday night after a free show. They used to have free shows in Branford on Friday nights and in

Mayo on Saturday nights. The town merchants would pay a guy to advertise for them, so the show was free to anybody. Some people took their own chairs, and others sat and watched from their cars, kind of like the drive-in theaters that came later.

Ozie and Daisy and all the kids had gone to the free show in Mayo that night, and they were on their way home when it happened. Mae was sitting up front between her Mama and Ozie, and the younger kids were in the back seat with Oleta. As they were going through the swamp, a bunch of men came out of nowhere in a dark truck, waylaid them—pushed them off the road—and shot Ozie right in front of his wife and all the kids. One bullet went into Mae's hip and crippled her for life. Oleta had to get up front, push Ozie over, and drive.

Mr. Marvin Warren[54] and Daddy helped them get Ozie out of the car that night, after they finally made it home.

At the trial, the evidence presented said that blood and bits from Ozie's shoulder ended up splattered all over the windshield. The ones that were accused of his murder said they were "just intending to give Ozie a good whipping—to straighten him out, but when he reached for his own gun, they had to shoot him.

Oleta, on the other hand, didn't see things unfold the night of the shooting the way the accused men said it did." [iii]

[iii] "Ozie never reached for his gun," Oleta said, years later. "Ozie never had time; it happened too fast. I had to push Ozie over so I could drive. Mae got in the back seat. I drove to Mr. Warren's house, and when I drove up, Merine was sitting in her daddy's truck listening to the radio (I don't think they had a radio in the house then). I jumped out and she saw my yellow crepe dress, spattered with blood, and wanted to know what had happened to my dress. 'Get your daddy,' I told her. Mr. Warren drove home with us, and he got Mr. Rye to help him get Ozie out of the car. There was no need to take Ozie to the doctor. He was dead. Mae wasn't taken to the doctor until after Ozie's funeral. When she died, years later, she still had that bullet in her hip."

I Knew Daddy Was Mad

Harold and I had gone over to Mayo to the same free show that Ozie and his family had gone to that night. We went there with the Herrings—Barney and Louise—and the Robins boys, who were living in Mayo then (Mr. Robins was out of jail and running a fish market in Mayo).

After seeing the show, we drove out to Alton Mills Lake and were playing the car radio real loud. Barney had rigged up a radio using a stick or a bottle and some wire for an antenna. Somebody on the other side of the lake started hollering at us, and we hollered back several times. We didn't know who it was, so after a while, we headed on home. I found out later that it was George Frederick, Osmond Palmer, and C. G. Howell; they were over there drinking Coca-Colas and roasting wieners.

When we drove up at home, Daddy came running out to the car. I knew he was mad because we were late getting home. But Daddy just asked if everything was okay. Then he said he was *glad* we were late. He knew that—to get home from Mayo—we had to travel through the swamp on the same road where Ozie had been killed.[55]

Halloween Night

We had been to a Halloween party at Ladyland School the night Granny had her accident. Our whole family always went. Everybody would dress up in something so that it was hard to guess who everybody was; then we played games. Granny loved to have a good time, and she had a good time that night.

When we all started walking home in the dark (it was about three-quarters of a mile home), we were still cutting up, singing, and skipping along the dirt road—Granny was skipping too—when all of a sudden, she got her feet crisscrossed, tripped, and fell hard on the ground. It was a so dark that night, no moon to speak of, that we had to feel to find Granny.

She said she couldn't get up—that she was hurt. We knew she was hurt if she said so, because Granny never complained. Somehow, we finally got her home and Daddy went after Dr. Green in Mayo. When he got there, he saw the problem and started giving orders.

"Delma, sew up two cloth bags the length of Dosia's leg and fill the bags with sand."

He placed a sand bag on each side of Granny's broken leg, and then placed boards next to the bags of sand. He tied that up to form a brace. Then he attached a pulley and an iron (one we used for ironing clothes; it was made of heavy wrought iron) to give weight to her foot and keep her leg stretched out.

Poor Granny had to lay like that for weeks and weeks. She couldn't get up to take a bath or get on the pot. I was a teenager then—still slept in the same room with her and Granddaddy Tip—so I was the one to help get a bed pan under her at night.

Granny had broken her arm before that, and it had healed, but her leg never did. Finally, though, she got so she could hobble around pretty good with the use of a crutch under one arm. She could sweep the yard and floors and things like that.

Granny had always been a good dancer, but after that night, Granny was never able to dance again.

Tip and Dosia Lanier (she, on a crutch) standing by their home

Our Bottle of Beer

I never cared for beer. It stinks too bad. But I did taste it once, when it had just come out, after prohibition. I was out again that night with Louise Herring, who was one of my best friends, her brother Barney,[56] and Jack Robins. We were in Live Oak, parked by the railroad tracks, and the boys said they were going to get themselves a beer. They wanted to know if Louise and I wanted one. We told them we would share one.

Daddy happened to be in town that night too, and I was holding that bottle of beer in my hand when he walked up.

"What ya doing, Mutt?" Daddy asked.

"Well . . . umm, the boys decided they wanted a beer a-piece, and Louise and I had never tasted it, so we told them to get us a bottle to share."

"Well, how is it?"

"I don't like it."

"Well, let me see it."

I handed it over to Daddy.

"Well, if you don't like it, honey, you don't have to drink it," Daddy said.

He held the bottle out at arm's length and turned it upside down. All of us watched, not saying a word, as the stream of beer flowed, foamed, and soaked into the ground. After that, I never did want any more beer.

High School Classes

My favorite class in high school was Home Ec [Economics]. My teacher, Miss Stribbling, had a rule that sewing projects were *not* to be taken home. She insisted that we work on our projects only in class so she could make sure everything was done right. But after she saw I knew how to sew—Granny had already taught me—she started letting me take my projects home to finish. Then, she got me to help her teach the others.

Another favorite teacher was Mrs. Shoppe. I had her for Speech and English. One of the girls in speech class was Mary Lunberg.[57] Her mother wanted to go to speech class, too, so Mrs. Shoppe said she could.

Almost every day somebody had to give a speech, and after a student finished with the speech, we were supposed to critique it. Mary's mother could *really* critique, and she was especially critical of the speech Mary gave. Then Mrs. Shoppe called on Mrs. Lunberg to give a speech.

"Oh, I don't want to *give* a speech," she said, "I just want to observe."

Mrs. Shoppe told her if she was going to stay in the class, she would have to give a speech, so the next day, she did; and after she finished it, we all got to critique *her* speech. We evidently did such a good job that she learned a lot. After that day Mrs. Lunberg never came back to class.

Mrs. Shoppe was really a good teacher, but I don't know what in the world she saw in her husband, the principal. One day I had to go to his office to change a class or something. He told me to have a seat on the couch in his office. While I sat there, he went in the bathroom next to his office and never even shut the door! From where I sat, I had a pretty good view of the man.

Curfew

I never really had a curfew, but I knew when to be home. One Sunday night, I went to the Pine Grove Church of God with Jim Johnson. Jim didn't have a car, so we rode with L. C. Moore, who was dating Jim's sister; they rode in the front, and Jim and I rode in the back.

When we got to the church, L.C. stopped his car, and Jim and I got out to go in the church, but L.C. and Jim's sister just sat there. Then, as soon as Jim closed the back door, they took off in the car.

When church was over, Jim and I went outside and looked around for L.C.'s car—expecting to see it parked somewhere—but it was nowhere to be seen. We waited around for a long time. Everybody else was leaving, so Jim and I finally started walking home. We had walked about a mile when L.C. drove up beside us with Jim's sister sitting real close to him. We got in and they drove me home, but I got there later than Daddy expected, and he was waiting. I knew right away that he was mad.

I tried to explain, but Daddy wouldn't listen.

"You won't be going anywhere anymore with L.C. Moore at the wheel."

That was the end of the discussion, and since Jim didn't have a car, I never got to go out with him again. He was the nicest boy I had ever gone with. He was a lot nicer than that Robert McDougal that I got paired off with one time.

I had gone to a party—there were a bunch of us—J. D., Ernest, Jim Johnson—but, somehow, I got paired off with Robert McDougal. He kept trying to put his arm around me, and I kept pulling away. Then he leaned over and whispered to me.

"There's something I'd like to tell you, and if I could write it down, I would."

I didn't like him a bit, so the next day I wrote him a note and told him I didn't want to go with him again.

There was another boy in school I didn't like—couldn't stand! It was C. G. Howell. I hated him from when he sat behind me in school and was always sticking pencils up my curls—before I finally got that teacher to cut my hair. Then, after I started in the ninth grade at Suwannee High School, he rode my bus, and every time he could, he would get in a position to tickle me—especially my knees. I was so ticklish—still am—and he knew it and took advantage of it. It made me so mad!

New Year's Eve

There was one other time that Daddy got mad with me for being out late. It was one New Year's Eve when a bunch of us went to a midnight show at the outdoor theater in Live Oak, and I didn't get home until two or three o'clock in the morning. I went inside and was about to get in bed when Daddy came in the room and wanted to know why I was coming in so late—way past midnight! I had to explain to him that the show *started* at midnight; it wasn't *over* at midnight like he thought.

"Well then, since you're up," Daddy said, "you can just go ahead and cook my breakfast."

He was leaving that day to head for Georgia to bring Granny's niece, O.D., and husband, Fred, down. They were going to move in and live in Granny's kitchen, so that Fred could help on the farm. (O.D. was the one that was born at Granny's house after Granny rescued Aunt Minnie so she wouldn't have to eat her husband's yellowhammer soup.)

I never did get to go to bed that night—or morning. By the time I cooked Daddy's breakfast, Mama got up and said it was time for me to help her get the kitchen ready for Fred and O.D.[58]

We moved the woodstove into what had been Harold's bedroom on the *back* porch. (Daddy had closed in one side of the *front* porch, and Harold's things had been moved from his room on the back porch to the front.) Then we moved the table and chairs over to the center of the back porch which Daddy had closed in to make a dining room.

Helping Mama move everything and get the old kitchen turned into a house for Fred and O.D. took all day long. Boy! When that New Year's Day was over, nobody had to show me where my bed was.

&~ 5   I Had a Lot to Learn (by C.G.)

When I came home from school one day, a bunch of women in the community—Dora Mills, Louise Lord, Ruby Hingson, Aunt Ethel, Aunt Lizzie, and Mae Starling—were all sitting around a quilting frame with Aunt Daisy, working on a patchwork quilt.

"Y'all can make me one of them quilts!" I said as I passed by on my way to put my books away—joking, you know. Well, when they later finished that quilt, they gave it to me! That really surprised me.

I was studying hard to try to finish high school, and for a while, everything at Uncle Clarence and Aunt Daisy's house seemed to be going good. But then one day, things kind of blew up.

I was helping Uncle Clarence reset some tobacco. We were about half done and it was getting late in the day, when Uncle Clarence said we should quit. After we got to the house, he said that I would need to help him finish it the next morning. I told him I couldn't the next day—that I needed to go to school that day because I had a test to take. He got real mad.

"If you can't do what I say, you can get out of my house!"

So, I went and started packing my clothes.

Aunt Daisy came in the room and asked me what I was doing. I told her I was packing up to leave. She started crying and begging me not to go, but I was too mad at Uncle Clarence to stay. I don't know what I would have done if he had crossed me again right then. I wanted to cut his guts out. I was that mad.

I took my clothes and left. Joe Hingson had said I could move in with him if it got bad. It was bad. I was twenty years old but still hadn't graduated from high school.

My Friend Joe

Joe was dating Ruby Lanier[59] when I moved in with him on April 5, 1936. I remember the date because it was on that same date, seven years earlier, that we had moved to Jacksonville when Mama got her very first job there.

Not long after I moved in with Joe, he and Ruby decided to get married. When I heard about it, I told Joe I would move out—maybe even move back to Jacksonville. But both Joe and Ruby told me they wanted me to stay. So I took them up on it because I really wanted to finish school at Suwannee High.

Of all the people in my life,

Joe Hingson

I think Joe Hingson had the most influence on me. He would sit and counsel me, and I learned to respect Joe's opinion and his attitude. He was real good to me.

Later on, when he worked for the ASCS,[60] I was his chain man. I held the end of the chain when he was measuring agricultural land—crop land.

Sometimes Joe would loan me his car, and a group of us would go out together. One night, I picked up a bunch of friends and drove out south of Live Oak and parked under some big oak trees. It was cool, so I left the lights on so we could gather up some wood to build a fire. Later, as it was getting late, we got ready to leave, but I couldn't start Joe's car. It wasn't uncommon for an old battery to run down if you kept the lights on too long or listened to the radio a long time, because the batteries were wet-cell. But I knew Joe's car had a good battery. So, all the kids—boys and girls—got behind the car and started pushing, with me at the wheel. They pushed and pushed, but the car wouldn't start. After a while they said they had to stop and rest. I reached over to turn the switch off while they rested, and when I did, I realized I never had turned it *on*!

I never let on what the trouble was. But when they started to push again, I made sure that switch was *on*. That time the car started up before it went ten feet.

Older Than Most

While in high school, in addition to earning a little money in the National Guard and serving as Joe Hingson's chain man, I earned some by helping people in the community, like Curtis Gamble. I plowed his crop using his mule.

I was older than most of the kids in my class because I had gotten behind when I had to stay home to help with farmwork, like when we lived on the Pennington place and when my family was moving from place to place. But when I *could* go to school, I studied hard, and during several school terms I moved up more than one grade to make up for falling behind.

Finally, I became a senior. That year, there was a 4-H Club that had started up, so I joined it—and the next thing I knew, the members elected me as the first Suwannee County 4-H Club Council President.

Also that year, the school gave a big science test—a competition. Anybody could take it, but Cornelia Marable and I were the only ones that did.

In January of my senior year, I turned twenty-one.

My First Bank Loan

Toward the end of the school year, I was getting dressed one morning and noticed that the seat of my pants was wearing thin. So I went up to the Commercial Bank to see if I could borrow a little money to buy some clothes. They let me have ten dollars. J. L. McMullen, who worked at the bank, signed the note with me. I took the ten dollars and went over to Seward Fleets and bought myself some new clothes.[61]

* * *

An Interview with C.G.

"What gave you the drive and determination to keep going—to finish high school?" C.G. was asked. "Your father was dead. Your mother wasn't around. Neither of them went past the seventh grade. Your Uncle Clarence didn't finish school. Neither did your friend, Joe. Your older brother, Mernest, quit school to go to work."

"Well, I just looked around me," C.G. replied, "and it looked to me like the people that got ahead in life were the people who had an education. But it wasn't easy—and at twenty-one, I still had a lot to learn.

"When that note for the ten dollars was coming due at the bank, I didn't have quite enough to pay it back—nearly enough, but not quite. Then I did something stupid.

"Just a few days before it was due, I went out one night with Curtis Gamble, Joe and Oliver Hingson, and Barney Lanier Jr. We went to Brooker's Bar; Suwannee County was a wet county then. The man that owned the bar had a slot machine, and that night he set a bottle of Scotch on the counter and said he'd bet that bottle of Scotch that I couldn't trip the jackpot. Now if I hadn't already been drinking that night, I would have known better than to try. But I started playing the slot machine, trying to throw the jackpot, and I ended up losing every bit of money I had.

" 'You stupid idiot!' I said to myself going home that night, and I vowed then that my drinking was over."

What C.G. Didn't Tell

In 1937, *The Suwannean,* the Suwannee High School yearbook, the name *C. G. Howell* appears often. Seniors were asked about their memories of their junior year, and this was C.G.'s response:

I remember that we lost only two games the whole football season . . . Mr. S. N. Reeves's beautification program . . . that the football field was completed and named The Reeves Field . . . and giving the seniors a Banquet.

The yearbook also listed these tidbits about C.G.:

Chief occupation: Cracking dumb jokes
Favorite expression: "You're two of them."
Probable destiny: Einstein's capable assistant

In addition to being known as a jokester, C.G. had a reputation as a science whiz. On *The Suwannean*'s Scholastic Leaders' page was the following notation:

C.G. had a B or better average in three units of science and by virtue of his accomplishments led in the scoring on a group of science achievements tests.

C.G., ready to receive his diploma

In June of 1937, when C.G. received his high school diploma—the first in his family to do so—it was announced that he had won the Bausch & Lomb Honorary Science Award. He was singled out as *the* student among sixty-seven seniors to be "remembered for his skill and knowledge in the field of science."

A Graduation Gift
When C.G. graduated, his mother gave him a poem that she—with only a seventh-grade education—had written for him. The poem, "A Mother's Dream Come True," left no doubt about how proud Clara was of her son.

And how did C.G. feel about this gift from his mother? One can only guess, based on the fact that he put the poem in his wallet and kept it there until the paper on which it was written was falling apart at the folds.[62] The poem appears below, with no changes or edits:

A Mother's Dream Come True

Heres to my boy who would never say die,
But who's watchword was ever, I'll try.
To fight my way to Victory,
And justify man's faith in me.

Hard has been the battle,
Dark has been the way;
But, now for you, the sun is shining
For you won the fight today.

With your school-mates you are standing
While teachers look on with pride
On this class of '37,
Their faith in you is justified.

On this, your day of graduation
With Diploma in your hand
And with other hard-won medals
You upon the stage do stand.

On your brow a look of Peace,
Fiery determination in your eye
To surmount every future Obstacle,
Be them ever so high.

In my heart is songs of gladness
Of your victory, justly won,
In my eyes, tears of happiness,
As I clasp your hand, My son:

Boy, on this day, which means so much to you,
Saw a mother's dream come true.

Mrs. C. E. Midgett

🐎 6 C.G.'s Intentions

The first time I went out with Ethel," C.G. said, "we double dated with Barney Lanier and Merine Warren. It was in April of my senior year in high school. After our first date I knew I wanted to date Ethel again—I intended to!—but she wasn't always available since she was still going to school. So I would occasionally find another girl to go out with."

Making Change
"After I'd graduated from high school," C.G. said, "Leroy Grove hired me as a car attendant at his Pure Oil station in Live Oak. The job included a little bit of everything—from pumping gas for customers, changing tires, patching inner tubes, sweeping and mopping floors, cleaning rest rooms, greasing cars—to accepting payment and making change for customers.

"Joe and Ruby had been real good to me, letting me live with them while I finished school. So, as soon as I knew I had the job at the Pure Oil station, I told them I would be moving out. I got a room in Colonel Henry's Rooming House in Live Oak. It was a boarding house where a bunch of fellows lived, and Mrs. Henry prepared our meals. All of us got to be real friendly.

"One day a new fellow moved in, so we decided to play a joke on him that night. At the supper table, every time he asked for something to be passed, we said, 'We ain't waiters!' So the new fellow would get up from his chair and go around the table and help his plate. After a few days, though, he was just one of us; then he would help us play the same joke on the next fellow that moved in.

"Soon after I started the job with Leroy Grove, Bob Holmes came to the gas station one day and asked if I'd go to work for him at his Sinclair station. I didn't take him up on it that day, but a few days later I wished I had.

" 'Looks like I *might* have to let you go, C.G.,' Leroy Groves said to me when I got to work one morning—but he didn't say why. I asked around and found out the money had been checking up short; I think another guy that worked there was taking it. In any case, I didn't want to stay where I wasn't trusted, so I walked down the street to see if Bob Holmes's job offer was still good. He said it was, so I went to work at his Sinclair station."

Edna Was a High Roller

"I was working at Bob's filling station," C.G. continued, "the time Edna Lanier gave me a good mauling. I had gone out with her a few times. (She was the youngest daughter of Tip Lanier's brother, France.) That Edna was a high roller! She believed in having a lot of fun. She was very open and cut the fool a lot—and strong as an ox.

"She came in the station one day when I was at work, and we got in a tussle. Somehow, I got out of balance and she got me on my back and rolled me all over the desk in that gas station. Bob Holmes just stood off and laughed.

" 'C.G.,' Bob said to me later, 'that old girl knew how to handle you.'

"I didn't work for Bob too long before I decided to move back in with Joe and Ruby and help Joe with farming. Joe said he would pay all expenses for the crop that year and give me a third of the crop if I would work with him.

"I also contracted with Uncle Joe Boatright to pull up his tobacco stalks to get rid of knot root. We agreed to five dollars an acre, but the crabgrass was real bad, and I soon realized it would be a lot bigger job than I expected. So I went back to Uncle Joe and asked to use his mule, Babe. I told him I would do the job for four dollars an acre, with the use of his mule. He agreed and I got the job done with the mule and a Dixie plow point."

Ethel Was Different

"One night that summer," C.G. said, "after National Guard drill, Murphy Touchton told me that Milton Rye (Ethel's Daddy) had a barn full of cured tobacco that he needed to take down and pack to get it to market the next day, the last day of the market—his last chance to sell it.

"So, I borrowed Joe Hingson's car and headed for Mr. Rye's. I got there about ten o'clock that night. The barn of tobacco was still hot; so we had to take the sticks of tobacco out of the barn and hang them in racks in the open to cool before we could take the tobacco off the sticks and pack it up. We worked all night long—finished up about daylight—and I got in good with Mr. Rye! A good thing, since I had already decided I liked his daughter.

"Ethel was very different from Edna, and we started going out more and more. I had known Ethel for a long time—ever since grade school when I would aggravate her by sticking pencils up her curls. She hated that. But she got me back one day.

"It was after we had started dating a little more, and we were sitting on the Lanier's closed-in back porch, eating Sunday dinner. Mrs. Rye was standing there telling something or other, so I was looking up at her, listening, with my mouth open. That's when Ethel sopped a piece of biscuit in cream and—before I knew what had happened—she poked it right in my mouth. I purely hated cream and Ethel knew it! I still hate cream to this day.

"For some occasion, maybe her birthday, I bought Ethel a Waterman ink pen. Paid five dollars for it."

Ethel Rye, after she and C.G. started going out together

"It was a Sheaffer's fountain pen," Ethel corrected. "It had iridescent pearl on it.[63] You bought me a dresser set too—a comb, brush, and mirror. I think it was a Max Factor set."

"Yeah, I paid five dollars for that too."

Playing Cupid

"I think it was the summer after C.G. helped Daddy unload the tobacco barn," Ethel said, "that we tried to hook Mary Catherine Cheshire up with my cousin Buck from Baltimore. Uncle Alonzo and Aunt Ethel and their sons Buck and Wilbur had come down for a visit. One night when C.G. came over, he brought Mary Catherine to be Buck's date. Mary Catherine, Buck, and I were all about the same age.

"We all went out together and had a real good time. But the minute we got back to the house, Aunt Ethel marched out on the porch and insisted that Buck get inside the house that minute. I think she was afraid her city boy might get involved with a country girl. After that night, if Buck wanted to go out with us, Aunt Ethel would have a pure conniption.

Buck Lanier, Tip Lanier, Wilbur Lanier, and Alonzo Lanier

"Aunt Ethel did not want Buck out of her sight, and the same went for Wilbur, who was a little younger than Buck.

"Wilbur liked to play with the chickens—the Rhode Island Reds. He would catch them and cradle them in his arms. But Aunt Ethel (my namesake) was constantly calling to him. I can still hear her, 'Wibbie, Dear! Wibbie, Dear!' I got so sick of hearing her voice. Wilbur wasn't a baby. He was ten years old.

Wilbur Lanier

"Then one night, I overheard her begging my Uncle Alonzo: 'Please, Pete'—she called him Pete—'Please take me home to my beautiful home in Baltimore.'

- 115 -

"I don't know if Aunt Ethel knew I heard or if she cared, but I never had much use for her after that."

The Deeds Were Transferred

Tip Lanier had not wanted his daughter to marry Milton Rye, and in the early years of that marriage, Tip had not gone out of his way to be friendly with his son-in-law.

Everyone in the family agreed that Tip was normally a friendly and generous person, but nobody in the family denied that he could be, at times, downright demanding and impossible to please.

To keep peace in the family, Milton likely, in the early years of his and Delma's marriage, had to bite his tongue a few times—not that he was a weak or timid man. He had, after all, guarded convicts, run moonshine, and wrestled gators caught in fishing nets.

No, Milton would not cross Tip because Milton loved Delma dearly, and he knew that she was crazy about her father. Besides, it was Tip's house where he, Delma, and the children often had to return for food and shelter when he couldn't find another job to support them. In fact, by the time Ethel and Harold had reached their teen years, they had come to think of the Lanier homestead as their permanent residence.

By that time, of course, Milton had gained the respect of Tip Lanier, and Tip was allowing Milton to run the farm. So it wasn't surprising to anybody when Tip announced one day that he was going to deed half his place (forty acres) to Milton and Delma. The other forty, he would deed to his son, Alonzo.

The deeds were transferred in 1938.

Alonzo, content with his life in Baltimore, let Milton continue farming the whole place in exchange for Milton's paying all the taxes.

Ira and Oleta

"That date we fixed up with Buck and Mary Catherine[64] didn't work out," Ethel said, "but things turned out a bit different the night C.G. brought his brother Ira with him when he came to pick me up for a date, and Oleta 'just happened' to be at my house.[65]

"Oleta and I had become good friends, and we spent lots of time together, mostly at my house. We would polish each other's fingernails and pull each other's eyebrows.

"She often took care of her brothers, Ellis and Clyde, so they would be with her when she came to visit. I remember one day Clyde was begging Oleta to go home. Ellis looked at us—still pulling eyebrows—and tried to get his brother to be patient. 'Just one more hair, Clyde. Just one more hair!'

"The night when C.G. brought Ira with him, Daddy had just picked Oleta up from work. Her family had been through a lot, and after her stepfather was murdered, she had dropped out of high school and taken a job as a housekeeper at the little hotel in Branford (she had heard about the job though Granny's niece, Nellie Brown, who lived in Branford). I think Oleta only worked during the week. She had no car, so that Friday, Daddy had gone over and picked her up.[66]

"When Ira saw Oleta that night, they fell in love at first sight. We didn't know it yet, but they would end up beating C.G. and me to the altar!"

On His Knees?

"Did C.G. get on his knees and propose to you?" Ethel was asked.

"Heck, No! I would 'ave slapped him over!"

"Why?"

"Because I don't like that kind of stuff."

"I don't remember exactly how it happened," C.G. jumped in. "It's been so long ago, now. Many people had us married before we were! A rumor got around that we were already secretly married.[67] One day Mr. Rye asked me if it was true. 'When we get married,' I told Mr. Rye, 'you and Mrs. Rye will be the first ones to know.' So, later, after Ethel and I decided we wanted to get married as soon as she finished school, I went and told Mr. Rye. 'There's only one thing I want to tell you,' he said. 'If you and Mutt don't get along, don't you ever get mad and hit her. You just bring her home.'

"Mr. and Mrs. Rye had known me and my family for a long time. Mrs. Rye had even known my daddy. He had boarded with the Laniers when he was helping with the construction of the Drew Bridge, and he pawned a watch to Tip—or maybe he gave it to Tip in return for board. Anyway, after Ethel and I started going together, Mrs. Rye gave me that watch—a lady's watch—one that a woman would wear pinned to her dress. I carried it with me for a while in my pocket, but it was too delicate for me. Before long the crystal broke, and I lost one of its hands.[68]

"Yeah, Ethel and I were really *ready* to get married, just as soon as she finished high school.

"Remember when we went up to Mr. and Mrs. Warren's place one day?" C.G. asked Ethel. "Remember what Merine's mother said to me?—'You and Ethel might go together, but when Ethel gets married it will be to Jack Robins!' "

"I remember," Ethel said.

"But *I* married Ethel," C.G. bragged. "Jack Robins went into the service and married a woman from England. Then, after bringing her back to the States and living with her a number of years, they divorced, and he married somebody he had dated before going overseas."[69]

Class of 1940

The 1940 Suwannee High School yearbook,[70] the *Suwannean,* included this line about Ethel: *Come what may her serenity is never shattered.* The yearbook also included a Class Song, penned by Ethel's friend, Merine Warren:

CLASS SONG

Oh! Suwannee High, our future fields are calling
From morn 'til night as thru the days we go,
We've started out on life's long unknown journeys.
We'll go, we'll go until the end we reach,
But when we go we feel a pang of sorrow,
And with these words we'll try to make it clear.
We'll think of you in sunshine and shadow.
Oh! Suwannee High, Oh! Suwannee High,
    we love you so.
                Merine Warren—'40

Ethel Rye, Jack Robins, Merine Warren, and Harold Rye

Ethel and C.G. on the Hal W. Adams bridge, the day of her senior class picnic

"On the last day of school," Ethel said, "our senior class went on a picnic. It was at Telford Springs. Leo Land[71] drove our bus. And C.G. joined us at the picnic; by then, we were making plans to get married."

Wedding Day

About three months after Ethel received her high school diploma, class of 1940, and a month before she turned nineteen, she walked down the aisle to marry C. G. Howell. It was not a fancy wedding, and they did not exchange rings, but they did dress for the occasion.

"The flower on my hat was a rose," Ethel said, "and the necklace I wore came with the dress, bought especially for the wedding. The day I walked the aisle, I weighed only 108 pounds."

C.G. weighed just 135 and showed off his trim physique in a charcoal grey suit (see cover photo).

"That was the only tailor-made suit I ever owned," he said. "I didn't have to buy it just for the wedding. I already had it. I had it tailor-made by a fellow named Dutton in Live Oak. He measured me and ordered it—one just like Joe Hingson had. It cost me thirty-five dollars."

The wedding ceremony took place at eight o'clock on Sunday morning, the eighth of September, 1940.

Back at the Lanier place, Ethel and C.G. posed for a photo while Ethel's grandfather commented to a friend, "The smartest thing on this place got married this morning."

An announcement in the *Suwannee Democrat* a few days later provided details:

> The Rev. Harold H. Link, pastor of the church, performed the ceremony. The bride and groom entered alone and were unattended. The bride's dress was of blue crepe made with a fitted bodice and pleated skirt. Her hat was of navy blue felt, topped with a red flower, and her other accessories were of navy blue.

Mr. and Mrs. C. G. Howell on the day they said, "I do"

The newspaper article did not mention Ethel's slight limp.

⤌ 7   We Bought the Farm

Ethel's limp on the day of her wedding was temporary—
the result of stepping on a broken bottle with a bare
foot. The glass had cut into the Achilles tendon above her
right heel. Since the injury was not a near-death experience,
she had seen no doctor; and on the day she became Mrs.
C. G. Howell, her foot appeared to be healing just fine.

After the ceremony, the bride and groom went with the
church congregation to a baptismal service at Running
Springs and then returned to the church for Sunday school
and the morning church service.

They ate a noon dinner at Tip and Dosia's place before
returning to the church at two-thirty that afternoon for a
study course. It was not until after training union and the
evening church service that the newlyweds were alone,
inside the house C.G. had secured for them.

"It was Barney Cheshire's tenant house," C.G. said,
"the house I had lived in when I was a little boy. It was the
house Daddy died in. When I asked Barney about renting

the house, he said we could live there rent free if I would just clean up around the place. So I had cleaned up around the outside, and Ruby Hingson and Mrs. Mamie Cheshire helped me clean the inside.

Setting Up Housekeeping

"When we married," C.G. continued, "we didn't have a pot to pee in. But we bought one! And as time went along, we accumulated a few other things.

"To furnish the house—it had three rooms, plus a front and back porch—I bought a used bedroom suit for forty-five dollars, a used dining set that had a table and five chairs, and a brand-new woodstove. We put the stove in the kitchen, and everything else, including the bed, went in the front room where the fireplace was. We used the third room for storage. In there, we stretched a piece of wire across one corner for hanging our clothes.

"On our first trip to the grocery store, we spent $11.43, buying things like matches, salt, sugar, grits, meal, flour, a pound of bacon, two cans of English peas, two cans of corn, two cans of tomatoes, and toothpicks."

"We also bought an oil lamp," Ethel said, "and Mama and Daddy gave us an Aladdin kerosene lamp—one that Daddy had given Mama before they married. I wonder whatever happened to that lamp."

"It might be out there in the barn," C.G. replied.

"The pump at that tenant house didn't work," Ethel said, "so we had to tote our water—for cooking and for taking baths—from the hand pump at the Cheshires' house, which was a good distance from the tenant house."

"Ethel had given me the impression before we married," C.G. said, "that she didn't know how to cook, telling me she had 'just made a few cakes.' But I knew cooking wouldn't be a problem since I had been batching with Joe Hingson and had learned how to cook. It was a big surprise after we married to see that Ethel did know how to cook. And she was a good cook!" [See Appendix A for a few of Ethel's recipes.]

Playing Pranks

"When we first married, we didn't have the money to do much," C.G. said. "We didn't even have as much as the price of a deck of cards, and we didn't drink. Some people would get drunk and go out and create their own fun.

"I remember hearing about Gordon Moses and his friend going to Matt Marable's house one night when it was freezing cold—called themselves having fun. Gordon was drinking and thought it would be funny to get Matt out of bed, so he started calling him—'Matt!'

"Matt got up and went out on the porch in his long johns and answered him, 'Yaw?' But it was dark, and at the exact same time he answered, Gordon yelled again, 'Matt.' When Matt answered again, 'Yaw?' Gordon was calling his name again and it drowned out Matt. Finally, Gordon said, 'Matt, my friend here just bet me ten dollars that I couldn't get you out of bed, and I've proved him wrong and just won myself ten dollars.'

" 'Gordon,' Matt replied, 'I done answered you till I'm 'bout froze to death! I bet ten dollars if you wait till I get my shotgun, you won't wake nobody *else* up!'

"It's a wonder tragedy didn't come from some of the pranks and things that were pulled—like, some people got a kick out of moving the flambeaus at the river when the new Hal W. Adams bridge[72] was being built to take you across the Suwannee River into Lafayette County. Where Highway 51 approached the river, the construction crew had set up kerosene flambeaus to alert people that the bridge was out to keep them from running their cars in the river. But, at night, pranksters would go there and move the flambeaus. I heard that my brother Ira and my cousin J. L. Hingson did that one time, but I wasn't there so I don't know for sure. Luckily nothing ever happened with the flambeaus moved—no tragedy."

A Can of Kerosene

"Before Ethel and I married," C.G. said, "I found a farm I wanted to buy in the Bakerville area—an all-black community not far from the Ladyland community—but Ethel said she wouldn't marry me if we were going to live in Bakerville. So I kept looking and asking around about another place to rent or buy; I wanted us to have a place of our own.

"When we got married, I was still farming with Joe Hingson, but I was to start a temporary job two weeks later that was to last through October. It was with the ASCS, measuring agricultural crop land for the allotment program; Willie Hingson was to help me, like I had helped Joe Hingson. (When I did the same thing the next year, I got DeWitt Johnson to help.)

"After I started the ASCS job, Ethel went one day to return some kerosene (we used kerosene in our lamps) that we had borrowed from Sam Stinson. She took the can of kerosene and walked over to their place; but when she got to their gate, she could tell nobody was home. Instead of walking all the way back home with the heavy can of kerosene, she decided she would set it up on one of their gateposts where they would see it when they got home. Well, when she set the can on the post, the Stinsonses' dog came after her. She turned and took off running, and when she did, she re-injured the foot she had cut before we married. At the wedding, her foot had looked like it was healing, but I guess that tendon inside had not yet healed. After running from the Stinsonses' dog, she developed a huge knot on the back of her heel, and she could hardly walk for a month."

Harold's Colt

"If I was going to farm the next year," C.G. said, "I needed, not only some land to plant the crops on, but also a mule or horse to help till the ground and plow the crops. Ethel's brother, Harold, had a colt that I thought he just might be willing to part with, so I went one day and talked to Harold.

"It turned out that I had a typewriter Harold wanted, so we agreed on a trade. I figured the horse was worth about seventy-five dollars and the typewriter wasn't, so I added a few dollars and we had a deal. We also agreed that I could leave the horse there on the Lanier/Rye place with him until I found some land to farm."

Frost on the Rooftop

"In November after the ASCS job ended," C.G. said, "I got another job, along with Joe Hingson, Oliver Hingson, and Barney Lanier, at Camp Blanding. We were, what you might call, wood butcherers—when we were supposed to be skilled carpenters. As soon as I knew I had the job, I ran to town and bought myself some tools. (Joe loaned me the money.)

"The man that was to be our boss was a pretty good-sized man that we ended up calling *Forty Broad*. When he saw me walk up that morning with a new saw, a new hammer, and a new nail apron, he cracked, 'By God, I bet it's a brand-new carpenter we got here too!'

"There was frost that morning, and Forty Broad put me on the housetop to work. Talk about scared—with frost on that roof! A little while later, I heard Forty Broad call, 'Hey, you up there.' I thought sure I had done something that didn't suit Forty Broad. But, he just told me to 'nail some one-by-six strips by the rafters to keep the birds out.'

"After Forty Broad got fired, a fellow by the name of Red Lindsey took over. About the second week in December, Lindsey said to us, 'I got to pink slip three of my employees.'

"I needed to quit anyway because I wanted to get ready to plant a crop the next year and still needed to find some land to rent or buy; so I asked for Lindsey's first pink slip and got it.

"I left Camp Blanding and headed back to the Cheshire house where I had left Ethel, but when I got there, Ethel was gone. The house was empty. Empty! No furniture! No clothes! No nothing!

"As it turned out, Ethel had told Ruby Hingson, Joe's wife, to tell me why she had to leave. She knew Ruby would see me when I got home, since their house was nearby. The reason Ethel had left was that Barney Cheshire had asked her if we could move out by Christmas because he needed the house for his new sharecropper. Rather than wait for me to get home right before Christmas, Ethel had gone ahead and packed up, and with her daddy's help, moved everything down to the Lanier/Rye place—in with Tip, Dosia, her Mama and Daddy, and Harold. After Ruby told me what had happened, I went and found Ethel and everything was okay.

"Our new living situation at the Lanier/Rye place was supposed to be temporary—just until we could find another place—but we ended up staying there longer than we expected because Mrs. Rye had hurt her back and needed Ethel's help."

I Rented the Ward Place

"Soon after I got back from Camp Blanding," C.G. said, "I heard that the Ward place, which joined Mr. Rye's land, was going to be available for rent after the first of the year.

"As I mentioned before, Edward Ward had left Daisy pretty well off when he died, with 260 acres that was paid for (land that Uncle Tip said included 80 acres he had once owned, before trading it to Dave Tomlinson).

"After Daisy's second husband, Ozie, was killed, she had married again. Her new husband, a man by the name of

Overstreet, had promptly cut all the high timber on the place—oaks and pines that could be used for making railroad ties—and as soon as he got paid for the timber, he took all the money and left town. Daisy had seen neither hide nor hair of him since.[73]

"After Overstreet ran off, Daisy had made a deal with a Richardson family to sharecrop her place. They were to live on the property and do the farming and get half the profits when the crops were sold, the customary arrangement. But instead of having the Richardsons live in one of her *tenant* houses, Daisy had let the Richardsons move into her *own* house (I don't know why); and she and her children had moved into one of her one-room tenant houses (the one to the north, that had been used as a school).[74]

"My understanding was that Daisy's deal with the Richardsons was ending, and they were moving out of her house at the end of the year. That was evidently Daisy's understanding too. When I went to talk to her about renting her 260 acres, she said that she was moving down to Clearwater, but she agreed to rent the place to me, beginning on January 1, 1941. We both signed the rental note, so I assumed she expected the Richardsons to be gone by New Year's Day.

"A few days after we signed the papers, Daisy took her family and headed for Clearwater. A couple of weeks after that, during a cold snap, the Richardson kids stopped in at Granny's house as they often did to warm themselves by the fireplace before walking on over to Ladyland School. Granny knew about my rental agreement with Daisy and was talking with the kids as they got warm. 'Well. I guess y'all gone be moving soon,' she said to them.

" 'Oh, no ma'am' one of the kids replied. 'We ain't gone move. Daddy's buying the place.'

"It turned out that the kids' father, Carl Richardson, hadn't even talked to Daisy about buying the place. He was planning to get the place by paying the back taxes. I did some checking around and was told that taxes on some of the land hadn't been paid in thirteen years.[75]

"I heard that Gus Smith had agreed to loan Richardson enough money to pay the back taxes on 160 acres. I also heard that Richardson told Gus Smith he didn't have any idea how to get in touch with Daisy. But he *did* know. What he knew was Daisy was in Clearwater and wouldn't know anything about what he was doing until after he got a tax deed in his name for 160 acres of her land. She wouldn't get a dime for it. I also heard that Richardson had tried but couldn't get a bank loan for paying the taxes on the whole thing—all 260 acres.

"I wrote to Daisy in Clearwater and told her what I'd heard—that Richardson was trying to get her place under the Murphy Act by paying back taxes on it, and that she was going to lose the place. I told her she needed to get back to Suwannee County and see what was going on. She did and found out the taxes on the place were about $365.

" 'C.G.,' she said to me, 'there's no way in the world I can raise that kind of money for the taxes.' I told her that I would really like to own the place, instead of renting it. She said if I could figure out a way, she'd sell it to me.

"I went and talked to Mr. Rye. We both decided to start trying to see if we could borrow the money. We agreed that if he could get the money to buy the 260 acres, he'd buy it, keep just 80 acres, and sell me the rest. Or, if I could get the money, I'd buy it, keep 180, and sell 80 to him. The eighty acres that Mr. Rye wanted had once been part of Uncle Tip's homestead, before he had traded it to Dave Tomlinson for a mule."

Getting the Money Together
"After Mr. Rye's and my discussion about buying the Ward place," C.G. said, "I went and talked to Daisy.

" 'If either you *or* Milton can get the money together,' Daisy said, 'I'll sell the place to either one of you.'

"So I went to the Commercial Bank in Live Oak, to see if they would loan me the money. I had borrowed ten dollars from them when I was a senior in high school and another thirty-five the next year. For that last loan, I needed a cosigner. Daisy Ward's brother-in-law, Mr. Will A. Ward (people called him *Glass-eyed Will* because he had a glass eye) is the one that agreed to co-sign the note with me. I had paid both loans back on time, so I had established a good credit history.

"Problem was, when I went to the bank to see about borrowing the money, they asked about Daisy's husband's whereabouts, saying Overstreet was legally entitled to half of any sale of the place. Daisy didn't know where old man Overstreet was. She hadn't heard from him since he left with her timber money. She wanted to divorce him but didn't have the money to pay for a divorce.

"Well, getting the money together so Daisy could get a divorce, pay her taxes, and sell the place was a roundabout mess, I'll tell you!

"Daisy had been made administrator of the estate when her husband Edward had died, so she could sign off for her minor children, but the older ones, Oleta and Mae, were, by then, married. Oleta had married my brother, Ira; and Mae had married Joseph "Buster" Lyle. To allow Daisy to sell the place, they would need to agree to sign quitclaim deeds. They did."[76]

A Scuffle and a Shooting

"The Richardsons were still living in the house, and I was still in the process of negotiating with Daisy and the bank about buying the place when a terrible thing happened in that house.

"It happened the night Carl Richardson came home from Camp Blanding. He didn't have a car, so he got a ride home with a fellow by the name of Bonds and another man.

Then, of course, they had all stopped on the way home for a few drinks.

"We heard that as soon as Richardson walked in the door that night, his wife asked him for money, knowing he had just been paid. She had a new sewing machine and maybe she wanted to buy some cloth to make the kids some clothes. (She had one boy when they married, and the rumor was that her father had paid Richardson to marry her, but I don't know if that is true; there was always some rumor going around about something or somebody.) Anyway, that night, Richardson claimed that he didn't have any money left.

" 'Them boys that brought me home done robbed me on the way home,' he told his wife.

"Richardson then proceeded to get his gun, a single barrel shotgun, 'so I can get my money back,' he told his wife—with him drinking and in a stupor!

"Well, he ended up getting in a scuffle with the fellows, and in the tussle over the shotgun, several shots were fired. His stepson, who was standing in front of the fireplace, was shot in the knee.

"Wess O'Neill's son[77] was visiting the Richardson boy—spending that night with him—and I think he saw the boy get shot. The Richardson boy was hurt and bleeding bad—yet (according to Wess O'Neill who told us about it later) the boy was more concerned about his mother's sewing machine than himself, saying 'Mama, don't let the blood get on your new machine.'

"To escape the gunfire, the Bonds fellow chose to exit the door, and the other man jumped out an open shutter—a window—while Richardson was reloading his gun. Hanging on the wall outside that window, there was an old three-bushel rusted tub with the bottom falling out (where a hen had a nest). How that fellow didn't hit that rusted and jagged metal tub and get all skinned up when he jumped, I don't know! Maybe he did. But somehow he managed to escape into the dark where Richardson couldn't see him.

"The men drove off, probably not even knowing the boy had been shot. Richardson then walked the quarter of a mile to Mr. Rye's house, saying just that his boy was hurt; and he wanted Mr. Rye to go to his house and get the boy and take him to the doctor—not explaining what had happened at all—just saying the boy was hurt. Mr. Rye was in bed, sick with pneumonia, and wasn't in any shape to go out. Plus, his old car had a bad tire on it, and he was afraid it wouldn't make it to town and back. Not knowing the boy was hurt bad—had been shot!—he told Harold to drive Mr. Richardson over and see if Lot Herring or one of his boys would take the boy to town to the doctor.

"When Harold went out to get in the old car, he saw that Richardson had a shotgun. He made some excuse and ran back in the house and said, 'Daddy, Carl's got a shotgun.' Then he ran right back out. Mr. Rye didn't know anything about the shooting, but knowing Richardson had a gun scared him. He dragged his sick self out of bed to see what was going on, but by then Harold had gone off with the man. Well, Mr. Rye was about scared to death because he had let Harold, not old enough to even be driving, carry that armed man off in the car. Plus, from just briefly talking to Carl, Mr. Rye knew Carl had been drinking.

"Harold took Richardson to the Herrings, and the Herrings went and got the boy and took him on to town to the doctor, but he was pretty far gone from loss of blood by the time they got him to the little makeshift hospital in Live Oak. I can't remember the doctor that was there then. I thought he was a quack. But, the boy had probably lost too much blood by the time they got him to the doctor, quack or not. The boy bled to death.

"Mr. Rye felt real bad about it, wondering if they could have saved the boy. If only he had known."

The Papers Were Signed

"After word got around in the community about what had happened that night," C.G. said, "and people found out that Ethel and I were planning to buy the place, they started trying to talk us out of it. 'Oh, I wish ya'll wouldn't buy that place' they said, 'there's all kind of things happened down there.' Some even told us the place was haunted. But we went forward with our plans, moved in the house in early March of 1941; and by the end of May, all the papers were signed.

"To pay for Daisy's divorce, the back taxes on the place, and something to her for the land, it cost me about a thousand dollars. That might not seem like much money today, but it seemed like a lot to me back then. I had to assume responsibility for a bank note, to be paid at the rate of a $150 a year, plus six percent interest.[78]

"Daisy seemed well-satisfied with the deal, and after the taxes were paid and the divorce was paid for, she ended up with more than nothing, which is what she would have got if Richardson or somebody else had taken her place under the Murphy Act."

After C.G. bought the Ward place, he reneged on his promise to sell eighty acres to his father-in-law. Instead, he let Mr. Rye farm the designated eighty-acre tract until the day that he could *give* it to him with no mortgage and no strings attached.

C.G. and Ethel's New Place

A small tenant house stood in the shade of a Chinaberry tree on the eastern edge of C.G.'s acreage (see map, p. 135). Another small tenant house (not shown on map) was on the eighty acres C.G. turned over to his father-in-law. But neither of these frame tenant houses was ever occupied again, and both eventually rotted to the ground.

The large farmhouse, which C.G. and Ethel had moved into, stood in the shade of large oaks (photo, p. 262). The house was situated on the north side of the farm, facing the Lanier/Rye place. When built, the cracker-style house consisted of only two rooms separated by an open hallway, plus two wide porches across its front and back; and behind the house was a kitchen that was connected to the back porch by a boardwalk. But, Edward and Daisy Ward had enclosed both sides of the back porch to create two bedrooms, albeit small ones.

"By the time we moved there," C.G. said, "the small bedroom of the southeast corner had been converted to a kitchen, and the old stand-alone kitchen was gone. But whoever tore it down had the good sense to leave the boardwalk, and having that was a real convenience. We could stand on the boardwalk to pump our water to take in the house, rather than having to stand on the ground and then track sand in the house.[79]

"Facing the house from the front, the two rooms on the right of the open hall were the bedrooms; Ethel and I slept in the front bedroom since it was bigger. Left of the hall was the living room, which had a fireplace, and the kitchen where we put our woodstove—though later on, we switched to a two-burner oil stove and eventually to a four-burner kerosene stove.

"Just as soon as we got our furniture moved in," C.G. said, "I found a good high place to store my shotgun—in the open hall up over the door going into our bedroom—so it was out of reach of any kid that might visit us. Then, I headed back down to Mr. Rye's place to get my colt that I had traded Harold for. I planned to break him and train him to plow. I had named him Rex. I put Rex in the cow lot west of the house, next to the old crib. But I eventually tore that old lot and crib down and built new animal pens on the east side of the house, behind the packhouse."

This arrangement put more distance between the house and the flies, gnats, and odor that went with animal pens.

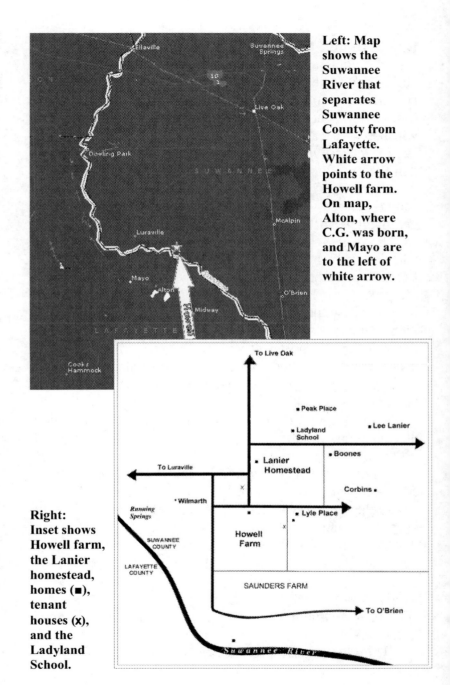

Left: Map shows the Suwannee River that separates Suwannee County from Lafayette. White arrow points to the Howell farm. On map, Alton, where C.G. was born, and Mayo are to the left of white arrow.

Right: Inset shows Howell farm, the Lanier homestead, homes (■), tenant houses (x), and the Ladyland School.

Bump! Bump! Bump! in the Night

"A few nights after we moved into the house," C.G. said, "Ethel and I were in bed and I heard a noise. 'Bump . . . Bump . . . Bump.' Ethel must have heard it at the same time. She reached over and touched me. 'You awake?' she whispered. 'Yeah,' I whispered back, 'did you hear that?' 'Yeah, reckon what it is?' (I could tell she was scared.) 'I don't know,' I told her, 'but I'm fixing to go and find out.'

"I crawled out of bed as easy as I could. The noise sounded like it was coming from the open hall. I needed to get my gun. But it was out there in the hall over the door!

"Ethel and I were imagining all kinds of things. But when I finally got to the door and eased it open just a crack, I could see in the moonlight that it was nothing to be afraid of. It was Kent Thomas's dog gnawing on a big hambone.

"After supper, Ethel had left a baked ham on the kitchen table, covered with a cloth, like she was used to doing before we got electricity and a refrigerator. The dog had evidently smelled that ham and helped himself. The kitchen door wouldn't stay shut because the old wooden latch on it was broken.

"That dog was evermore enjoying himself as he rolled that hambone around on the floor. He had about finished off all the meat.

"I hollered at the dog and he took off down the back steps—left his bone behind. So, I picked it up and threw it out in the yard, set a chair up against the kitchen door to keep it shut, and went back to bed.

"After that one time, I don't remember that we ever heard any more bumps in the night."

The Visiting Baptist Preacher

"Our back bedroom went unused," C.G. said, "except when we stored tobacco there."

"Until that Baptist preacher visited!" Ethel corrected.

"Oh, I forgot about that," C.G. replied. "I think he was preaching a revival at Philadelphia, and we offered for him to spend a night with us."

"We hadn't slept in that room," Ethel said, "and I don't remember where I got the bed frame and mattress to put in there, but anyway, I made the bed for him and thought he would be plenty comfortable.

"The next morning, he was up before daylight—dressed and ready to leave. He wouldn't even stay for breakfast! I couldn't figure out what in the world was wrong until after he left and I went in that room where he had slept and saw blood spots all over that white sheet. Bedbugs had feasted on him good.

"That room, like the kitchen, didn't have a ceiling in it. It was built of old slab lumber, and bats that can carry bedbugs could get in there. The walls had lots of cracks and crevices where the bedbugs could hide during the day, so I didn't know they were there. But they had sure been out that night. They ate that preacher up! We never did see the likes of him again.

"To get rid of the bedbugs in that room, I took the mattress out and aired and sunned it, and I scrubbed that whole room down—walls, floors, and all—with lye soap. After that we never had any more problems with bedbugs or with our company leaving early."

We Had Some Catching Up to Do
"My brothers and one of my sisters got ahead of Ethel and me in starting a family," C.G. said. "Back when we were dating, my brother Ira met Oleta and fell head over heels in love. When Ira first told me he wanted to marry Oleta— 'right away,' he said, I tried my best to convince him that they should both finish high school first. He was living with Aunt Ethel at the time. I told him that I would pay for his school supplies if he would stay in school. But my words fell on deaf ears.

"He and Oleta married on October 7, 1939. They moved into another house that Aunt Ethel owned, but living there didn't last long, because Aunt Ethel tried to tend to their business.

"Our brother Mernest was already married. He and his wife, Eloise, lived in an apartment in Miami and offered for Ira and Oleta to move in with them, so they did. Mernest even let Ira have his job, which was then at Swift Meat Company, and Mernest went and found another job.

"Eloise and Oleta were both pregnant at the same time. I can't quite imagine those two pregnant women—different as night and day—living in the same house together.

"Mernest and Eloise's son Donald and Ira and Oleta's son Jimmy were born just five days apart."

"When Jimmy was born," Oleta said, "we were on what you would probably call welfare, because we had no money and no health insurance.

Eloise and Mernest Howell. Mernest is holding his nephew Jimmy Howell (left) and his son Donald (right).

After Jimmy was born, we moved out of Mernest and Eloise's place and in with the Midgetts—Ira's mother and her husband, Charles. They were renting a house on 1st Street in Miami. We paid them fourteen dollars a week for room and board. Ira's job then was driving a soft drink delivery truck. Every day he had to drive all the way to Key West and back. One day I put Jim in a stroller and went down to the A&P grocery for milk. I saw a *Help Wanted* sign in the window. So I went in and talked to the meat manager. His name was Swann. 'I see you want to hire

- 138 -

someone,' I told Mr. Swann. 'I have a boy to feed, and my husband really needs a better job, and you should hire him!' 'Well, send him in,' he told me. So when Ira went into the store," Oleta said proudly, "he was hired on the spot."[80]

"Meanwhile," C.G. said, "my sister Clara Mae had married Bob Midgett, her stepbrother. They had a baby boy they named Loren,[81] and Mernest and Eloise had another baby[82] on the way, so Ethel and I had some catching up to do!"

Clara and C. E. Midgett. Clara is holding her first grandson, Donald.

Laura Howell (C.G.'s baby sister)

"C.G.'s youngest sister, Laura, was just seventeen," Ethel said, "when she came up from Miami for a visit. It was the summer after we got settled in our house. I wasn't feeling good when she got there, and she guessed why.

" 'Ethel,' Laura said, 'I'll bet you're pregnant! If it's a girl, name her after me!' "

- 139 -

Baby Patsy

"Dr. Price came to the house and delivered the baby," C.G. said. "I had paid him his standard thirty-five-dollar fee in advance."

"Since it was a girl," Ethel said, "we named her Laura Patricia, after Laura, and called her Patsy. Dr. Price weighed her on his draw scales, and she weighed eight pounds even.

"Mama was there to help. Then she cooked breakfast, and Dr. Price stayed and ate.

"Upon seeing our new baby," Ethel continued, "Susie Allen got me back for something I had said about one of her babies a long time ago. I had said it the day she took her new baby boy over to Granny's house to show him off. Her husband Newt drove her there in their horse and wagon, a conveyance that had no cover to shield them from the sun. Most mothers would know to shield a baby's face from the hot sun, but evidently, Susie didn't.

Patsy Howell

"When they got there that day, her baby's little face was red as a beet—blistered from the hot sun. What I wanted to say to her was, 'Don't you know you should cover that baby's face!' But instead I just tried to call her attention to it so maybe she wouldn't let it happen again. All I said was, 'My goodness, Susie, the baby's little face sure does look red.'

"It was a few days after Patsy was born that the Allens came to see Granny and Granddaddy Tip, and I was there with the baby. Susie Allen took one look at Patsy's face and said, 'Well, ain't her head long!' The funny thing is, Patsy's face was as round as a ball!

"And that reminds me of something Daddy said to Susie's husband, one time," Ethel continued.

"Newt was always bragging about Susie, and I guess Daddy got tired of hearing it. One day Newt said, 'It's a good thing all men ain't alike or all of 'em would-a wanted my Susie.'

" 'Well,' Daddy replied, 'if they was all like me, they wouldn't have had her.' "

Left to right: Clara Mae with Loren; Oleta with Jimmy; and Eloise with Donald and Ruth (in arms). C.G.'s brothers and sisters were definitely way ahead in the baby department.

⌒ 8   Rooted in Florida Soil

When C.G. made the decision to buy the Ward place, he had a willing partner in Ethel Rye Howell. She was deeply rooted in the southern soil of north Florida. Ancestors of her maternal grandfather, Tip Lanier, arrived in the area before Florida even became a state.

Dates in Florida History

1821   *Florida became a territory of the U.S. government.*
1845   *Florida was recognized as the twenty-seventh state, a slave state, on March 3, 1845. Florida's population at that time was 66,500.*
1861   *Florida seceded from the Union.*
1888   *Phosphate became a major industry in Florida.*

And public records show that the ancestors of Ethel's maternal grandmother, Dosia Dees, were living in north Florida when the South seceded from the Union.

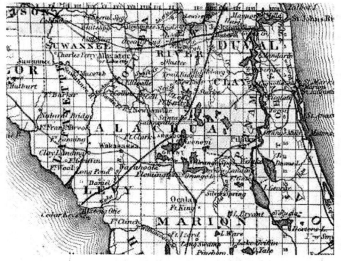

Northern Florida, 1864
Courtesy, Alachua County Library District
http://heritage.acld.lib.fl.us

Lanier Homestead (arrow) by S & S Railroad
1899 Map, courtesy, the private collection of Roy Winkelman
Florida Center for Instructional Technology (FCIT)
http://etc.usf.edu/maps

Dosia Dees's Family

A small scrap of yellowed paper, torn from a ruled tablet, that Dosia kept tucked within the pages of her Bible, provided this information about her father and mother:

March 14, 1928

Lewis M. Deas[iv]
Born February 8, 1816
Died April 12, 1902

Lydia Deas
Born October 6, 1829
Died September 29, 1894

When found after Dosia's death, the scrap of paper was falling apart at the folds, the result of being folded and refolded so many times. That is the only written information about Dosia's family that she left, but John and Maude Renfroe, her nephew and niece, wrote the following (note that they wrote—not Lewis Deas—but Louis Dees):

> Our grandfather, Louis Malonie Dees, and family were one of the first settlers in what is now Lafayette County. They settled at Cooks Hammock, near Calf Creek early in 1850. They moved in 1862 to Hamilton County, but moved back to Lafayette County in 1876, settling at Daytown where they lived the rest of his life.
>
> He was called to the Civil War and was on his way to the battlefield when the war ended. He gave beef-cattle to help feed the soldiers. Our grandmother knitted socks, gloves, made coats, etc., to help the soldiers. She spun and made wool for their clothing and made palmetto hats.

[iv] On the scrap of paper in her Bible, Dosia spelled her parents' last name D-e-a-s; but on her marriage certificate, it is spelled D-e-e-s, and other family members spelled it D-e-e-s.

Our grandfather grew corn, cotton, potatoes, cane and vegetables. He also fished and hunted.

The entire country was covered with large, yellow pine. The settlers built their houses with the small trees.

Our grandfather made his cane mill out of wood, also his barrels, pails, and bread trays. He started his fires by striking flint and steel together using cotton or rags to catch the sparks to get the blaze started. Matches were very scarce then. Some of the settlers used oak wood to keep their fires going from day to day. Tallow candles and lightwood fires were the only means for both lights and warmth.

They made their own shoes from tanned cow hides.

The hand mill was used every day for grinding corn for meal and grits.

Schools were taught by private teachers, and to begin with, were taught in the settler's home, moving from one neighbor's home to another, day to day. Later small school houses were built from small logs and the children sat on hued logs for seats.

Their method of travel was by oxen, horses, and carts. The way our grandfather got salt to use was by going by horse and cart to the coast and making it from the salt water, which took several days to get a supply.

Census records show that in 1860 there were 567 slaves in Lafayette County. Lewis M. Dees owned one of them.

Members of his generation said he treated the slave like a brother. If Lewis had lived in a different time and place, perhaps he would have agreed with the statement made centuries before by Plato—*A slave is an embarrassing possession*—and recognized that no matter how good the treatment, one person should never be owned by another.

Lewis was fifty-one and Lydia was thirty-seven when she gave birth to Theodosia Dees (Dosia) on January 24, 1867, near Daytown (Day), Florida.

Lewis and Lydia already had three children: seven-year-old Samuel, four-year-old Ella Louise, and two-year-old Lewis Summer. (The children were called Sammy, Lou, and Summer.)

After Dosia was born, Lewis and Lydia went on to have two more daughters: Minnie and Mary Ann.

When Dosia reached the age of nineteen, she married Tip Lanier. (Her sister Lou[83] had already married Tip's younger brother Lee.)

Tip's Grandparents, Benjamin and Sara

Tip never spoke of any of his grandparents; likely, all were deceased when he was born. But public records provide the following information about his paternal grandparents.

Benjamin Lanier, was born in 1786, before the U.S. Constitution was written, in the area that later became Duplin County, North Carolina.

At the age of nineteen, Benjamin married Sara Pridgen, the daughter of Luke Pridgen and Amelia Bowen Pridgen. Their marriage was recorded on September 24, 1805, in Bulloch County, Georgia. It was there, near the town of Savannah, that they started their family.

Sometime before 1845, Benjamin and Sara moved to the territory of Florida. There, when the very first statewide votes were cast—votes regarding statehood—on Monday, May 26, 1845, Benjamin Lanier served at the Courthouse in Madison as one of three election inspectors for precinct number three.[84]

Benjamin and Sara had eleven children, including Rowan (Tip's father).

Benjamin died in Madison County in August of 1854 at the age of sixty-eight. He had lived to see his son Rowan marry, but the birth of his grandson Tip was still about a decade away.

The date of Sarah's death is unknown.

Tip's Parents, Rowan and Emmaline

Tip's father, Rowan Johnson Lanier, was born in Bulloch County, Georgia, on April 6, 1826.

Tip's mother was born on April 9, 1833, in the area that became Madison County, Florida, but at the time of her birth, Florida had yet to be recognized as a state. Emmaline was nearly twelve when that happened.

At the age of twenty-four, Rowan married seventeen-year-old Emmaline. After their marriage (1850), they settled in Madison, the area of her birth.

The Civil War

By the time the first shots of the Civil War were fired at Fort Sumter on April 12, 1861, Emmaline and Rowan had seven children: three boys and four girls.

Whether or not Rowan served in the Confederate army is not known. Under the first Southern draft laws, passed in April of 1862, he would have been exempt. The law then

Emmaline and Rowan Lanier, Ethel's great-grandparents

stated that able-bodied men, ages eighteen to thirty-five, were liable for three years' service. At the time, Rowan was over the age limit; he was thirty-six.

But the draft laws were later modified to include men from seventeen to *fifty*! Under the new laws, Rowan most certainly would have been eligible, and two men from Florida by the name of R. J. Lanier are listed on the U.S.

Interior Department's website as having served in the Confederate Cavalry. If Rowan served, he likely fought for only a short period (not that it would have seemed short). A

Asbery (Tip) Lanier

short period is assumed because two years into the war, on June 15, 1863, Emmaline gave birth to Asbery (Tip),[v] and two weeks after the war ended, she gave birth to their ninth child, whom they named Robert Lee, after the famous General.

Rowan and Emmaline went on to have a total of fourteen children: seven boys and seven girls, but their tenth child, daughter Patia, died as an infant (see Appendix B).[85]

Tip and Dosia

Tip and Dosia were married on January 6, 1886. Tip had never attended school and could neither read nor write. Dosia said she would teach him. They set up housekeeping in a one-room cabin—a shack really— but that was temporary.

Nine months and one day after Tip and Dosia married, Dosia went into labor, but the

---

[v] Tip Lanier's correct name is a puzzle. Some genealogists believe his full name is Asbery Thomas Lanier (as shown on Ethel Rye's Ancestry, p. xiii); others believe it is Asbury Tipton Lanier (as listed in Appendix B). Tip himself was no help. He always signed his name: *A. Lanier.*

baby, a boy, died during childbirth. Later on, when Tip and Dosia referred to their firstborn, they called him Lloyd, but no one is sure where the baby was buried. The following (unedited) inscription in the family Bible, thought to be written by Dosia, lists all three children:

Loided Lanier was
Borned October the 7 1886

Lonzo Lanier was
Borned October the 10 1891

Delma Lanier
was bornd September the 2 1896

Although the name of Tip and Dosia's second son was recorded as *Lonzo* in the family Bible, he later signed his name *Alonzo*.

Whether or not a midwife assisted Dosia with the delivery of Lloyd and/or Alonzo is not known either; perhaps not, since Dosia herself was a midwife. But during the summer that Dosia was expecting her third child, she arranged for a black midwife in the community to assist with the delivery.

As soon as Dosia's labor pains started, on the second day of September, the midwife was summoned. After she arrived, labor dragged on and on. Having lost one baby during childbirth, Dosia grew concerned. The midwife, frustrated as well, finally blurted—

"Dat baby's just too big to come out! Dat baby just can't be born!"

"Put your fingers down under *dat* baby's armpits!" Dosia replied, "and pull it out!"

When Dosia retold the story later, she said. "When the midwife weighed the baby on a set of hang-me-down scales, the needle bounced back and forth before settling on the fourteen-pound mark!"

Dosia and Tip named the baby Queen Delma Lanier. However, the name Queen was not recorded in the Bible—and since Delma hated the name—she never used it. As for the date of her birth, she was told it was September 2, 1895 (though her mother wrote *1896* in the family Bible).

Dosia, Delma, and Alonzo Lanier

Note in the photo at left that Alonzo has his pants legs rolled up and wears no shoes, but he is *dressed up* in a double-breasted coat. He wears a pained expression that says, *How soon can I take off this hot jacket?*

After this photo was taken, baby Delma caught scarlet fever and lost all her hair. When it grew back, it came in dark and naturally curly,[86] and her father, Tip, decreed then that it should never be cut. It never was, as long as Tip Lanier lived.

The Lanier Homestead
In the late 1800s, under the U.S. Homestead Act, Tip applied for a parcel of public land offered by the U.S. Government—free land—as if anything is ever free. In this case, the one requirement was that the land be cultivated

for a period of ten years.

One hundred and sixty acres of land was deeded to Asbery Lanier by U.S. President William McKinley on May 12, 1899.[87] The land was in the middle of a Florida wilderness—untamed land, sandy loam that had to be cleared of trees and scrub before it could be cultivated; and clearing such land required sweat, manpower, and/or horsepower. Tip owned no horse and had no money to buy one. But his neighbor Dave Tomlinson had a mule. So, Tip bargained with Mr. Tomlinson for the mule and signed a note agreeing to pay for the animal at a later date.

Alas, when the note came due, Tip still had not the cash to pay Mr. Tomlinson. So, in lieu of cash, he signed away half of his 160-acre homestead to Mr. Tomlinson. Eighty acres for a mule! But at the time, both parties agreed it was a fair trade, since the land had cost Tip nothing other than a ten- or fifteen-dollar application fee.

On the western front of the remaining eighty acres, Tip erected a log house. By today's standards, it was small (one room for eating, sleeping, and living), but its walls were solidly constructed of sturdy logs chinked with clay.

The home had no indoor plumbing and no electricity, but Tip and Dosia had a hand pump for drawing water, a kerosene lantern for evening light, and a fireplace that heated the house and served as Dosia's stove; with those amenities, they lived as well or better than their neighbors.

Family and Friends

Alonzo and Delma did not get to know their Lanier grandparents, nor did Delma know their Grandmother Dees (Lydia died at the age of sixty-four, when Alonzo was about three, before Delma was born); but Lewis Dees, fifteen years older than his wife, lived until Alonzo was nearly eleven, and Delma was six. As for aunts, uncles, cousins, and friends, Alonzo and Delma had plenty of those.

Every now and then, Tip and Dosia took a trip to the

Gulf by way of the old Salt Lake Road. This excursion took them through Lafayette County and past the home of their friends, John and Cora Rye. They never passed without stopping to visit; and the Ryes would return the favor by visiting the Laniers at their home near Wilmarth. As a result, the children became good friends, especially Alonzo and Milton.

One day at the Laniers' home, Alonzo and Milton were palling around together when Milton went up and stood in front of the Laniers' bureau, his chin barely reaching the top of the chest. He picked up a comb and straightened his hair; then, after eyeing his reflection in the mirror just above the bureau, he turned to Alonzo and said, "I'm going to marry your sister someday!"

When school was in session, Alonzo and Delma walked a quarter of a mile to the one-room Ladyland schoolhouse where they studied reading, writing, arithmetic, and spelling using a *Blue Back Speller.* The school went through the eighth grade and so did they.

Alonzo was nearly grown and Delma was a teenager when a new baby came into their lives. His name was Cary.

"Cary's mother died during childbirth," Ethel said. "Some of his aunts tried to care for him for a while, but he was about to die when his daddy, Mr. Neely, went to Granny and asked if she would take the baby. Of course, she said she would. The Neelys were not blood related, but were related through marriage. (Cary was the nephew of Tip's sister Millie; that is, he was Millie's husband's brother's child.)"

Cary was a tiny baby—probably premature, so Dosia fed him with an eyedropper for the first few weeks. Delma said that her new brother got diarrhea one time, and they like never to have got that stopped, and every time she had to wash one of his diapers, she lost every bit of her appetite.

During World War I

Alonzo helped his father on the farm until he was twenty-six years old. Then came World War I.

On June 26, 1918, Alonzo enlisted in the Army. When he went to complete the paperwork, he saw that the forms asked for his full name, including his middle name. If his parents had ever given him a middle name, they had never told him. So on the application, he wrote: *Lanier, Alonzo nmn* (*nmn* stood for no middle name, without which, he was told, his form would be rejected as incomplete). Where the application asked for his occupation, he wrote *farmer.*

Alonzo's impending departure was soon announced in the *Suwannee Democrat.* The article, clipped and saved by his family, read:

> Twenty-one white men of Suwannee County are to leave for Camp Jackson, Saturday. The list is as follows: Jas. C. Adams, Ottis Oliver Hurst...and Alonza [*sic*] Lanier.[88]

While in the service, Alonzo was stationed at the Ordnance Depot in Curtis Bay (port of Baltimore). The Army was there to guard ships and vehicles and load munitions and cargo onto ships bound for France.

No doubt the Baltimore winter was a shock to Alonzo, accustomed to Florida's mild weather. Before the winter ended, he contracted pneumonia. The Army sent him to recuperate at nearby Fort McHenry, which was being used as a hospital.[vi]

During his active duty, Alonzo served as a cook at Curtis Bay. There, he got the nickname Pete, given to him by his sergeant—perhaps, some speculated, because the sergeant thought the name Alonzo not tough enough for a

---

[vi] It was at Fort McHenry that Francis Scott Key wrote "The Star Spangled Banner" during the War of 1812, when the Americans were battling the British.

soldier. As it turned out, Alonzo never saw combat. He was discharged on March 29, 1919. His discharge papers describe him as having blue eyes, brown hair, a dark complexion, and 5 feet 7½ inches tall.

Tip and Dosia thought their son would come home when he was released, but Alonzo had a reason to stay in Baltimore. He had met a tall redhead by the name of Ethel Severn, a sister of one of his buddies; like his buddies, she called him Pete.

With Alonzo far away in Baltimore, Tip and Dosia's foster son, Cary, became a big help to Tip on the farm. Cary had grown into a robust, jolly fellow, belying his precarious start. As time passed, Tip taught Cary to play the fiddle, something he had never had the time, or taken the time, to teach his biological children.[89] After Cary mastered the instrument, Tip started letting Cary switch off with him at the square dances.[90]

Delma, as a Young Lady

As a young lady, Delma wore her long dark hair pinned up on top of her head, in a bun, similar to the way her mother wore hers. But whereas Dosia's straight hair stayed put (it was always slicked down tight, away from her sun-damaged face), Delma's wavy hair did just the opposite. Her curls were always springing loose so that soft tendrils framed her fair face, a face she was extra careful to protect from the damaging rays of the sun.

In the photograph shown on the next page, she stands close to Ed Randall, a young man who worked for the railroad and—some said—was the perfect suitor for Delma. She appears happy, decked out in a wide-brimmed hat and a white voile, ankle-length dress with lace-trimmed ruffles extending from her waist, across her bosom, and over her shoulders. The fleur-de-lis pin at her shoulder secures a gold watch, perhaps the one that Clarence (Bud) Howell pawned or traded to Tip in exchange for room and board.

In this photograph, the face of the watch seems much too close to Delma's face for her eyes to focus on its dial, and that is probably just the way Delma wanted it. Never a stickler for time, she likely wore the watch more for decoration than for the time of day. If she wound the watch at all, she likely never bothered to lift its gold cover to check the exact time.

Delma did not marry Ed Randall, the man in the photograph, but they became friends for life.

Ed Randall and Delma Lanier

Delma Takes the Cake

Delma was a popular young lady, a fact supported by an article published in 1916 in the *Suwannee Democrat*:

> The big box supper at the Ladyland school house Friday night came off on scheduled time and was a pronounced success from every standpoint. A large crowd was in attendance, evidencing the splendid spirit of interest in school affairs of the Wilmarth people. It is to the credit of the Ladyland people that they have taken more interest in their school for the past session than ever before . . . .

The box supper was an outgrowth of this spirit, it being necessary to provide for the ever increasing needs of the school. Much credit is due to the efforts of the principal, Mr. Trexler, for the success of the undertaking, as well as to Mr. Peacock, the assistant. Twenty-nine beautifully decorated boxes were then bid off, the amount of $21.20 being realized from the sale. Then came the popularity contest, the prize given was a handsome cake. For every five cents contributed, the giver was allowed five votes for his choice. A great deal of interest was shown in this contest, the leading lady being only a few votes ahead at any time. The contest soon settled down between Miss Delma Lanier and Miss Lena Miller. As the contest proceeded, the leadership alternated between these two young ladies and the result was in doubt until the last count, which showed Miss Delma the winner of the popularity contest and cake. The final vote stood: Miss Lanier 1,335; Miss Miller 1,270.

News Item from Wilmarth Florida
Published August 18, 1916 (Vol XX, No ll)
The Suwannee Democrat

Although Miss Lena Miller had reason to be jealous of Delma's popularity, she never gave any indication of it. The same could not be said for Susie Allen.

Newt and Delma
As good neighbors do, Newt Allen and his wife Susie often stopped by to visit with the Laniers and sometimes brought garden vegetables or some other item to share. Once they even gave Tip and Dosia half of a goat.

One day when Newt and Susie dropped by, Delma was outside by the rail fence, washing clothes in tubs of water. Newt went over to talk to Delma instead of going inside the house with Susie to see Dosia—and he must have lingered by the fence in conversation with Delma a bit too long. Susie, who had gone inside, watched him through a window and soon marched out to the porch.

"Ain't y'all puhr-ty things—or not?" Susie hollered to her husband and Delma in an accusatory tone.

Having absolutely no interest whatsoever in Newt Allen, Delma said she was taken aback by Susie's remark. Newt was, after all, nearly old enough to be her father! Besides, she was already wearing a ruby ring,[91] presented to her by Milton Rye, a fellow who'd had his sights on Delma since his chin reached the top of the Laniers' bureau.

A Man Who Gained Respect

Tip was not happy about his daughter's engagement to Milton Rye.

"In Granddaddy Tip's eyes," Ethel said, "no man would have been good enough for her. Granddaddy thought Mama hung the moon."

It is often said that a woman chooses for her husband a man who reminds her of her father. But in Delma's case, that did not ring true. Tip was a tall man, a man whose demeanor seemed to command respect when he walked into a room. Milton, on the other hand, was a man of small stature, but one who gained respect the longer he stayed.

Considering Milton's looks—his small frame, his sandy hair, and his blue eyes—he didn't look the part of a convict guard, the job he held at the time he married Delma. In fact, Milton's quiet presence evidently gave the convicts he guarded a false first impression.

"If I was to run, boss," one convict asked him, "you wouldn't really shoot me, would you?"

"Try me," Milton Rye replied, turning his gun up and shooting at a squirrel on a tree branch overhead. The dead squirrel landed at the prisoner's feet.

Milton said he had to repeat this demonstration only when a new prisoner was added to his gang. He also said that no convict ever escaped on his watch, and he never had to shoot one.

Milton and Delma Marry

Milton had no transportation of his own in those days. But, when he wanted to see his fiancée—his Delma—his *Shug* (short for sugar), he caught the train—practically to her

front door, without even having to buy a ticket! It was a freight train that hauled phosphate. It traveled on a track that ran right in front of the Lanier place. When the train slowed in preparation for its next stop at Wilmarth, Milton hopped off.

Four months after Delma won the popularity contest at Ladyland, she became the bride of Milton Rye. The wedding was held on December 3, 1916, at the home of her parents. It was reported later that Delma's father did not watch

Milton and Delma Rye (Her dress was red satin with rhinestone buttons.)

as The Reverend M. H. Touchton pronounced Delma and Milton "man and wife." It was just more than Tip Lanier could take.

Grandchildren for Tip and Dosia

Delma and Alonzo took turns presenting their parents with grandchildren. Although Alonzo was several years older, Delma took the lead.

Milton was still working as a convict guard in Taylor and Lafayette counties when Delma became pregnant. Unfortunately, their firstborn, a baby boy, was stillborn. The couple never talked about this much. The baby was never named, the birth date is not known, and none of the family knows where the baby was buried. Perhaps it was in a grave near where they lived at the time.

In 1921, five years into their marriage, Milton was working with his brother Raleigh, operating a garage and filling station in Macclenny, when Delma discovered she was pregnant again. Milton was then twenty-eight and Delma twenty-five. As her due date drew near, she asked her mother, Dosia, to come to Macclenny for the birth.

On October 1, 1921, Dosia assisted Dr. Brown in the delivery of a baby girl, born at four o'clock in the afternoon. They named her Ethel Macie Rye—Macie,[92] after one of Milton's cousins that he was crazy about, and Ethel after Alonzo's tall, redheaded fiancée, Ethel Severn.

Dosia thought the baby was beautiful, and in years to come she told little Ethel about the day of her birth.

"When you was born," Dosia said to her little granddaughter, "you was *so* pretty! Your face was all covered with hair! But you was so pretty!"

It was a story little Ethel would ask her Granny to repeat again and again. But, after Ethel was older and was asked to provide more details about her birth, she had few words—"I was born. That's enough, ain't it? I have no idea how much I weighed, and I doubt I was measured. They probably couldn't keep me still long enough."

Three months after Ethel's birth, Delma's brother, Alonzo married Ethel Margaret Severn. The ceremony took

- 159 -

Alonzo and Ethel Severn Lanier

place on December 21, 1921, in the Fort Avenue Methodist Church in Baltimore. Alonzo's Florida relatives did not attend, but his family gave their blessings.

Alonzo and Ethel then moved into a row house at 1523 Covington Street in Baltimore, a few blocks from Fort McHenry where he had recuperated from pneumonia while serving in the Army.

"Buck" Lanier

Their first child was born on September 13, 1922. They named him Severn Eugene Lanier, using his mother's family name *Severn* as his first—not that he used Severn or Eugene. After some of the kids on the block began teasing him about his girly name, he nicknamed himself *Buck* after his movie hero, cowboy Buck Jones, and that became him.

Now it was Milton and Delma's turn to have a baby.

After the garage job in Macclenny ended, Milton

went back to guarding convicts and moved his family to Alton in Lafayette County. It was there that little Ethel got herself a baby brother. He was born on February 13, 1924. Milton and Delma named their son Harold Milton Rye. In addition to having his father's name, the baby had his father's blue eyes.

Wilbur Lanier

Delma and Milton were then one up on Alonzo and his wife, but it would eventually even out.

Tip and Dosia got their fourth and last grandchild a few years later when Alonzo and Ethel had another son, whom they named Wilbur Bruce Lanier.

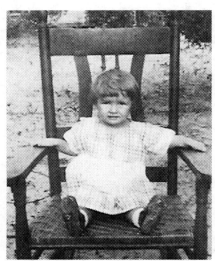

Ethel Rye

He Asked![93]

Soon after Harold was born, the Rye family moved back to live with Tip and Dosia on the farm.

Floyd Lanier, Tip's nephew who lived nearby, thought little Ethel was the cutest little thing that ever was. He dearly loved to hear her talk. So he would ask her questions just to listen to her response.

"What does your Granny do when she gets up every morning?" he asked one day, knowing full well the answer: Dosia got up and milked the cow.

- 161 -

"P-sh-sh-sh-sh-h-h-h-h-h-h-h-h-h-h-h-h-h," little Ethel answered, illustrating—not the sound of milking the cow— but the sound her Granny made when she peed in the pot.

Tip's Brothers
"Granddaddy Tip was close to several of his brothers," Ethel said. "I think he was closest to his brother Lee, probably because they were the most alike. When they were younger, I think they had a lot of fun together."

Bernice Lanier, Tip's niece and Lee Lanier's granddaughter, agreed and told the following story about them.

"They were headed to a frolic over in Lafayette County one night. I guess it was before Grandpa Lee or Uncle Tip got married. I heard that Uncle Tip got all dressed up in a white suit, whereas Grandpa Lee was wearing overalls. When they got to the river where they had to cross, Tip got in the boat and was waiting for Lee, who was taking his sweet time. Tip turned around and said to Lee, 'Aye God, buddy, if you're gonna go, then get in the damn boat!' So Lee sailed into the boat, and when he did, he turned it over. They finally got the boat turned upright and paddled on across the river, but they were both soakin' wet.

"After they tied the boat up, Tip wanted to stop at a friend's house before walking on to the frolic—and did—to freshen up and let his clothes dry a little. But Lee didn't want to stop. He was ready to party! He left Tip there and walked on to the frolic with his clothes dripping wet."

"Uncle Lee was a mess," Ethel said, when she heard Bernice's story.

"Yeah, he was a mess," C.G. said. I heard about him getting a trick played on him one day—but he started it! He was taking some corn to the mill at Luraville, to get it ground into grits and meal. To get there, he had to pass by the Joe Miller place. That day the Millers were out in their cane patch cutting and stacking stalks of cane for grinding to make syrup. Lee got down off his mule, set his sack of corn on the ground to let his mule rest, and climbed over the rail fence to help himself to a stalk of the Millers' cane, without even speaking to the Millers. Then, after helping himself, he climbed up on the rail fence and started cutting off and chewing pieces of their cane.

"When he finally climbed down off the fence, Mr. Miller walked over where he was and spoke. Uncle Lee responded with not much more than a 'Howdy' as he put his sack of corn back on the mule. As he mounted the mule, he didn't see Joe Miller reach down and pick up a fresh pine cone that had fallen from a tree. Just as Uncle Lee got settled on his mule and was adjusting the sack of corn, Mr. Miller lifted the mule's tail and clamped it down on top of that prickly pine cone. That mule let loose, and Uncle Lee slid to one side of the mule and the sack of corn slid to the other. When the sack hit the ground, it split wide open and his corn spilled everywhere. But neither one of the men was mad. Uncle Lee just got up and laughed as Joe Miller started calling his hogs to eat the kernels.

"Then Uncle Lee had to go back home and bag up another sack of corn for the mill."

"After Uncle Lee and Aunt Lou had so many kids— they had eight—" Ethel said, "then Uncle Lee didn't have as much time to cut the fool. But Granddaddy and his friend John Morgan, a teacher at Ladyland that boarded at Granny and Granddaddy's, liked to go visit with Uncle Lee. When Granddaddy left home, he would tell Granny he was going to Lee's to *set watch*, whatever that meant. What they were really doing was going over there to tell jokes.

"Their visits with Uncle Lee got longer and longer. They would stay late into the night. The next morning, Granddaddy Tip would say, 'John was dragging for me last night,' which meant he was keeping him up half the night. Well, Uncle Lee finally got tired of them staying so late at his place when he had work to do the next day. So, one night he came over to visit Granddaddy Tip and stayed late—I mean, real late! He finally left, but after he got out to the yard gate, he turned around and came right back in the house and sat down again. He kept Granddaddy up all night!

Lee and Lou (Dees) Lanier's family

"Uncle Lee's place was close by," Ethel continued, "but he got so busy with his big family that we saw less of him and more of Uncle Lewis and Uncle France.

"Uncle Lewis's family is the one we saw the most of because Mama and his daughter, Ernestine, were real good friends.

"Uncle Ed was another of Granddaddy's brothers, but we didn't see much of his family, even though his wife and Uncle Lewis's wife were sisters. But I did get to know two of his children who went to our church, Mamie and Slim.[94]

"We saw a lot of Uncle France's family too."

"Yeah, I heard that your Uncle France borrowed a cultivator from Doc Boatright one time," C.G. said, "and kept it eight years!

"As the story went, France bought a tractor but didn't buy a cultivator to go with it. He needed one, and somebody told him that Doc Boatright had one he wasn't using (it had come with his Farm All tractor). So, Uncle France went over and asked to borrow it, telling Doc he needed to use it just until he could get himself one. Well, eight years later, France still had it. When Doc was going to sell his tractor, he told the buyer he had a cultivator to go with it, and went over to get it. Uncle France said, 'Doc, you ought not to a told that man that you had a cultivator. Now what am I gonna do for one?'

"Uncle France had a saying, 'If anybody loans me anything, they can figure on coming to get it when I get through with it because I barely had enough time to borrow it, and I shore ain't got time to take it back.'

"I also remember hearing about one of Uncle Tip and France's bird-hunting episodes," C.G. continued. "Uncle Tip always believed in giving wild game a fair chance. Well, that day France hauled off and shot into some birds on the ground and killed several. When he headed toward the birds to pick them up, Tip said, 'Aye God, buddy, you didn't even give them birds a chance—shooting 'em on the ground like that. I'm gonna whip you.'

"I heard they had a regular dogfight out there in the woods; but then they got up, brushed their clothes off, and went on hunting."

"Yeah, Uncle France and Granddaddy Tip used to go hunting a lot," Ethel added. "They liked to go fishing too, in the Suwannee River; and if somebody said, 'Good Luck' as they headed out, Granddaddy would say, 'Ding the luck! Now I won't catch a thing!' He thought that just mentioning good luck would bring bad.

"Uncle France had eight children:[95] four boys, Chandler, Rowan, Lucian, and Malcolm (Mutt), and four girls, Abby, Erma, Verdie, and Edna."

"Uncle France took in a girl by the name of Mott and raised her like she was his own," Bernice Lanier said. "Mrs. Mott, the girl's mother, was a Hart before she married; I don't know what the circumstances were that she had to give the girl up."

"Then there was Uncle Porch," Ethel said. "He married Eliza Cheshire.[96] They had eight children: three sons— Lucian, Arthur, Barney—and five daughters—Bertie, Dora, Eva, Rosa, and Mary."

Porch and Eliza (Cheshire) Lanier's family
(Photo, courtesy of Denise Lee, Porch's great-great-granddaughter)

The Philandering Lanier Brothers

The word around town was that Tip's brother Porch was a man about town. One rumor said that Porch had fathered—in addition to his eight legitimate children—at least one bastard child. Porch's granddaughter, Ruby Lanier Hingson said she could neither confirm nor deny these rumors, but she knew only about her Grandpa Lanier's legitimate children.[97]

There were also rumors that Tip had, not just one woman on the side, but two. It was said that he had an affair with a Bonds woman he hired to help on the farm, to plow and help drive cows to the dipping vat. Some said she gave birth to a child after she left his place and that it had to be Tip's child.[98]

Then there was the rumor about Tip and Mrs. Tempie Boone, a neighbor woman who had a husband but never had any children.

"Granddaddy Tip never failed to take Tempie his first mess of greens from the garden," Ethel said, "even before Granny got to cook any. He would deliver them to Mrs. Boone personally. But Granny never seemed suspicious of anything. If Granny ever suspected anything, she never let on. She worked so hard, she might have been glad to share him with Tempie *and* the Bonds woman."

"I heard about Tempie and Tip on more than one occasion," Bernice Lanier said, "and Uncle Tip's horse was often seen tied up in front of Mrs. Boone's place—when it was perfectly obvious that Mr. Boone was not at home. I think Aunt Dosia was aware of it.

"Granddaddy Lee had his affairs too," Bernice continued. "People said his horse knew the way to Tempie's house the same as Uncle Tip's did, but he would put his horse out in the field behind Tempie's house and let it roam, instead of tying the horse up right at her front gate, like his brother did.

"Tempie—or Tippy as some of us called her—was quite a character. She built her own house. It was on the plot of land southeast of the Ladyland School, not far from us. One day we ran into her on the road between our house and hers and she was drunk—Tippy fell down right in the middle of the road and her frock flew up, and it was quite evident she wore no underwear.

"One day we went to help at the Boone's hog killing," Bernice continued. "My daddy [Lee's son, Floyd] knew how to cut up hogs, and he was cutting up some meat, and somehow he nearly whacked off one of old lady Boone's fingers. She cussed my daddy out real good."

Speaking of Whacking

"Back then," Ethel said, "most women shaved their husbands. Men had to shave with straight razors, and there was less chance of a cut if they let somebody else do the shaving. They probably couldn't afford barbers. I saw Granny shave Granddaddy Tip—a many a time."

One has to wonder, with all the talk about Tip's shenanigans, if he could totally relax when he leaned back in his chair at home and let Dosia place the sharp blade of the straight razor on the skin of his neck and drag it ever so slowly upward.

9 Harold's Generosity

W hen C.G. and I married," Ethel said, "Harold was still living at home, going to school, and helping Daddy with the farm, but he was anxious to get away, to get out on his own. He and Daddy got along well, but he and Granddaddy Tip never did, maybe because Grand-daddy Tip had teased Harold so much when he was little."

When asked about this, Harold said, "Yeah, about all Granddaddy ever did was order other people around. Plus, I knew there had to be a better way to make a living."

"One day I went to town to sell some corn for Daddy," Harold continued, "and Mr. Howland told me it took eighty-two bushels of dry corn to equal a ton. I knew it was more like fifty-two, or even less, but he argued with me about it, and he told Daddy later, 'That son of yours is a smart aleck.'

"Huffman, of Huffman and Gilmore, used to say, 'You know, farmers are like bees; if you don't rob 'em once in a while, they don't work.'

"One summer, I got a job in Live Oak at the tobacco market; my job was to walk behind the buyers and write down the prices on the tickets, that is, the top bid. The Florida tobacco market was one of the first markets to open, and I think at the time Suwannee and Columbia were the only counties where tobacco was being grown. On some days, up to eleven thousand dollars worth of tobacco was sold in the warehouse where I worked.

"While working there, I got to know Jack Calhoun, one of the auctioneers. He tried his best to get me to go to auctioneers' school. I didn't do that; but the summer when I was fifteen, I went and worked with Uncle Ellis in Green Cove Springs. I worked there for two summers, and when Uncle Ellis and Edward started talking about signing up with the War Department, I told them I wanted to go too."

Harold's Mind Was Made Up

"Yeah, when Harold found out that Uncle Ellis and Uncle Edward were planning to get jobs with the War Department," Ethel said, "he was packed. Mama and Daddy tried their best to talk him out of it—to get him to finish school first—but his mind was made up, so they let him go.

"About the time that Harold left, Buddie Rye moved into his room. Buddie's mama and daddy, Uncle Ellis and Aunt Daisy, had been having marital problems for some time. (Aunt Daisy was the one that wanted Grandmama Rye's silver 'tay' pot.) So, when Uncle Ellis decided to join the War Department, they split up and sent Buddie—a teenager then—to the farm to live with Mama, Daddy, Granny, and Granddaddy Tip.

"When Harold left, Mama sure hated to see him go. But he promised to write—and did."

Harold's first letter home cost him three cents to mail, but to his mother, the letter was priceless. On the outside of the envelope was his temporary return address: 1045 N.W. 1st Street, Miami, Florida.

September 5th 1942
Miami, Florida

Dear Mama, Daddy, and all:

How are you all getting along these days? We are doing alright so far. I had to go to Jacksonville the other day to get a certified copy of my birth certificate so I could get my passport. The one I had wasn't any good because it didn't show your maiden name and Daddy's name and my name.

I got back to Miami Saturday about two thirty in the evening, and the company told me that I would probably leave for Nassau about Wednesday. Don't write me any letters until you hear from me in Nassau. My address will be Milton Harold Rye, Care of Pleasantville Constructors, Inc., A.P.O. 618, care of Postmaster, New York, N.Y. Don't address any mail to Nassau, because it has to go to New York to go through a censor office.

Well how are the rest of the folks these days, and how is Buddie getting along in school. I think he will like it alright once he gets acquainted. Uncle Ellis is going to go to Nassau I think. I sure hope he does, because it will be a lot better for me if he does. Edward has not got his release from his draft board yet, but I still think he will make it.

Well, I guess I had better close for this time, and I will wire you just as quick as I land over there.

Lots of love to all,
Harold

September 8th 1942
Miami, Florida

Dear Mama, And Daddy:
I am sending you a form to fill out in the presence of a notary public and send it to the address on the back of it as soon as possible. Take it to a lawyer and he will show you what to do with it. If nothing happens I will leave Miami for Nassau tomorrow on a plane.

How are all of the folks getting along up there now? We are getting along just fine, so don't worry about me one minute. If anything happens you will know about it in due time and if I cannot stand it I can come on back home. I met a fellow in Green Cove the other day who had spent a lot of time in Nassau and he said that he liked it fine over there. He gave me the address of a lot of people over there and told me to look them up, so I think that I am going to like it fine.

Well I guess I had better close for this time and get this in the mail as soon as possible. I opened an account in the bank this morning, and as soon as I get there I will send you a check.

Tell Buddie, and Ethel and C.G. that I will write them as soon as I get settled down.

Lots of Love,
Harold

P.S. Mail this paper as soon as possible

September 12th [1942]
Miami, Florida

Dear Mama and Daddy:
How is everybody up there now? I am going fine so far except that I am a little nervous from taking some shots, outside of that I am fine.

Say did you all fill out the paper that I mailed to you to be filled out and mailed to Washington. If you didn't I would appreciate it if you would get it ready as soon as possible because they want it for some information on my passport.

Well I got my ticket today and I will leave for Nassau Monday morning so you all can start writing me any time now that I am sure that I am going. Tell Buddie and all the rest of the folks Hello for me and I will write to them as soon as I get settled down in Nassau and tell them all to write to me too.

Well I guess I had better close for this time, but I will write more as soon as I get to Nassau.

Your son,
Harold

P.S. I am sending back the old original copy of my birth certificate so that you can keep it. The date of birth was wrong on it, it is on the state board of health records February 12th so that must be right.

Letters from Nassau

Harold's letters from Nassau bore the return address: A.P.O. 618, New York, N.Y. Some had an additional notation, *Pleasantville Constructors Inc.*

Harold was under strict orders not to divulge his exact location with the War Department.

When each letter arrived at Route 4, Box 245, Live Oak, Florida, its envelope had a strip of brown tape across one end, evidence the letter had been opened and inspected, but each envelope also bore a stamped message, *PASSED BY ARMY EXAMINER.*

9/16/1942,
Nassau, Bahamas

Hello Mother, and Dad,

How are you all getting along these days? I am getting along fine. I was going to wire you as soon as I got here, but there is no place to send a wire around here, so I am sending you this letter airmail. I got here Monday afternoon about 2:30 o'clock. The place is very pretty, and I like it fine, I sure do wish you all were here to enjoy it with me. The only thing that I can't get used to is this money here, because we have to use English money.

Well Edward couldn't get a release from his draft board so he could not come over here, and I had to come by myself, but I have plenty of company here. Edward is going to join the Army Engineering Corps. Boy he really did want to come over here when I came, but he didn't make it.

Say how is Granny, and Granddaddy, and Ethel, and C.G. getting along, and is Buddie liking school any better.

Say Daddy if you are going to fix the house, go ahead, and start on it, and let me know how much money you will need, and I can start helping you out in about a week.

Well I guess I had better close as I want to write to Buddie.

Lots of Love
Harold

9/21/42
Nassau, Bahamas

Hello Mama, Daddy, and all,

How are you all getting along now? I got your letter tonight. I had been to town to take a shot, and I sure was glad to get it.

You all asked me about my work, and if it was hard. Well it is the easiest job I ever had. I have been running a wobble wheel roller, but today I started driving a tractor, it reminded me of home. I have a swell boss man, and he seems to like me a lot. If there is any favors he can do me he is always glad to do it. I am making about ninety dollars a week, and I think it will get better.

I am liking the place better every day. All the stuff you hear about this being such a bad place is just a bunch of bull so don't believe anything you hear about it. The only thing wrong is that you all are not here. So don't worry about me working too hard, or not having enough to eat, because the food is really good.

Say, what is the reason that Buddie can't hear from

his folks. I wrote Uncle Ellis, and told him to write to Buddie, because I know how it makes me feel when you all don't write real often. Tell Buddie that I will write, and send him some pictures of Nassau about tomorrow. Tell him not to let that new girl friend of his interfere with his school work. You all said Uncle Ellis was coming to Nassau, well I have been looking for him every day, but I haven't seen him yet. I was lonesome for somebody I knew at first, but I know a lot of fellows over here now.

Say Daddy about the lumber. Investigate it, and find where and how you can get good smooth lumber, free of knots, fairly reasonable, and make a deal for it. We don't want a house built of sorry lumber. Get enough to fix it just like you want it. Paint, and everything. After this coming Saturday I can send you a check. Last Sat. I only got paid for two days, and I am drawing out $10.00 a week over here, so that only left about ten dollars to go to the bank after my board was taken out.

The good part about it over here, we don't have to pay for haircuts, or medical care. We can have our teeth filled, pulled, or cleaned free of charge. That saves a lot of expense.

Well I guess I had better close for this time. Tell Buddie, and Mutt, and C.G. if they don't write, I am going to get mad. Also tell Granny and Granddad hello for me.

Lots of love to all,
Harold

9/26/42
Nassau, Bahamas

Hello, Mother, and Dad,

How are you getting along now, and did you get my last letter I wrote you? Well at last I am sending you a check. You probably thought I had forgotten about it. The money that I send home is for you all to use, and there is plenty more where this came from. I want you all to have anything you want. If I come home, and find you all trying to save any of this that you don't need I am going to spank both of you.

Listen Daddy when you find out about the lumber, and how much it will cost let me know how much it will be, and I will mail you a check for it. Don't get any old bad lumber no matter how much good one cost. We want a good looking house. Get someone who knows about a circulating heater, and if you want that we will get one instead of a fireplace.

Say Mama you asked me if I was staying at the hotel. Well I have been sleeping at the barracks, but there are so much noise at nights from drunks coming in that I cannot sleep so I am moving to town tomorrow to an apartment house, but my address will still be the same.

How is the rest of the folks getting along, and tell them all hello for me. Tell Buddie if he can quit thinking about his girl long enough to write me.

Well I guess I had better close for this time. Answer real soon and let me know all the news.

Your son,
Harold Rye

P.S. enclosed is a check for $50.00

9/30/42
A.P.O. 618

Hello Mama, and Daddy,

How is everybody at home these days, and what are you doing now? Say the other day I wrote you all a letter, and sent a check in it, and haven't heard from you as to whether you got it, or not.

Mama you asked about sending me some chicken, and cake. Well as much as I'd love to have it, you had better not send it. It would be alright to send some candy if you can. I would love to have some chocolate fudge.

Say Mom you all had better turn in my sugar card, as you might get in trouble about it. You asked me if I was boarding at the hotel. Well I am staying at the barracks, and living like a soldier, but I like it. Uncle Ellis isn't here yet but his tools are. He may come in today.

Well I guess I had better close for this time. You will have to excuse this writing as I am in a hurry. Tell all of the folks hello for me.

Love,
Harold

10/2/42
A.P.O. 618

Hello Mama, and Daddy,

How are you all getting along these days? I would have written you sooner, but I have been on the move for the past week, and couldn't get a chance to write you.

I think before long Uncle Ellis and I will both be living in the same room at the hotel.

Well I was sure sorry to hear about the wreck. Buddie was sure lucky not to get hurt any worse than he did, tell him I will write to him a little later.

Say those pictures you sent me are really cute. Lady looks a lot like Bell did, I only hope she is as good as Belle was, and I bet Daddy does too.

Listen Daddy if you can't get the frame on the truck fixed, see what kind of a trade in you can get on a 40, or 41 ford truck, because after all you have to have one. I am still waiting to hear about the lumber.

Well I guess I had better close for now as it is getting late. Tell Mutt, I will write soon. Tell the rest of the folks hello for me.

Love,
Harold

The photograph at right is probably the one that Delma sent to Harold—of Milton, Delma, and Milton's new bird dog, Lady.

They are standing in front of Milton's "new" car, a 1936 Ford.

The old log house is shown in the background, but it would not stand much longer if Harold had anything to do with it!

The next letter, dated the same day as the one above, was to Harold's sister, Mutt.

Milton, Delma, and Lady (dog)

10/2/42
A.P.O. 618

Dear Mutt,

How are you all getting along these days? I am still going strong. Say those pictures of Patsy are really cute.

I had a letter from Mama last night, and she said that you had made me some candy, but it hasn't got here yet. I can taste it already.

How is the daughter coming along now, and is she walking, and talking yet she probably will be when I see her again. Well how did your corn crop turn out this year, and is the price any good. Boy I would give a hundred dollars for a breakfast of grits, ham, and eggs. I haven't eaten any egg since I left home.

Well I guess I will stop for now as I am getting sleepy, but will write more later.

Your bud,
Harold

10/5/42
A.P.O. 618

Hello Mutt, and C.G.,

How are you all getting along these days? I am getting along fine right on.

Say I received the candy the other day, and it is really good, thanks a million for everything. I wish I could keep a supply of it all the time.

I am sure sorry to hear about the wreck the Georges had, but I expected it sooner because they sure do handle

a car rough. Buddie was sure lucky to get out of it
unhurt.

Mutt you asked about the money, I will be glad to let
you have it, but there will be no interest on it. Anytime
you need any money just let me know I only get ten
dollars a week of my money over here, and the rest goes
to the bank, and so far I haven't had to draw any out for
myself. I am sending the check to you, and I hope you
won't have any trouble getting it cashed.

Well I guess Patsy will be walking, and talking when
I see her again, I guess I will stop for this time as news is
out.

Your bud,
Harold

10/12/42
A.P.O. 618

Hello Mama, and Daddy,

How are you all getting along now? I received your
letter tonight, and was really glad to hear from you all. I
am getting along fine, and hope you are the same. Uncle
Ellis is here, and had a letter from aunt Daisy the other
day, and she said that she was going to take Buddie back
over there. I guess they are there by now. Boy it is really
raining over here now. I sure wish it would fair off for a
while.

Say Daddy you can run on a cash basis next year
without going off and working. Just remember that as
long as I make it you don't have to worry about where
yours is coming from. Daddy if I was you I wouldn't
plant any tobacco next year as it will be so hard to get

any hands to take care of it, and it would cause you all to have to work too hard. Put the time, and money on hogs, and you will get more money for less work. If you want to fertilize some corn, go ahead, and put in your order for your fertilizer, and I'll see that you get the money to pay for it.

Say Daddy you didn't say whether Dixie said you could get the trees, or not. Be sure, and find out if you can, or not, and go ahead, and have them cut, and let me know what the cost is. We are going to have a new house if there is any possible chance.

Daddy find out from mister Drew what he wants for his whole place, and what kind of terms he will give us, for Uncle Ellis wants us to buy it together, and I think it will be a good investment for the two of us. We plan to follow this work as long as we can.

Tell Mutt I wrote her the last letter, and that my address is still the same too. How is Granny, and Granddaddy getting along, tell them hello for me. Tell the George boys hello for me too.

Well I guess I will stop for the time being. but [write] real soon. In the meantime all of you be good, and write to me real often. Listen Daddy, see if you can get somebody to gather your corn.

Lots of love,
Harold

P.S. Tell Buddie I would appreciate a letter from him. Here is my new address:

A.P.O. 618
C/o Postmaster
Miami, Florida

10/17/42
A.P.O. 618

Hello Mama, and Daddy,

How are you all getting along these days? I received your letter tonight, and was very glad to hear from you. The pictures are real cute. I am growing me a mustache, and I am going to have some pictures made with it, and if you want some to go in your garden just let me know.

Say Daddy how long has Buddie been back, and what does he think he could get a job doing. Tell him to go to school, and stay on the farm, for that is what his Daddy wants him to do.

Say Mama tell Daddy he had better not stop eating, or I'll catch him in weight. I am out growing all of my clothes.

Well as for us coming home for Christmas, I don't think now that we will, because it would cost us about one hundred and fifty dollars each, and we would only have about three days to stay so we are not going. I guess we will stay the six months and then come home. We will have about two, or three weeks then.

Daddy I am sending you a check for $75.00, and then you can get straight with Sears, and have some left. If we can't get terms in town we had better buy from Sears. Have you found out yet what the lumber will cost us, When you do, let me know.

Well I guess I had better close for this time.

Lots of love to all,
Harold

P.S. You will have to excuse this bad writing for I have just had another shot, and I am nervous from it.

11/16/42
A.P.O. 618,
Miami, Fla.

Hello Mama, and Daddy,

How are you all getting along?

I had a letter from Mutt yesterday, and she said that you all hadn't heard from me in over two weeks. Well I am positive that I have mailed two letters if not three in the past two weeks. They just didn't go through.
Anyway I am still fine, and healthy. Don't worry about me for if anything was wrong the company would notify you.

Say is Aunt Daisy and Buddie still there? Uncle Ellis is sure upset about Buddie. She won't leave him alone.

Say Mama thanks a lot for the gifts they really came in good.

Well I guess I had better close for this time with lots of love to all,

Harold

P.S. Daddy is the Land place still for sale? If it is how much is the payments?

On the Move Again
A picture of the Hotel Tamiami, a six-story hotel, was incorporated into the return address of the next letter Harold wrote from Miami.

12/18/42
Miami, Fla.

Hello Mom,

How are you all getting along now, I am still getting along fine. Well I am back in Miami, but don't know when I will be home, but don't answer this letter, I have another job which will pay me about a hundred, and thirty-five dollars a week.

I was talking to Oleta last night, and she said you are planning to make a trip down this year.

Well Mama, I am going to close for now, and hoping to see you soon.

Harold

2/17/43
Miami, Fla.

Hello Mama, and Daddy,

How are you all getting along now? Hope Daddy is better by now.

Well I got to Miami Tuesday about seven o'clock, and believe me I was all tired out. It took eleven hours to go from Jax. to Miami.

Well I went to the office today, and everything was alright. I will leave here tomorrow, or Friday night on a north bound train, but don't know just where we will sail from. I will write you all along, and as soon as I get to South America I will send you a cable message, and let you know how everything is. It may be some time before you will hear, but don't worry, because everything is going to be alright. If anything bad happens, the company will let you know, so please don't worry.

As soon as you find out about the house, let me know. I am going to send my money to you all so it will be handy for you.

Well I guess I had better close for now, but will write you all along. Tell all hello for me.

Lots of love,
Harold

2/18/43
Miami, Fla.

Hello Mama, and Daddy:

How are you all getting along these days? I guess you are surprised to hear that I AM STILL IN Miami, but you know how the war department does business. I may get out of here by Sunday, but don't know for sure yet. I checked one of my suit cases to Trinidad today, so I know it won't be very long now. Will let you know all along how everything is.

Well I am finishing my letter now that I started a day or two ago, and I still haven't left Miami, by the way today is Sunday. Boy I am disgusted with this place. It costs $3.00 a day for a room, and about $2.90 a day for eats, they told me yesterday that we might get out Tuesday night, or Wednesday morning.

Say Daddy how are you getting along now. You can send a letter to 1348 N.W. 7th St., and let me know how you are. That is where Ira and Oleta live. They want me to move out [there] with them, and I think I will for it will save a lot of expense.

Well I guess I had better close for this time, and if this letter doesn't make sense you can lay it to my present state of mind and boy that is plenty mixed up. Hoping this finds you all o.k.

Your son,
Harold

2/26/43

Hello Mama, and Dad:

How are you all getting along now? I am doing fine, and having a wonderful trip. It is not permissible to tell where we are, but everything is O.K., so don't worry about me.

How are you getting with your cold, and how is Ethel, and C.G. now? Let me know about everything as soon as you write to me. I don't know yet what my address will be yet, but will let you know as soon as I find out.

Well I guess I will close for now, but will write you as soon as I get a chance.

Love,
Harold

The Substitute Postman

"Mama and Granddaddy Tip were always watching for the postman to come by," Ethel said, "in hopes we would get another letter from Harold. All of us shared the mailbox at their house."

"Yeah, our mailbox was real big," C.G. added, "big enough to hold small packages. We ordered a lot of things through the mail back then—clothes, baby chicks, seed. When a big package came, one that was too big to fit in the box, the mail carrier would take it up and leave it on the Rye's front porch.

"But one time we got a substitute mail carrier, and that fellow was a big, fat, sloppy, gobby thing! He made Ethel—when she was pregnant with Anetha—go out and get a big heavy package (a bushel of seed corn we had ordered) out of his car trunk! He was too lazy to get out of his car and carry that bag to the porch. He was one sorry piece of humanity! The sorry bastard!"

Where Exactly Was Harold?

When Delma received a letter from the War Department postmarked March 6, 1943, she tore into it like a kid with a bag of candy. The letter itself was not dated and was brief:

War Department
Office of the Division Engineer
Caribbean Division
Caribbean Defense Command

Mrs. Delma Rye
Live Oak, Fla.

Dear Madam:

You are informed that Milton H. Rye has arrived safely in Trinidad.

For the Division Engineer:
J.W. Sawyer
Major, Corps of Engineers
Executive Assistant

Delma Was Disappointed

Delma had hoped the letter from the War Department would provide a new address for her son. It didn't. So she wasted no time in writing back to Mr. Sawyer.

His reply follows:

War Department
Office of the Division Engineer
Caribbean Division
Caribbean Defense Command
March 12, 1943

Mrs. Delma Rye
Route 4, Box 245,
Live Oaks, Florida.

Dear Madam:

Reference is made to your letter dated March 10, 1943.

Airmail letters addressed to your son at APO 868, C/o Postmaster, Miami, Florida will reach him.
For the Division Engineer:

J. W. Sawyer
Major, Corps of Engineers,
Executive Assistant

Yet Another Address

The return address on Harold's next letter, which was slow to arrive, was:

> United States Engineering Department
> A.P.O. 889 C/o Postmaster
> New York, N.Y.

Harold continued to write home, most often in longhand using blue or black ink, writing on tissue-thin, unruled, airmail paper. His lines were straight, his penmanship good, and he seldom crossed through a word. Letters were mailed in red-white-and-blue-bordered, 4"x7" airmail envelopes, preprinted and embossed with 6¢ U.S. POSTAGE VIA AIR MAIL. He usually addressed both his parents in his letters, but the envelopes were always addressed to his father only:

> *M. M. Rye*
> *Route #4, Box 245*
> *Live Oak, Florida*

3/5/43
U.S.E.D.
A.P.O. 869
C/o Postmaster
New York, N.Y.

Hello Mama, Daddy, and all,

How is everything with you all now. I arrived safely, and what I have seen so far, I like it alright. It took us ten days to get here.

They have some real high mountains, and they also have monkeys. And parrots, too.

Say Daddy I will send my checks to you as soon as I get them. I will have to endorse them before they leave here, and I will write the words, for deposit only so that no one else if they got it could cash it, then you can deposit it, and write checks on it as you need it.

Well I guess I had better close for this time, but will write again as soon as I know what I am going to do. Let me know how Mutt gets along.

As ever,
Harold

3/9/43
A.P.O. 869
Miami, Fla.

Hello Mama, and Daddy,

How are you all getting along now? I am getting along fine and hope you are the same. I went to work the other day, and I have a swell boss man. So far as I can see there isn't anything wrong with this place.

Well, how are you, and C.G. coming along with the crop, and how is Mutt getting along now, and don't fail to let me know how everything comes out.

Say I heard the other day that after March 21st they were going to let you drive all you wanted to.

Well I guess I had better close for this time as there isn't much to say, so you all be good, and tell Granny, and Granddaddy Hello for me.

Love,
Harold

United States Engineering Dept.
A.P.O. 869, c/o Postmaster
Miami, Florida

3/14/43
A.P.O. 869,
Miami, Florida

Hello Mama and Daddy,

How are you all getting along now, and also how is Mutt. It seems to me that I should have heard from you all by now but haven't heard a word yet. You had better write me pretty soon as I am going to get mad.

Listen Daddy I am enclosing a check, and you can deposit it in the bank, and explain it to the bank so that you can write checks on it when you need it. I wrote "for deposit only" so that if it gets lost in the mail nobody else could cash it. I want you to pay my income tax out of it. As soon as you find out about the house, why let me know.

Say have you heard from Glen and Howard [George], and do you know if they went into the Merchant Marine or not?

Well I am going to close for this time and will write again in a day or two.

Love,
Harold

3/19/43
A.P.O. 869
Miami, Fla.

Hello Mama, and Daddy,

How are you all getting along now? I received your letter today, and I sure was glad to hear from you. Tell Granddaddy he could sure have a lot of fun here.

Listen I am sending a couple of checks, so be sure and let me know if they come, and don't forget to pay my income tax for me. Tell Granny, and Granddaddy, also Mutt, C.G. and Patsy hello for me, and I will write to them later. Tell Mr. and Mrs. Robins hello for me.

Well I am going to close for now, and get some sleep, and will write more, later.

Lots of love,
Harold

3/23/43
A.P.O. 869
C/o Postmaster
Miami, Fla.

Hello Mama, Daddy, and all,

How are you all getting along now? I received your letter this afternoon, and sure was glad to hear from you. I know you do feel bad about the tobacco bed, but those things just have to happen so don't feel too badly about it.

Say I am sorry I forgot all about your birthday, but I was so busy, it just slipped my mind. Since I can't send you a present, take $25.00 out of what I sent, for a present.

Well I guess Howard and Glenn wishes they would have come with me now. How is Bud getting along with the farming now?

Listen don't forget to let me know how Mutt gets along, and how is Patsy getting along. [How are] Granny and Granddaddy getting along, tell them hello for me.

Well I guess I had better close for now, so be good and Write real often.

Lots of love,
Harold

P.S. let me know if you have found out anything about the house yet.

3/25/43
A. P.O. 869,
C/o Postmaster
Miami, Fla.

Hello Mama, and Daddy,
How are you all getting along these days. I received two letters from you this afternoon, and I sure was glad to hear from you. I am writing so often now that I can't think of very much to write about.

Listen when you write tell me if you get the checks or not. I sent two in one letter, one was for $115.80, and one for $59.63, and here comes another for $76.13, so be sure, and let me know when you get them. They are taking out a third of my pay until they get $175.00, but I will get it back when I start home.

Well I will close for this time, but will write more, later, so don't forget to let me know how Mutt gets along. Tell Oleta hello for me, and also Granny, and Granddaddy.

Lots of love to all,
Harold

3/28/43
A.P.O. 869,
C/o Postmaster

Hello Mama, and Daddy,

How are you all getting along now? I received your letter the other day, and sure was glad to hear from you. Sure was sorry to hear about Granddaddy. I sure was glad to hear that Mutt made the grade O.K. for I was worried about her.

Listen about the checks. When you receive them be sure to write me, because if they don't get there I can have payment stopped, because I know the numbers of them. So far I have sent four home and you only mentioned one you received.

When you go to Punta Gorda, take all the money you need. Write me, and tell me how Granddaddy is, and also send me Edward's address for I want to write to him.

I guess by now your tobacco bed is over the blue mold, I hope so anyway.

Well I am going to quit for now, but will write more later.

Lots of love to all,
Harold

3/1/43
A.P.O. 869,
C/o Postmaster
Miami, Florida

Hello Mama, and Daddy,

How does this find you all getting along; I am still

well, and getting along fine. Today is payday so I am sending my check home. It sure does look small, because they are still taking out thirty-three, and one third per cent, but they will only do that for two more weeks

Listen Daddy I am trying for a higher paying job, and I have to give some references, so I want you to ask Mr. Hinley and Mr. Kierce if they will give me a recommendation, and let me know right back. The job is on a rubber plantation, and it will be almost like farming back home. It pays a lot more than what I am doing.

How is the farm coming along now? I guess by now you are setting tobacco, and I sure hope you get a good stand. Did you get the transplanter? If you can, it will save you a lot of work. Say, have you ever found out anything about the house yet. When you do, let me know.

How is Mutt, and her family getting along now, also Granny and Granddaddy? Tell C.G. that it will be alright for him to eat anything he wants including Collard Greens.

Listen, if you remember I ordered a catalogue of farms in Oregon before I left. If it has come, or when it does I wish you would send it on down to me.

Are Oleta and Jimmie still there? If they are, tell them hello for me.

Well I am going to close for now, but will write more, later, so everybody be good, and whatever you do don't work too hard.

Lots of love to all,
Harold Rye

4/8/43
A.P.O. 869
Miami, Fla.

Hello Mama, Daddy, and all,
How are you all getting along these days? I am still on the go, and feeling O.K.

I guess by now you are through planting corn, and setting tobacco. Sure hope you get a good stand, and also a good price for it. How is C.G. coming along with his farming, and how is the new daughter getting along now.

Well I am sending another check, for $59.60. After next week they won't be taking out as much. Listen Daddy if you will, give Bob a check for ten dollars, and sixty-five cents. It is some I owe him yet on the old Buick, I had forgotten all about it. Have you paid my income tax yet, If you haven't you had better do it, as they will have me in the federal penitentiary.

Say did you find out about the recommendations for me? If you didn't, find out as soon as you can, and let me know, because I will need them pretty soon.

Well I will close for now, but will write again soon.

Love,
Harold

4/16/43
A.P.O. 869
Miami, Fla.

Hello Mama, and Daddy,
How are you all getting along these days? I guess by

now you are all through planting the crop. Listen Daddy I don't see what you are planting cotton for; you know you are not able to pick it, and there is no money in it either.

Mama you ask about using some of (our) money to buy an oil stove with. That makes me want to spank you, for you know the money is yours when you want it, so go ahead and buy yourself an oil stove, and be sure you get a good one if it takes all the money. I am sending another check for $64.63.

How is Granny and Granddaddy getting along, also Mutt, C.G., and their family? Tell them I will write to them later.

As soon as you find out about the house, let me know, and did you find out what Mr. Drew wanted for the place, and what his terms were. Did Uncle Ellis say whether or not he wanted to buy it.

Well I am going to close for this time, but will write again later.

As ever,
Harold

P.S. Mama you said you were sending me some gum, well I can buy plenty of gum over here, but you can send me some of that tooth powder, and a couple of heavy duty brushes.

4/30/43
A.P.O. 869

Hello Mama, and Daddy,

How are you all getting along these days? I am still O.K. and hope you are the same. Are you through setting tobacco yet? I sure hope you get a good price for what you have. I don't see why you want to plant cotton for as you are not able to pick it.

I am sending a check of 94.63, so let me know if you get it or not. The bank account should be strong enough to stand the pressure of a new house if they will let you build one.

So, Bob is joining the Marines? If he wants a job, tell him he can get one down here, and won't have to be eighteen. He can come down as an office worker, and learn to run some machinery after he gets here.

Listen Daddy, if you don't mind it I wish you would go to the local board, and tell them my address, I wrote them, but evidently they didn't get it. I got the classification card O.K.

Well I am going to close for this time, but will write again soon. Tell everybody hello for me.

As ever,
Harold

5/8/43
A.P.O. 869
Miami, Florida

Hello Mama, and Daddy,

How is everybody getting along up on the farm now? I am still holding my own, and feeling O.K. I guess you are having plenty to do, but whatever you do don't work too hard, because you don't have to as long as I have a job, and when the job runs out I will come back, and farm for you.

Say dad you had better take some money out of the bank, and order a pair of those hogs you were talking about if you haven't already got them. As soon as you find out if they will let us build a house or not, let me know. If they will, then we will buy the Drew place, and if they won't, then we will buy the Land place, and cut the timber, and build anyway. Try to get them to let you build if possible, and if they will it will be better, for I had rather have the Drew place than the other, and I know you had, for it is the best hog range, and maybe we can get the land that Cow and Running Springs are on pretty cheap. Inquire, and see who it belongs to and what they want for it.

Say, what is the reason they wouldn't let you send that real estate catalogue to me?

You say it is dry up there. I sure wish you had some of this rain we are getting down here, that's why my pay check is so small this week. I am sending check for $81.63, and money order for $15.00 so let me know if you get it. Maybe I will get to make some money if I ever get what they promised me.

How are Mutt, and C.G. and family getting along, and also Granny and Granddaddy? Hope Granny is feeling better now.

Listen, Mom, you asked me if I got the classification card, well I did, but I don't see why they sent it to Miami for, because I wrote them a letter as soon as I landed here and told them my address. If you can I wish you would straighten them out for me.

Well I am going to close for this time, as I am getting sleepy.

Lots of love,
Harold

If Bob wants a job in Brazil tell him to go to 7th Avenue, and 54th Street in Miami to the office of Faulk and Coleman.

5/10/43
A.P.O. 869
Miami, Fla.

Hello Mama, and Daddy,

How are you all getting along now? I received your letter tonight, and sure was glad to hear from you and that you are all O.K. Speaking of the dry spell you are having, well, it is just the opposite down here. When I first came here I laughed at all of these little streams that they told me were rivers. Most of them had no water in them at all, but now they are overflowing and where they come out of the mountains it is swifter than the Suwannee is.

Well. Mama, yesterday was Mother's day, and I am sorry I couldn't send you anything, but I will just send you my best wishes, to you and Granny.

You mentioned about the oil burners for the tobacco barn. Well Daddy if I were you I would go ahead and get them. Give him a check for them with my compliments for you know how bad it is to sit up[vii] so by all means get them, and if you have to go after them take out money from the bank for that too.

Listen Daddy have you heard from the bureau of internal revenue about the income tax yet. You said something in your letters about wanting to know how much I sent with the report. Well I left it there for you all to mail for me, and I hope you mailed it if you are not

---

[vii] With wood-burning stoves in the barn, there was the chance of a fire destroying the whole barn of tobacco, so Milton often sat up all night, when his barn of tobacco was cooking (a common practice).

sure write to them and see for I don't want to get into trouble about it.

As soon as you find out about the house don't fail to let me know.

Mama you said you were sending me a box of stuff. Well you needn't send candy for I can get that here, but if you can I wish you would get me a couple of pair of boat pants, size 30"w—L-25". Get the army khaki if possible, and also a rain coat size 38, or 36.

Well I am going to close for this time as I am getting sleepy so be good, and be sure and get those burners.

As ever
Harold

Tell Mutt and C.G., and Granny and Granddaddy hello for me.

5/14/43

Hello Mama, and Daddy,

How are you all getting along now? I am still able to work, and eat all I can get, boy we really get it.

Well I am sending another check for $94.63, and I hope you get it. Say did you buy the oil burners you were telling me about yet, if you haven't, you had better hurry before someone else beats you to it.

How are your crops, and hogs coming along now? I sure hope you make good on them. Say I never ask you before but how is the tractor holding up, and do you ever see Markey. I wonder what he is doing for a living now.

I wrote to Uncle Ellis the other day, and I haven't heard from him in some time, I don't know if he is still there or not. Do you think he and Daisy will go back together? If he does he's crazy.

How are Mutt and C.G. and the family? Tell them I will write them tomorrow nite. Are Granny and Granddaddy getting along O.K.? Tell them hello for me.

Well I am going to close for this time so be good and write real often.

Lots of love,
Harold

5/18/43
A.P.O. 869
Miami, Fla.

Hello Mama, and Daddy,

How are you, and the rest of the family? I am still working, and eating, and I feel fine too.

Well I guess you have your new cookers for the tobacco barn by now, and what do you think of them. I am sure you will like them when you start using it, no more sleepless nights, and boy that is something.

Listen when you find out if you can build a house, why don't you look at some plans, and pick out one just like you want, and let him figure with you on it, and see if he will bring it under the F.H.A. for us. If he will, it will be better for him and for us, and if he can't we will see what else we can do. If the F.H.A. will handle it we can buy new furniture and a lot of other things we need. If not we will buy it outright. Don't forget the tile floors, and walls for the kitchen, and put it in a position where we can build a nice garage beside it. We are going to make that a beautiful place. Listen Daddy look in the catalogue, and see about a Delco system, and figure up

the number of lights you will have in the house, and all
electrical appliances you will have including the pump,
and see what [a] plant will cost that will handle it, and
get the easy payment rate for the engine, and pump, and
the batteries is. If it is not too much we will go ahead and
order it, and then we will have that. We want an
automatic load control too, don't we?

I guess you think I'm silly to write all this crap, but I
want to help plan for this dream home.

Well I am not sending a check home this week for I
lost a lot of time on account of rain, and I am buying a
radio for company as there is no place to go very much.

Well I am going to close for this time as I am getting
sleepy, so write real soon and all the news.

Lots of love,
Harold Rye

6/2/43
A.P.O. 869
New York

Hello Mama, Daddy, and all,

How are you all getting along now? I am still doing
fine, and getting plenty to eat.

I am sure glad you are getting a good stand of tobacco,
and how is it doing now, and also the rest of the crop?

Say Daddy what have you done about the Drew
place? If we can make a deal for it we can sell the timber
off, and pay for the place, and have enough left to build
the house too, at the present price of lumber. That is
very cheap for that kind of land. Say what is Uncle Ellis
doing about this land, or have you heard from him yet? I

had a letter from Joyce, and she said he had been on a trip, but didn't say where.

How is Granny, and Granddaddy getting along now? I am going to write Mutt and C.G. tonight so they will know I haven't forgotten them.

Say I hadn't told you before but I think I am going to be transferred, but can't say where. I will make about twice the money I am making if I go.

Well I am going to close for this time, and don't you all work too hard because you don't have to now, so be good, and write real soon.

As ever,
Harold

P.S. Am sending money order for $75.00.
Send mail to New York from now on.

6/8/43,
A.P.O.
New York, N.Y

Hello Mama, and Daddy,

How are you all getting [along] now? I am still doing fine. I received your letter yesterday, and I sure am sorry that you can't send the pants and raincoat, but don't send them back yet for I think I can get a permit for you to send them yet for I need them.

I had a letter from Mutt also the other day, and she tells me that Rex is about all in. I sure am sorry to hear of that as he was such a nice little horse, and they need him so badly. I guess he can get another and pretty reasonable. Say do you all still have Willie Wilson's horse?

Listen Daddy when you go to town I want you to go to the draft board and talk to them, and see if they will give me another six months deferment if the office here sends them form 42-A. If they won't I am coming back to the U.S.A. and go to a Military school. I hope they will for I want to get a little more so we can buy that house, and pay for land too. Say did you hear from Uncle Ellis yet? And have you done anything about the place yet? I believe the timber would more than pay for it.

How are the crops coming along now since the rain started? I guess you will soon be ready to barn tobacco.[viii] Say have you set up the oil burners yet and how do you think you are going to like them? They will save you a lot of work, and I believe you will get a better cure on your tobacco. Listen you all don't work too hard, because you don't have to as long as I have any money, or a job.

You said you went to Lake City Sunday. I sure would like to have been there, and seen Uncle Raleigh and Aubrey. What did they have to say?

How are Granny and Granddaddy getting along? Tell them hello for me, and I sure would love to see you all. I had some pictures made Sunday. I will send you some when I get them.

Well I am going to close for this time, but will write again right away as I want to send a money order so be good, don't work too hard, and keep your nose clean.

Lots of love to all
Harold

From now on, send the mail to New York.

[viii] To "barn tobacco" meant to put the tobacco in the barn to cook or cure it.

Rex

"The first year after I got Rex, my horse," C.G. said, "I used him to plant corn, tobacco, peanuts, and cotton."

"And that was when we almost separated," Ethel said. "I told C.G., 'I am *not* gonna pick cotton!' and I meant it."

"I used Rex for two years," C.G. continued, "but then he got sleeping sickness—encephalitis—and I couldn't work him. I never will forget how I was needing to clean out the peanuts—to plow the weeds out—but with Rex real sick, I had no way to plow.

"Well, Aunt Lizzie Boatright came down one day with her boys and girls in a wagon that was hooked up to their tractor, a John Deere that had replaced Babe, their mule. All of them got out of the wagon and stayed at our house while Aunt Lizzie had Pete take the tractor and go all the way back home and get their plow so he could come back and plow my peanut patch.

"When Rex didn't get any better, I went and got the vet, and he drove out to see about him. But it was too late. The vet couldn't save my horse."

6/14/43
A.P.O. 869
New York, N.Y.

Hello Mama, and Daddy,

How are you all getting along these days? I am still doing fine, and hope you are the same.

Say I got the pants Saturday, and I sure am proud of them for I really needed them, and they are just a perfect fit. I sure do thank you for them.

You wrote me that C.G. and Ethel had finally lost the horse, and I sure am sorry to hear about it for I know they needed him. If they want it you can let them have the money to buy another one if he can find one he wants.

Listen I just remembered that tomorrow is Granddad's birthday, so take ten dollars, and give it to him for me, and he can buy what he wants, and tell him I hope he has a happy birthday, and many more of them.

Mama you asked me if I sent a check in the last letter. Well I didn't, but I am sending one in this one for $100.13, and as soon as I have a chance I want [to] buy a money order for last week.

Say Daddy what have you done about the place, and the house? You never seem to answer any of my questions.

I don't know if I told you or not, but I had some pictures made, and [I'll send them] as soon as I get them developed. I was not in my dress clothes, but it is me anyway.

Have you heard from Uncle Ellis yet? It has been some time since I heard from him, but I hear from Joyce quite often.

Well how is the farming coming along? If you all don't quit working so hard I am going to have you shipped down here where I can keep an eye on you, for it worries me for you to work so hard for you don't have to you know.

Well I am going to close for this time as I am so sleepy I can hardly see. Tell Mutt and C.G. hello for me.

> Lots of love to all,
> Harold

Planting by the Signs

"After my horse, Rex, died," C.G. said, I got a mule that I named Jack. He helped me plant twenty-five acres of corn and tobacco. Then each year, I would plant a few more things, like cane for syrup, peas, watermelons to eat and sell, and oats and rye for our cows and hogs to graze on.

"To know when to plant the crops, I always went by *The Ladies' Birthday Almanac.*"

"That's the best almanac there is," Ethel added. "Granddaddy Tip used it, and Daddy used it."

"It tells you how to plant according to the signs of the zodiac," C.G. explained, "Pisces is the feet. When I started planting tobacco, I would try to plant when the signs were in the breast or in the feet. That was supposed to be a water sign, and the plants would take root and start off better. The *Almanac* tells you when to plant aboveground crops like mustard, beans, peas—and belowground root crops like turnips and rutabagas. You plant when the moon is growing. The Almanac is set up according to the time zones, so we always looked in the Eastern zone.

"As for marking and branding cattle, we would do that when the signs were in the knee or below, so the animals wouldn't bleed as bad. We had to brand our cattle back then because it was open range. Later on, after people started putting up fences, it wasn't necessary."

6/16/43
A.P.O. 869
New York, N.Y.

Hello Mama, and Daddy,

How are you all these days? I am still fine, and hope you are the same.

Boy that sure was good news about the house because that is what I have been looking forward to and I imagine you have also. You asked me which I had rather have, well as for me I think the concrete blocks would be the best, and the cheaper in the long run, but if you all want one of lumber it suits me O.K. for I want you to be pleased with it. What kind of plan do you plan to use? And does this fifteen hundred include everything? If you build one of concrete blocks it would make the place look more up to date. Have you found out if they will give us terms or not so we can buy a light plant, too?[ix] I also would like to get some new furniture for the dining room, living, and kitchen anyway.

Say did you go to the draft board, and ask about that deferment, if you haven't I wish you would.

Well how are the crops doing now? They should be doing fine in the hot weather. Boy this climate down here is really nice. There is a nice trade wind blowing all the time.

Well I am going to close for this time, and will write again Thursday. Tell all the folks hello for me.

Lots of love to all,
Harold

...869
.....York

Hello Mama, and Daddy;

How are you all getting along these days, I am still doing OK.

Well Daddy, I got your letter today about the Drew place, and boy was I surprised to hear how much they wanted for it. Well I don't know what Uncle Ellis will want to do, but I say lets grab it while we can for if Saunders gets it we may as well move to some other place. The only thing I know to do is to go to the Commercial Bank and tell them what you have, and see if they will make up what we don't have. If Uncle Ellis will come across, we can make up over half of it. Then

---

[ix] Harold knew that electric power/wires did not extend to the area where his family lived and probably wouldn't for some time.

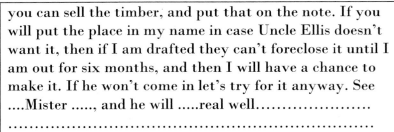

you can sell the timber, and put that on the note. If you will put the place in my name in case Uncle Ellis doesn't want it, then if I am drafted they can't foreclose it until I am out for six months, and then I will have a chance to make it. If he won't come in let's try for it anyway. See ....Mister ....., and he will .....real well.....................
....
so let me know what you do. If anything develops, why, let me know. You can send me a cable. I think I am going to be transferred, if I do I can make twice the money I am making. So sit tight, and let me know what you can do.

Tell Granny and Granddaddy hello for me and also Mutt, C.G. and family hello for me.

Lots of love to all,
Harold

The omissions in the letter above were not the work of the censor's office, but the result of being stored where a mother mouse got to them and thought the tissue-thin airmail paper was the perfect material for making confetti for her babies' bed. (Harold's letter was about to end up like Tip's violin—eaten up by mice.) The letters that follow arrived in business-sized envelopes; and from here on, Harold addressed his parents, not as Mama and Daddy, but as Mom and Pop, and then Folks/Everyone.

8/15/43
A.P.O.
New York

Hello Mom, and Pop,
I received your letter yesterday, and sure was glad to

hear from you, and that you are getting along good. I am still getting along fine, and eating all that I can get.

You said that Mister Tedder got word from Washington that my papers had not been filled out right, and they had notified me. Well you can tell him that is a lot of stuff. I haven't received a notice yet, and they filled out the papers in the office here, and would not let us do it ourselves. Anyway I can see the Major, and he will get it straight for me, just don't say anything to Tedder about [it] until I let you know how I come out. If I can I would like to stay until November as I think we are going to start making 84 hrs. per week. Then I will come home and help you finish the house, and get the next crop in if you can get me deferred up to that time.

If I can get in two months at 84 hrs., that will almost pay for the house, and then we will be sitting pretty.

Sure am glad you got a good price for your tobacco, but sorry you didn't have very much of it.

Say have you found out yet how much the house is going to cost you, and just what you are going to build out of.

How are C.G. and Mutt and their family doing, also Granny and Granddaddy?

Well I am going to close for now, but will write again soon.

> Love,
> Harold

8/19/43

Hello Mom and Pop,

How are you all getting along these days? I rec'd.

your nice letter the other day, and I sure was glad to hear from you, and that you were getting along good. You said you had only rec'd. one letter from me since I have been transferred, well you should have another by now as I wrote you one just the other day.

I think that I am straight with them about my draft release now as I went to see the Area Engineer about it, and he said that he would get it straight for me right away. You see it is not that I don't want to come home, but I want to get enough ahead to fix the place up so that it won't be such a hard job to run it and now is my chance. I have an easy job and a good boss, and he seems to like me.

Say as soon as you get the estimation for the house, I would like to know how much it is complete including paints, and plumbing, and wiring, for I think it is a good idea to do it all at one time, or we may not ever get it done, don't you? Tell me if you think there is enough already in the bank, and by the way you haven't told me how many checks you have received yet. I wish you would let me know so that I would know if any have been lost or not. Am enclosing a money order of $200.00. This is the first pay I have had since I was transferred, and they still owe me $255.00 more. See if there will be any discount for cash on the house there should be.

How is the Howell family getting along, tell them hello, and I will write them soon. Hope Patsy is better by now, also tell Granny and Granddaddy Hello for me.

Has C.G. got his new tractor yet?

You will have to excuse such writing as I am using my suitcase for a table.

Say when you see Mr. and Mrs. Sharples, tell them hello for me, also Mr. and Mrs. McCarwick. Give the George family my regards too.

Well folks I am going to have to close for now as it is getting pretty late, and I have to work tomorrow, so you all be good, and write me all the news from home.

As ever,
Harold

P.S. Received your letter tonight asking whether I wanted boat pants or slacks. I had rather have slacks instead. Am sending home $316.00 instead of $200.00.

September 1ˢᵗ 1943
A.P.O. 418
New York, N.Y.

Hello folks,

How are you all getting along these days? I'm still doing [fine] and working every day. I received your letter the other day and I sure was glad to hear from you and that you were getting along fine.

You said that you were trying to get me oil treated boots, but so far you hadn't been able to find any of them. In a case of that kind I guess I will have to take a pair of the other kind, but I wanted the oil treated ones on account of the water and mud. You said in your letter that you had not received a letter from me last week, well I wrote you a letter and sent three hundred and sixteen dollars in it in checks, and I would like to know if you got it or not. Also let me know how many checks you have received up to now so that I will know if any of them have been lost on the way. If they have, why I have the numbers of all of them so that I can trace them up.

I guess that before long you will be living in your new

house or at least I hope that you will. Sure hope that you
can get it finished before winter begins as the old one is
so cold.

Well I am going to close for this time as news is
getting scarce, so write real soon and let me know all of
the news.

Love,
Harold

9/10/43
A.P.O. 418
New York, N.Y.

Hello Folks;

How are you all getting along these days? I guess you
are having some hot weather now, and it isn't a bit cool
down here.

I received your letter yesterday about the checks, and
according to your figures there is about four checks that
never got there. I am putting in a tracer on it. If you will,
you can go to the bank and find out the serial numbers
and the amount of each check for me so I will know just
which ones are missing. I would like to get them back for
that is a lot of money to lose.

Say does the price on the house include the plumbing,
and wiring for it too? Sure hope you can get it finished
before winter.

How are Granny and Granddaddy getting along?
Also Mutt and C.G. and their family?

Well I am going to close for this time, hoping to hear
from you all soon.

Lots of love to all,
Harold

9/14/43
A.P.O. 418,
New York, N.Y.

Hello Folks;

How is business these days? Guess you thought I had forgotten all about you, but have been so busy until I just couldn't get around to it.

How are you progressing on the new home? The plans you sent me look pretty good to me. Are you going to put French doors between the living room and dining room, if you can it will look a lot better. Also what color have you decided to trim it in? Are you going to paint it and varnish the floors before you move in? Say try and get one of those fancy glass doors for the front. I want to make one more suggestion, can you order a living room, and dining room suit from Sears Roebuck to have to put in when you move in? If you can, why, get it on the installment plan so it won't take so much cash. If you get one how would it suit you to get one of those Angora Mohairs; these will last forever, and look good too. And yourself one of those nice six piece dining room suits, with china cabinet and all, we might as well go high class while we are at it, we can get the bedroom suits later. Say is there going to be room for a piano in the living [room]? Cause you know Mama and me have to have one.

I guess you think maybe I am trying to run your business, but I just can't help having something to say about it for, I really want to see it finished. Then [it] will be the prettiest place in the country when you get a nice lawn, and some flowers planted around.

I guess you are pretty busy now, but don't do too

much, for you don't have to anymore. Sure hope you make good on the hogs and cabbage.

Am enclosing money orders for $177.50, let me know if you get them.

Tell Granny and Granddad hello for me, and tell Mutt, and C.G. I'll write them tomorrow night without fail.

Lots of love to all,
Harold

9/20/43
A.P.O. 418
New York, N.Y.

Hello Folks,

How are you all getting along these days? I am still getting along fine, and hope you are the same. I guess you wonder why I don't write more often, but I don't have very much time for writing, and there is hardly anything to write about, or that you can say in a letter, but don't worry about me for if anything happens the war department will let you know. I am sending two more checks, one for $72.00, and one for $55.00. Please write me when you get them.

Have you received the papers for the house yet, if so have you started to build yet?

You asked when I was coming home, well I guess it will be a while yet for they won't let me quit, and I can't get a leave until this job is finished. As much as I would like to see you all, so just sit tight and don't worry about me for I am fine.

Ask Granddaddy if he would just as soon have a leopard skin, or black panther as a bear skin as they don't have any bear down here.

Went to the beach the other day. Had a nice time, but it isn't as nice as the beaches in Florida.

How is your cabbage bed coming along? I think you will make some money on them, and please don't plant any more cotton cause it is only a back ache as you know by now. As long as I can work you don't have to plant anything if you don't want to, and don't forget that.

Give Mutt, and C.G. and family, also Granny, and Granddaddy my love, and I will try and write them tomorrow.

I will close for this time as I am getting sleepy so be good and answer soon.

Love to all,
Harold

P.S. received pictures O.K. they sure are good, and thanks for them.

9/23/43
A.P.O. 418
New York, N.Y.

Hello Folks;

How are you all getting along these days? I am still on the up and up. Sure is warm down here now. Guess it is pretty cold up there now. Sure would like to be there as I like winter. I was just looking at a picture of a couple of Bird dogs, and a hunter, it made my fingers itch. Do you have many quail, and squirrel this season?

Well I received the boat pants yesterday, and they sure are nice, and thanks for them, it must have been a lot of trouble. I am going to ask you to do me another favor. Try, and get me a Spanish book. Hugo's Simplified Spanish I think is the name of it, and a Spanish dictionary. You can get these from Sears. I am looking forward to the Xmas package. Wish I could send you all something but it isn't possible, the mail is too crowded. You all just take some money, and have a good time for me.

Well back to the subject of the new house. It should be nearing completion by now. It will be a beauty when you get it finished. I can't wait for a picture of it. I sure do like the plan, and the color. When we get a lawn fixed it will sure look good. As soon as I come home I want to rent a big tractor and clear the other land.

How are the rest of the folks? Tell them to take care of themselves.

Am going to close for this time so write me real soon.

Love to all,
Harold

P.S. Enclosed is money order for $227.50

9/29/43
A.P.O. 418
New York

Hello everybody;

How are you all getting along these days? I am still on the go. Boy it sure is hot around here now.

Well by now you should be started on the house. You sure will have to be on your toes to be finished by the first of Dec. Sure will seem good to come home and see a nice new home in the middle of the oak grove, send me a copy of the plans, I would like to look at it.

Say I am sending two checks in this letter for $127.50 each, be sure and let me know if you get them. We are only getting paid every two weeks now.

Say if you don't mind you can send Elouise's address

and I will drop her a few lines. Sure would like to have seen them. Say how about sending me Edward's address as I lost the one I had.

Well I am going to close for this time so be good and write.

Love,
Harold

Had to cut it short to go to work

10/2/43
A.P.O. 418
New York, N.Y.

Hello Folks;

How are you all getting along these days? I am still getting along fine, and hope you are the same. Hope the flu patients are O.K. by now.

How is the new building doing now? You should be about ready to wind her up. You asked about the porches. I think it would look more like a house to have the front porch made of wood, and have concrete steps, and pillars, It would be nice to have the back porch of concrete, of course you all build it the way you like it, for you are doing the work. About the living room suit. If you can get a good one with springs then I believe it will be a lot better, but if you can't, we will have to take one without them. If I were you I would go ahead, and order the dining room suit as it would look sort of funny to have the living room so nice, and nothing in the dining room, don't you think? You aren't going to put tile in the dining room are you?

Say you can tell Mutt that I wrote her the other day, and she should have it by now.

Well I am going to close for this time as news is scarce and so is paper, and you can't buy any here. Write real soon, and let me hear all the news.

Lots of love,
Harold

P.S. enclosed is money order of $222.50, sent one last week for $227.50.

11/15/43
A.P.O. 418
New York

Hello Folks,

How are you all doing these days? I am still getting along fine, and hope you are the same. Received your letter today, and sure was glad to hear from you. About the money order you said it was for $222.50. Well there was another before that for $227.58, let me know if you got it.

Well by now the new house should be just about completed. I can hardly wait to see it, but I guess I will have to. What have you done about the living room, and dining room suit? Say, you put tile on the kitchen, and bathroom floor didn't you?

You said that it rained there, sure is good on your cabbage patch. You should make some good money on them.

Well I am going to close for this time as news is scarce so answer real soon and tell me all the news.

Lots of love,
Harold

11/26/43
A.P.O. 868

Hello Folks,
How are you all getting along these days? I am still O.K.
Well how is the new home progressing these days, she should be just about finished by now. Also how are the cabbages doing? They should be a good price, hope so anyway.
How is Granny and Granddaddy, Ethel, and C.G. and family?
Well I am going to close for this time as I am in a hurry, so be good, and write real often.

Love,
Harold

When Harold's Job Ended

Harold had been unable to tell his family about all his comings and goings with the War Department, but when his job ended, he headed home to bring them up to date.

He was eager to tell his family about the jobs he had held as a heavy equipment operator, using drag lines and power shovels, motor graders, and bulldozers to build roads and airports in Nassau, Trinidad, and French Guyana (between Dutch Guyana and Brazil)—places they could only imagine.

Harold would tell them of seeing big colorful parrots, monkeys, and fourteen-inch spiders that could spin a web like a rope—strong enough to catch a bird they could eat! He would tell his family about the guy who made pets out of snakes, and about the day that guy and several others were trying to hold on to a snake that was at least twenty-seven feet long! And about how the guys started yelling at him—Harold—to help them, and he told them to "go to hell."

But, Harold was most eager to see the house his money had built, the house that had replaced his grandparents' old log home.

The House Harold's Money Built

While the main part of the old house was being torn down and the new house was going up, the Ryes and Laniers had lived in the old, detached kitchen.[99]

The new house stood on the very same spot of ground as the old log house had for half a century. Harold had seen no pictures of the new house, but he could close his eyes and imagine its grandeur.

In Delma's brown eyes, the new house was indeed looking like a mansion. Unlike the log house she had lived in most of her life, the new house (constructed according to a Sears and Roebuck plan) was painted. White! Inside and out. She liked the wide front porch with square columns supporting the roof, the living and dining room wood floors that were coated with varnish, and—perhaps most of all—the kitchen with its white built-in cabinets that had doors with panes of glass.

Wiring the House

Since the new house would belong to the Ryes, Tip had pretty much left all the decisions to Milton—except when it came to wiring the house for electricity.

"The very idea of putting live wires in a house!" Tip said. "Electricity! That stuff is dangerous. It could burn the whole house down and us in it."

To that, Milton turned a deaf ear. He hired Tom Morgan to wire the house.

Tip didn't let up, though. When Mr. Morgan actually started stringing the wires, Tip put his foot down where his and Dosia's room was concerned.

"Aye God, buddy," he told Milton and Mr. Morgan, "I don't want none of them wires run in mine and Dosia's bedroom. It could catch fire while we're sound asleep."

Milton ignored Tip's objections again. Wires were run to every room.

What Harold Saw

When Harold, having been exposed to big cities and a tropical paradise, set eyes on the house his money had built, he must have felt bitter disappointment. He had wanted block construction. It was frame. He had wanted a wooden front porch. It was concrete. He had wanted a fancy glass front door. It was wood panel, plus a screen door. He had wanted French doors to separate the living and dining rooms. It was open. *And where was the piano?* He had wanted a concrete back porch. It didn't exist; instead, unpainted boards led from the back door to the ground where a pile of rocks (that were supposed to eventually serve as the base for a back porch) littered the backyard. *Where was the lawn? The flowers?*

Harold had also expected a bathroom. There was a bath ROOM. *But, where were the fixtures—the tub, the toilet, the lavatory? Where was the water? Was there even a septic tank in the ground?*

Reality

While Harold had sent his family nearly every dime he had made, constructing a home was expensive. Money could be stretched just so far. On the positive side, the house had been wired for electricity. Mr. Morgan had installed electrical outlets, light fixtures, and even light switches. But when Harold flipped the switch, nothing happened. *Where was the power?*

It the early 1940s, having electric power connected to your house, if you lived in a rural area, wasn't as simple as paying a deposit. At that time, only about half of all rural homes in the United States had electricity because power lines did not extend there. That was the case for most of Suwannee County. There were no power lines within miles of the Ryes' new house.

But there was hope. The U.S. government's Rural Electrification Act of 1936 had provided federal funding for installation of electrical distribution systems to serve rural areas. It was a matter of time.

As it turned out, Harold had little time to worry about the house, its state of completion, or getting electricity connected to it, because his draft papers had arrived the day before he did.

Harold's friend Ernest Robins with his grandmother (everyone called her Grandmother Robins) in front of the Rye's new home

Inside the New House
Delma was proud of her new house and its furnishings. Milton's brother, Ellis, and his wife, Daisy, had given her their used, but good, living room suite as a thank-you for taking care of Buddie while they were separated. The set included an upholstered sofa and two matching chairs with rolled arms and backs, spoon feet—and springs within the cushions, just as Harold had strongly suggested.[100]

Delma also had a new dining room suite from Sears and Roebuck that included a table and six chairs, a buffet, and a china cabinet! In the china cabinet she had placed her treasured pink glassware, the serving pieces of her new Blue Willow dishes, and a green cookie jar she used for storing things like postage stamps and chewing gum.[101]

The old woodstove, which had been moved from the old house into the new kitchen, was only temporary. Delma had thought she wanted a new oil stove, but her husband had suggested she wait and get a modern electric one. Milton planned to shop for the best one money could buy— just as soon as they got electricity. But even without an electric stove, Delma thought her kitchen was near perfect.

On each side of the window were white, custom-built cabinets with clear glass-paned doors that showed off her new Blue Willow plates, bowls, cups, and saucers, along with her mother's durable crock-like bowls that she used for mixing and serving and for storing milk while cream was rising to the top.

Also in the kitchen was a small table that Milton had built. On it, Delma could roll out biscuit dough.[102] And, by the window to the left of the stove, he had installed a white dish towel rack with three swinging dowel arms; each dowel was tipped with bright red paint, giving Delma's kitchen a very modern look.

Under the other window was a white, five-foot-long metal cabinet, complete with a built-in enamel sink. For the time being, Delma still had to haul water in a bucket to and from the kitchen, but the sink was equipped with a faucet that would eventually bring cold running water, after they got electricity and an electric pump. Running hot water was, of course, another matter. But meanwhile, Delma still had her big teakettle. It was a pretty good water heater.

From the window over the sink, Delma had a good view of the clothesline as well as the washhouse that Milton was in the process of building. She planned to get a wringer washer for the washhouse too, just as soon as they got electricity.

Considering the situation with electricity and running water, the bathroom was temporarily furnished with a zinc tub for bathing, a washbasin atop a wooden cabinet for washing faces and hands, and a slop jar. (A porcelain sink, tub, and commode would be installed after they got electricity and running water.)

Each of the three bedrooms was furnished with pieces from the old house. Each had a bureau and an iron bed with wire springs and a striped tick-covered mattress. In addition, Milton and Delma's bedroom on the front of the house (as well as the back bedroom that was intended for Harold) contained a freestanding, mahogany-stained wardrobe that Milton had built and finished himself. Inside each was a high shelf, the perfect spot for storing hats, handbags, ammunition, or anything that needed to be kept out of the reach of children. Underneath each wardrobe shelf was a long row of tiny metal eyes that Milton had screwed into the wood. Each eye, perfectly spaced about an inch apart, would accept the crook of a wire coat hanger. (This seemed such a clever idea, but inserting a loaded wire hanger in one of those hooks in the custom-made mahogany wardrobes was more tedious than threading a needle.)

Tip and Dosia said they needed no big wardrobe in their bedroom, and they didn't. Their bureau and a metal trunk,[103] which they had owned since they were first married, stored about everything in the world they owned. So, instead of a wardrobe, Milton had their room equipped with a medicine cabinet, built right into the wall. A twist of its small wooden latch let the door open to reveal bottles of liniment, tonics, and Tip's spirits of medicine.

Of all the new furnishings and all the items that had been moved from the old house into the new, perhaps the most treasured of all were the letters Harold had written home. For safekeeping, Delma placed those in the top drawer of her new buffet, right next to the yellowed homestead deed signed by President McKinley.[104]

Harold in Uniform

Soon after Harold left for the service, he mailed his family a hand-tinted, eight-by-ten photograph of himself in uniform. Harold, they thought, had never looked so handsome!

After buying a frame for the picture, Delma looked around for a place to set it. The photo was too large to fit on the narrow mantel over the fireplace. Besides, the mantel already held two large photographs of Ethel: one of her wearing a long white gown that she had made and worn to her senior prom; the other was of her in her mortarboard cap and gown. So, Delma placed the newly framed

Harold Rye

photo on top of the large radio in the corner of the living room, where the rays of light shining through a south window put Harold in the spotlight.

❧ 10   Family and Farm Life

W hen Patsy was born," Ethel said, "I had only a dozen and a half diapers. That was enough to get by during sunny weather. But if it rained—and it did—I had to dry them on the wire that C.G. put up for me under the eave of the front porch."

When Dr. Price was summoned to the Howell residence for the second time in a little over a year, he delivered another baby girl—a healthy, nine-pound girl.

"Even though Patsy was just a little over thirteen months old then," Ethel said, "I already had her weaned and trained. I never wanted to have more than one baby at a time in diapers, and didn't."

The proud parents named the new baby Anetha Faye— Anetha, after a girl C.G. had admired in high school.

Ethel and C.G. holding baby Anetha and Patsy

"The girl's name was Anetha Truett," C.G. said. "We never dated, but she was smart and pretty."

"After Anetha was born," Ethel said, "I had a *time* with Patsy. She would bite Anetha for no apparent reason, kind of like Harold used to bite me; but I wasn't a tiny baby then and Anetha was.

"I was so afraid Patsy would bite Anetha while I was outside. I had to go out and milk the cow, even on cold winter mornings, and had nobody to watch them. So, I would tie Patsy to the bedpost. I hated to do it, but it was too cold to take them out, plus I couldn't milk the cow while holding on to them; and the cow *had* to be milked.[105]

"Looking back, I guess I fussed at Patsy too much. I never will forget how I was "after her" one day when she was a bit older—but not yet two. I don't remember now what it was that I was fussing and quarrelling about. But I was cross with her, and after a while she looked up at me and said, 'Mama, if you gonna whip me, whip me, and hush your karl-in.' "

Der She Go!

"When we bought the farm," Ethel said, "Allie and Kent Thomas—they were colored people—lived about a half mile due east, on the Morrison place (the Lyle place before the Morrisons bought it.) We thought a lot of Kent and Allie; we were always helping one another out. Allie would often walk down to our old house, and when she got there, she'd say, 'Now Miss Ethel, I come to love dem babies. You just go on and do whatever it is you gotta do today, and I'll just love dem babies.'

"We had a baby swing that Patsy and Anetha loved— Anetha, especially—and Allie liked to watch her swing. When Anetha was sitting in the swing, she could stand up so her little feet would be flat on the floor, but as she twisted herself round and round, just the tips of her toes touched the floor. Allie would watch her, saying 'Look at her, Miss Ethel, she's crankin' up a car, she's crankin' up a car, she crankin' up a car!' Then Anetha would jerk her little feet up and curl herself into a ball as the swing unwound faster and faster. 'Der she go! Der she go, Miss Ethel!' Allie would say as Anetha spun out and then giggled like crazy.

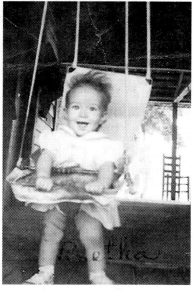

Anetha, in the swing she loved

"Allie would sometimes spend nearly all day at our house, and late in the day, she'd say to me, 'Miss Ethel, I wonder if you'd write a letter to my daughter fer me?' Allie didn't know how to read or write, so she would tell me just what she wanted to say, and I would put it down on paper for her.

"Besides their daughter, Allie and Kent had a son, Buster (they also had a grandson that stayed with them). Their son Buster was a good worker. When he came to help us, he would always get to our house real early—between daylight and sunup.[x]

"Later on, Kent and Allie moved closer to Live Oak and next door to another white family. I didn't know the other family at the time, but according to the way Allie described them, they were—well, Allie said they didn't often bathe, and they let chickens walk through their house. 'Lord a Mercy, Miss Ethel!' Allie said. 'What a sight that is! That rooster standin' up on dat kitchen table a-crowin', and dat woman sittin' at the back door, holding a slab a' bacon 'tween her legs, cuttin' it wid a knife.'

"After Kent and Allie moved off the Morrison place, John and Mertis Avery bought it. They moved into the big house, and Mr. Avery's parents, who were getting on in years, moved into the smaller one that I had once lived in. C.G. and I got to be real good friends with John and Mertis. They had two real nice boys: Billy, who was the oldest, and Donald Ray, who was the same age as Patsy."

Their Family Was Complete

C.G. and Ethel thought two children made the perfect-sized family. When Patsy celebrated her second birthday (she was already talking up a storm), Anetha was approaching twelve months. Ethel was not worried about becoming pregnant again; after all, she was still nursing Anetha, and a

---

[x] *Daylight and sunup* may seem redundant to some. But those who have lived on a farm know that much can be accomplished between daylight and sunup—chores like milking a cow and feeding livestock.

woman could not become pregnant while nursing, so she had been told.

When Ethel discovered she *was* pregnant, she was not pleased—three pregnancies in three years! C.G. was not overjoyed either. Times were hard.

But, as those who knew these two expected, both soon came to terms with the situation. Within weeks if not days, C.G. and Ethel were puzzling over names for the new baby.

"We should name him Clarence Alton," C.G. said to Ethel, "Clarence after my daddy, and Alton after Mr. Alton Raines." (Mr. Raines worked for the U.S. Department of Agriculture; C.G. had always looked up to him.) The matter was settled. Clarence Alton it would be.

Buddie's Skeeter

When the teenage Buddie Rye had gone to live with his Uncle Milton and Aunt Delma, he had arrived in his very own car.

"Buddie had told his daddy, Ellis, a mechanic, that he wanted a car," C.G. said, "and his daddy told him what to do. 'Go out there to the junk pile and build yourself a car.' So that's what Buddie had done. He had built his car from parts salvaged from his daddy's junk pile. That was the car he drove from Jacksonville when he went to live with Mr. and Mrs. Rye.

"While living with them, he had at least one accident with the car, and by the time his mama finally came and got him, after she and Ellis got back together, the car wasn't running too well; so when Daisy took Buddie back to Jacksonville, the old car got left behind."

The Spring of 1944

"Buddie's car hadn't been cranked since," C.G. continued. "It didn't look like Buddie ever planned to come back for it, and Mr. Rye wanted it moved; the relic had been sitting in his yard, idle and exposed to all the elements since

Buddie had abandoned it. We called it a cut-down skeeter. It was just a rusting chassis with no protective steel body to cover its engine and seats.

" 'C.G., you're a pretty good mechanic,' Mr. Rye said to me one day. 'You might be able to get that thing going.' So I started tinkering with it—put gas in it, cleaned out the gas line, checked the timing, cleaned the plugs and set the gaps in the plugs and the distributor, and put oil in it—oil that Mr. Rye had drained from his tractor, intending to throw it away. I didn't figure the used oil mattered, because when Buddie had the car running, it would blow the oil out the back in no time.

"After I started working on that skeeter in the spring of 1944, I had that thing running in about thirty minutes.[xi] After I found a string of numbers on it, I sent them off to Tallahassee to get the registration for it. Then I ordered tires from Sears and Roebuck.

"I remember that about the time I got that car running in the spring of '44, was when I heard the bad news about Thomas Lee Boatright."

Joe Boatright got word on April 13, 1944, that his son Thomas Lee, was missing in action in Germany.

"Early that summer, I found out that A. W. Ross Jr., had an old coupe—a Model A Ford body—that would fit over the chassis of Buddie's skeeter; so I asked A.W. about it, and he said he would take fifteen dollars for it. Before heading up to his house to get it, I found some bolts at home that I thought would work to attach the body to the chassis. I laid them on the floorboard and drove the skeeter to A.W.'s house. He and his brothers, Jack, Howard, and Thomas, helped me set the body over the frame. I dropped the pins in and bolted it, paid A.W. the fifteen dollars, and

---

[xi] Some might question C.G.'s estimate of the time, considering that he was well-known for losing track of it, especially when he was absorbed in an important activity like repairing a car—or visiting.

at last I had myself a car. But, it rattled pretty bad, so when I got back home, I measured the frame and everything to see exactly what I needed to get it tighter.

"A few days later, I drove the car to Live Oak and got some bolts that were the right size, some lock washers and grommets—big rubber washers—from Claude Hackney (he gave them to me). Then I rebolted the body to the frame, using the grommets between the body and frame to get rid of some of the shakes and rattles. It was a pretty quiet car when I got through with it.

"Later on, I took it to town and had the motor rebuilt—had the block rebored—to a bigger hole—and put bigger pistons and rings in it to replace the old ones that were scored. I also put new plugs in the motor (but not a new condenser and distributor), and timed it." (Photo, p. 245)

Our Farm Animals

"We raised animals for our own food," C.G. said, "as well as for market. To bring our cows—Jerseys, Guernseys, and Holsteins—and our one horse or mule through the winter, we fed them mostly fodder (corn leaves).

"When we were drying the fodder, if it came up a rain, we would have to run out and gather it up fast. If it got wet, it would rot. We also fed the animals hay made from pea vines, and corn. I would run the ears of corn through the hammer mill, cobs and all, to make feed. Then, during the warm months, the animals could graze on Bahia grass.

"We fed the hogs more corn than anything else. And of course they loved clabber and slop from the kitchen.

"Every fall, we killed hogs for us to eat. Mr. Rye and I usually butchered several at a time. We killed them by slitting their throats; that allowed most of the blood to drain out. Some people would catch the blood to use in sausage, but we didn't save the blood; we just let it run out on the ground. Then we scalded each hog in the sugarcane kettle so the hair would be easy to scrape off.

"After scraping the hogs, we cut the hamstrings on the two back legs of each animal, slid a strong rounded stick—one that was whittled to a point on each end[106]—through the hamstrings, and hoisted each hog up, suspending each one from its back legs. Then we slit each hog open along the underside of its belly so the bowels would fall down in a zinc washtub. The intestines would be stripped later to use for sausage casings. (Ethel tried boiling a few chitlins a time or two, but we didn't care much for them.)

"The fat was placed on large outdoor tables and the women would cut it into small pieces before it was put in a wrought-iron pot over a fire. Once all the lard was cooked out of the fat, we had cracklins.

"The slabs of pork were taken to town for curing. To cure the meat, it was kept under refrigeration, and a mixture of sugar and salt was rubbed into it daily for several days, then every other day for a period of time.

"Once the slabs were cured, we took them back home to be smoked. We rinsed off the sugar and salt, rubbed the meat down with borax and black pepper, and suspended the slabs in the smokehouse. Then we built a fire under them. Pecan limbs were preferable, but oak would do. We smoked the meat several days—maybe a week to ten days—until it turned brown. Curing and smoking wasn't necessary if you had a freezer, but we didn't have electricity yet.

"As for beef, we didn't cure or smoke it. We either ate it up fresh, before it spoiled, or we canned it. The best way was to use a pressure cooker if you had one.

"I helped my Aunt Lizzie can some beef once. I remember there was a man there, helping Uncle Joe out, and he ate dinner with us that day. He said to Aunt Lizzie as he helped himself to another big steak, 'That sure is good steak!' Their young son Carra, after looking at the big steak the man had put on his plate, said, 'I see it is!' Aunt Lizzie really got mad with Carra for saying that.

"When we first married, Ethel canned some pork sausage. But she never did can any beef.

"We didn't butcher many cows. They are so heavy that when we did butcher one, we had to suspend the carcass using a pulley and a chain. Once the carcass was hanging up, we pulled the hide off. The back legs were done first. Then we cut the head off and finished it up. We used a handsaw to help cut the meat into different pieces, similar to the way we cut up the hogs.

"Sometimes when cutting up our meat, we got creative. One day after I had cut up a hog, I took it to McMullen Food Bank for curing, and Helen McMullen started checking me in. She looked at the meat and she gave me a puzzled look. 'C.G.,' she finally said, 'you've got *two* sides, *no* shoulders, and *four* hams.'

" 'Yeah, Helen,' I said, 'I bred my hogs so they didn't have shoulders!' Of course, what I had done was—I had cut the shoulders to *look* like hams, just for the heck of it."

The Spoiled Pig

Occasionally, a sow births more pigs than she has teats for the pigs to suck, which means one little runty pig gets pushed aside at feeding time. When this happened, C.G. would give the runty pig to Ethel to fatten up. She would feed the baby pig with a bottle and then start adding solid food, as if it were her own baby. After she got the pig stronger, she would give him back to C.G. to put back with the others.

One day C.G. was complaining because one of Ethel's fattened-up pigs, now back with the other pigs, was turning up his nose—and that's not just a figure of speech—at the slop and grain C.G. was pouring into the pig trough.

"You've just spoiled that pig plum rotten," he told Ethel. "All that pig will eat now is cornbread and milk!"

Patsy, hearing this, corrected her father. "Daddy, That ain't all that pig will eat. He'll eat cake."

Big Ears

Although C.G. and Ethel worked hard on the farm, they took time off to visit with friends. C.G. really enjoyed having other people around, and it was well known that any time he had an audience, he could think of a joke to tell.

Ruby and Joe Hingson

"One night Ethel and I went someplace with Joe and Ruby," C.G. said. "They had Mary Frances with them, and we had Patsy with us. Anetha was probably with Mr. and Mrs. Rye, and Ruby and Joe had left their other kids with somebody. Patsy and Mary Frances liked to play together; they were the same age, two or three years old then. On the way home, the kids were asleep—or so we thought. Anyway, we all started telling jokes.

" 'I saw a man in Live Oak once,' I said, 'that had no arms and no legs, but he could chop wood!' I let that sink in before I asked, 'And, do you know how a man with no arms and no legs could chop wood?'

" 'No. How?' Joe, Ruby, and Ethel said together.

" 'He stuck the ax handle up his rear, and did somersaults!'

"Everybody started laughing. Then Pasty—I just *knew* she was asleep!—raised up and asked, 'Daddy, can you chop wood like that?' "

Payment for a Manicure

Patsy was not (and never would be) afraid to speak up. Such was the case when she went with her mother one day to Annie's Beauty Shop. On that occasion, it was Ethel that Patsy embarrassed.

The prices at Annie Mills's shop, if not Annie herself, made it the most popular beauty shop in town. The atmosphere there was electric. While Annie was cutting, curling, and combing hair, she was also chatting and chain-smoking. Her customers, one after the other, would be placed under one of the black dome-shaped hair dryers that lined the walls. While some flipped through magazines, others gabbed and gossiped in competition with the roar of the dryers blowing hot air.

Annie and her fellow beauticians kept pumping the pedals of their pneumatic chairs up and down, beautifying one customer after another like an assembly line. Annie stayed so busy coiffing and curling the hair of her customers that she neglected her own frizzy locks. But Annie was an energetic and likeable person and always had a smile on her face.

That day, after cutting and rolling up Ethel's hair and seating her under the dryer, Annie entertained little Patsy by painting Patsy's fingernails bright red. Annie expected no payment, at least no monetary payment.

After Ethel's hair was dry and combed out, she got up to pay for her do and also offered to pay Annie for little Patsy's manicure.

"Oh, I just need a kiss for the manicure," Annie said and bent down to collect her kiss from Patsy.

Patsy shook her head slowly back and forth.

"Why won't you give me a kiss?" Annie asked with a pout.

" 'Cause you smoke!"—came Patsy's reply.

Then it was Ethel's head that was going back and forth.

The War

"I spent over seven years in the National Guard," C.G. said, "advancing from private to corporal. I was still in the Guard when Ethel and I married, but after we bought the farm in the spring of 1941, I decided to get out because National Guard camp would take me away from the farm during the busiest season.

"After Japan bombed Pearl Harbor on December 7, 1941, so *many* men were called into service. But farmers who were producing necessary goods for survival—food crops and livestock—were given deferments. The government gave deferment points based on what type of crops and livestock a farmer produced. Some years I earned three points and some years I earned five and eight points, more than was necessary for a deferment. So, I was classified 2A, and with that, I was never drafted."

Victory Gardens[107]

"Mr. Steiner Kierce, the Agricultural Agent for Suwannee County, came out to the farm early during the summer of '44," C.G. said, "and asked me if I would go to work for him as the War Foods Administrator for Suwannee County. I had known Mr. Kierce since high school when I was the Suwannee County 4-H Club Council President, and I think he liked my work.

"With the war, everybody was being encouraged to grow Victory Gardens. It was part of the Agricultural Stabilization Program (ASP);[108] the idea was that everybody should learn how to grow their own vegetables. For a garden to be classified a Victory Garden, a person had to plant at least seven varieties.

"For years and years, people had grown their own food; they had farmed just to eat. But, farming got complicated when people got away from that and started trying to get rich and the government started trying to help. To keep prices of goods up, the government started the allotment program.

"After buying the Ward place, I was allotted—allowed to plant each year—just four acres of cotton, four and seven-tenths of an acre of tobacco, and eleven acres of peanuts for selling. I could plant more peanuts and corn for eating and for hay and animal feed.

"I planted cotton one year against Ethel's wishes. She'd had her fill of cotton before we married and knew we couldn't make any money at it. I planted it just that one year. Later on, I gave my cotton allotment away.

"As for tobacco, the government kept cutting down the allotment until I could plant just nine-tenths of an acre.[109] To keep insects from eating up that little bit of tobacco, we put Parrish Green Poison on it. At the time, we could buy that at the drugstore.

"The government also wanted farmers to plant certain crops to build [enrich] the soil and prevent erosion. To encourage that, they started paying farmers—sending conservation checks—if the farmer would plant certain crops, like crotalaria, hairy indigo, and blue lupin. I did some of that; and after experimenting, I thought blue lupin was the best. What I did was plant an acre of different kinds of seed to see what gave the best results. I also tried both oats and rye and used different kinds of fertilizer.

"As for the Victory Garden program, the government would pay a family an extra dollar and fifty cents. That money was added to their conservation checks.

"Mr. Kierce asked me to serve as the administrator of the Victory Garden program in Suwannee County. I took the job, which paid two-hundred dollars a month; but that also had to cover my gas. I drove my Model A and went around the county encouraging people to plant Victory Gardens. I drove many a mile with that old car. I think gas was about seventeen cents a gallon, then, and my Model A got about twenty-two miles to a gallon."

A Long Hot Summer
"Oh, it was hot that summer of '44!" Ethel said. "It was the first time I had been pregnant during a summer—and I was pretty far along by June.

"I never will forget the day I was helping in tobacco and Aunt Ethel Houck [C.G.'s mother's sister] was handing tobacco alongside me. We hadn't been at the job long before she leaned over to me and whispered, 'When's your baby due?'

"I told her 'October,' and knowing her daughter was expecting a baby too, I asked her, 'And, when is Edna's baby due?'

" 'My Gawd-a-mighty!' Mrs. Houck snapped, 'I don't ask my young'uns things like that!' "

The Fall of 1944
Since Dr. Price had delivered the first two Howell babies, Ethel was now visiting him regularly, for checkups. On one such visit, C.G. accompanied his wife and paid Dr. Price the full delivery fee in advance—forty-five dollars.

Like Ethel's previous deliveries, the baby would be born at home. The plan was for Ethel's mother to stay with her during her recovery, just as she had after the birth of the first two babies.

Unfortunately, as the due date approached, Delma found herself consumed with taking care of her ill mother, Dosia. So C.G. and Ethel started asking around the community, trying to find someone they could hire to help with the children. But time ran out.

"C.G., wake up!"

"Huh?"

"Wake up! It's time."

"What?"

"It's time. You need to go get the doctoh-oh-oh-ohrrr!"

C.G., realizing labor was underway, jumped out of bed, dressed, and helped Ethel get Patsy and Anetha up. Then the whole family piled into the car. C.G. knew Delma would take care of them while he fetched the doctor.

After dropping off his family at the Ryes', C.G. pointed his Model A in the direction of Live Oak and revved its engine. The car flew down the bumpy dirt road in the dark morning hours. C.G. knew it was eighteen miles to town and no shorter back.

As it turned out, C.G. and a man named John Fink were on a similar mission that predawn morning. At the same time, both screeched to a halt in front of Dr. Price's office, with each man requesting assistance for his wife who was in labor. *To which woman would the good doctor go first?*

"I'm sorry, Mr. Fink, I will have to go with Mr. Howell. He has already paid the bill."

By the time C.G. and Dr. Price arrived that early morning, Delma had gotten Ethel as comfortable as possible in the front bedroom of her new house.[xii]

Dr. Price, of slender build and slightly stooped, was bald except for a few wisps of grey hair. At Ethel's bedside, he went to work earning his forty-five dollar fee, all the while offering words of encouragement to his patient in his gentle manner, though of course childbirth was anything but gentle.

Delma was kept busy bringing in cloths and pans of freshly drawn water and, after the delivery, helping Dr. Price with the cleanup.

"You'll stay for breakfast, won't you?" Delma asked the doctor as he was finally finishing up.

"No, I'd best get on over to the Fink place," he answered, and headed out.

C.G., upon learning he had another girl, let go of the name Clarence Alton and said Ethel could name the baby anything she wanted. She chose Susie Jeannette, after nobody in particular. As it turned out, two-year-old Patsy couldn't get her mouth around *Susie Jeannette*. So before

---

[xii] In telling this story, C.G. bragged about how he rushed for the doctor, how the bill was prepaid, how he and Dr. Price "got back to Ethel in no time flat!" "It seemed longer than that to *me*!" Ethel replied.

long everybody in the family was calling the baby what Patsy did: *Susanette*.

Ethel declared, after this baby was delivered, that she was "*done* with having babies." C.G. accepted that he would never have a son, *but who was to say he couldn't have another male in the household?*

Tommy

On the same day Susanette drew her first breath, so did a litter of puppies belonging to a dog owned by Mr. Kierce's friend, Bob Miller.[110] One Sunday afternoon in November, Mr. Kierce picked out a male, brown-and-white pup with a blaze up its face, and took the Heinz 57 (mutt) puppy to C.G.

Instead of Clarence Alton, C.G. named the boy dog Tommy, after Bob Miller's son who had the same birthday as the pups and Susanette.

"Tommy turned out to be a really good dog," Ethel said. He wanted to be wherever the girls were. He would lie down on the floor beside Susanette when I put her down on a pallet. Even when she poked him in the eye, he would never snap at her. In fact, I don't think he ever snapped at anybody—except Michael Schemer—he bit him bad in the cheek. I sure did feel bad about that. I don't know what Michael did to Tommy to make him bite. Maybe he tried to take his bone. I don't know, but, I sure hated it."

Christmas in Miami

"We went down to Miami that Christmas in the Model A," C.G. said, "and because Ethel wanted to go see her Grandmama Rye, we went by way of Punta Gorda. About the time we got there, that car began to backfire; so I went to a parts place and bought a set of points and a condenser ($3.60 worth of parts) and replaced them. We drove on down

Cora Rye, Ethel's paternal grandma

to Naples and across the Tamiami Trail—the longest road!—forty miles with no curve. Gas was still being rationed because of the war, but I had saved enough ration stamps for the trip. On the way home, we were close to Green Cove Springs when the speedometer showed a thousand miles—or I knew it was a thousand miles since I had rebuilt the motor. People had told me that you had to change the oil every thousand miles."

As C.G. described the trip, Ethel butted in—and Ethel was not one to butt.

"That trip to Miami is the time I thought the most about leaving C. G. Howell," Ethel said. "Patsy was not yet three, Anetha—she was hardly walking—and the new baby was just three months old; I carried her on a pillow on my lap. Anetha and Patsy slept on the little ledge in the back behind our seat, feet to feet. The trip down there went okay. But when we headed back home, we left Miami before daylight, and when we got as far as Green Cove Springs, C.G. decided we would just 'have to stop and get the oil changed.' It was early afternoon, and he saw the car had reached the mileage for an oil change. I suggested he wait. He said, 'It can't wait until we get home.'

Clara Midgett with Susanette

"So, he stopped in Green Cove Springs or Palatka to have it changed. We had to get *out* of the car for them to

- 244 -

put it up on the rack, and boy did I have a time. Patsy and Anetha were so tired—and I tell you!—I never felt more like leaving C.G. than I did that day. I had to sit on the bathroom toilet to nurse the baby, and Patsy and Anetha were so tired I couldn't keep them from wallowing on the filthy floor. I used most of a roll of toilet paper trying to wipe them clean because there were no towels to be seen."

"Later on," C.G. jumped in, picking up where he had left off, with his mind still on his car and not Ethel's predicament—or how close he had come to being a divorced man—"I had some trouble with the gas line on that car breaking. So I got some copper tubing and some ferrules to go over the ends of the pipe. I used a longer pipe and bent it like a spring. After that, the gas line never gave any more trouble.

"I had nineteen-inch tires on that car. Man! I drove that Model A! Even after it ran hot and broke the engine block, I drove it. I just poured some liquid weld in the motor and that sealed it up."

**Patsy sits on the fender and Anetha serves
as the hood ornament on C.G.'s Model A.**

Farming

When C.G. was asked to describe his and Ethel's farming operation, he summed it up on a single sheet of paper:

January: We shelled seed corn and peanuts from the previous year to use for planting a new crop, or bought hybrid seed (they became available in 1942). We also made sure to keep our tobacco beds watered as the tiny seedlings were emerging.

February: We planted watermelons. In late February or early March, we transplanted the tobacco.

March: Between the 15th and the 20th, we planted corn.

April: We planted peanuts.

May: We put poison on the tobacco in early May and suckered the tobacco in late May.

June: We began gathering and curing tobacco.

July: We were still gathering and curing tobacco and cutting and loading watermelons.

August: We were taking tobacco off the stick, packing it up, and getting it to market. I counted up one time how many times a leaf of tobacco or stick of tobacco got handled by different people—before it was packed on sheets to haul to market for sale—and it was twenty-five to thirty times.

September: We plowed under all the past year's above-ground crop residue, in preparation for planting cover crops to build the soil.

October: We planted blue lupin, rye, or oats as a soil builder.

November: We prepared the seed beds by plowing an area and putting down a fumigant. We killed hogs and made syrup from cane.

December: We planted tobacco seeds.

Spare time: We wormed and marked livestock, repaired barns and other outlying buildings, and cleaned out the fence rows with a grubbing hoe. There was no rest for the tired or weary.

Straight Rows

"I was known for laying off straight rows," C.G. said. "Some people liked to lay off their rows using a stake, but I would just set my sights on a stump or some other landmark in the distance and go straight toward it. But, one time I got tricked. I thought I was looking at a stump, and it turned out to be the backend of a cow that evidently didn't stand still. That row ended up pretty crooked.

"After that mistake, I decided to make myself a row marker from an old weeder. I added three two-by-fours to it, so that as I plowed down one row, I'd be marking off two more rows, one on each side of the row that the mule was on. One year, I laid off all of Uncle Clarence's and Jimmy North's cropland—and mine—with that row marker and my mule.

"Ethel never laid off any rows or did any of the plowing, but she would help me with other things like the planting and hoeing of the crops. That reminds me [C.G. chuckled]. One time I said to somebody, 'Ethel is the best *hoer* I've ever had!' I was just joking around, you know. But she heard me and let me know later that she didn't think that was one bit funny."

"When I went out to hoe," Ethel said, "I would set up the playpen at the end of the rows and put the girls in it and then check on them every time I got back to that end of one of the rows.

"One time I couldn't figure out why Susanette kept crying and crying. I checked on her and couldn't find any problem, so I thought she was just tired and would fall asleep. Well, when I made another loop, finishing two more rows, she was *still* crying, so I went and checked on her again. I finally thought to take off her little booties that I had made for her, and that's when I found the problem. There were ants inside one bootie, and they had been stinging her. Her little foot was covered with big red welts. When I saw that, I wanted to cry too."

"The year after I fixed up the Model A," C.G. said, "I was able to buy my first tractor. I added lights to it—so when I got home from my day job, I could still see how to plow. I kept on working for Mr. Kierce during the day and farming at night. I also bought a row marker that had a disk on the end of it, and some years I would lay off all of Mr. Rye's rows and my rows with that. When Mr. Rye laid off his own rows, he used his tractor's tracks as his guide for keeping his rows straight."

Mr. Fixer-Upper

C.G. was known for his ability to fix just about any-thing. People in the

Susanette, receiving her first "fix-it" lesson from C.G. He holds a stilson and box wrench as he repairs his Farm All.

community were always asking him to help repair a car, a tractor, or some piece of equipment. He recognized that almost anything could be repaired. When Ethel cooked holes in her pots, he mended them with a Mend-X kit. On the rare occasion that he didn't know how to fix something, he knew who could.

"Our pump went out one day," C.G. said, "and I didn't know how to fix it, but I knew Marvin Warren did. So I went over to his house and asked for his help.

" 'Nope, C.G., I can't go today.' he said, 'I promised to put Sheetrock in Merine's room today. I've been promising and promising. Today I gotta do the job.'

"I explained to Mr. Warren that we couldn't get a drop of water, and I really needed his help, so if he would go with me and help me fix my pump, then I would go to his house the next day and help him with Merine's room. He agreed, and by the end of that day we had water; and by the end of the next day, Merine's room had Sheetrock."

Organic versus Chemical

"When I first started farming," C.G. said, "most people used cottonseed meal, what they now call *organic,* for fertilizer. When commercial fertilizer, the chemical stuff, became popular, I changed to that. But one of the problems with commercial fertilizer is that it can get the soil out of balance—the nitrogen [N], phosphate [Ph], and potash [K]. Sometimes I would put down 4N-10Ph-12K, other times 5-10-15 or 10-10-10 at a rate of about twenty pounds per acre. I also bought ammonium nitrate that I spread at the rate of about two-hundred pounds per acre, about forty-five days after I planted a crop. Then when a crop was done, I'd plow under what was left of it to help build the soil for the next crop."

Harold and Louise

In the summer of 1945, Ethel's brother Harold announced to his family that he was getting married.

Milton and Delma had been concerned when their son dropped out of high school and joined the War Department, but his work, travels, and seeking answers to questions based on his own curiosity had likely provided him as good of an education as a formal one—maybe better. After he was drafted into the military, he took an exam that qualified him for the Navy Air Corps. It was while he was with the

Navy, stationed in the Chicago area, that he met the woman he planned to marry—Louise Gaboian.[111]

Harold and Louise married on June 3, 1945.

Needing Money

C.G. was in need of extra money to get some of his fields stumped and didn't know where he was going to get it.

One day when he drove to Live Oak and got out of his Model A to go into his office, a black man on the street stopped to admire his car.

"That's a good-sounding motor," the man said.

"Yeah, it runs good," C.G. told him. "I've been driving it for a couple of years now."

"You wouldn't want to sell it, would you?"

"Matter a' fact, I would."

"What'll you take for it?"

"A hundred and fifty," C.G. answered, and before he knew it, he had made a deal for the sale of his car.

"Can it wait till Saturday week?" the man asked.

C.G. agreed to that, but the day the man paid him for and took his car, C.G. was left with no other transportation of his own to get home.

"I hitched a ride with Arthur Chauncey," C.G. said, "and asked him about riding back and forth with him to work for a while. I had the tractor, so I drove it every morning up to his house (just the other side of Leo Land's place—not quite half-way to town) and rode on to town with him, to my job at the Agricultural Office on Ohio Avenue. The office was in a two-story building next to the town's biggest hotel, at the intersection of U.S. 129 and U.S. 90.

"By then, Mr. Kierce had promoted me to office manager. It paid $165 a month, and none of that had to pay for gas since the job didn't require travel.

"Later on, Mr. Kierce offered me the job of Assistant County Agent—though it was temporary. He was honest with me when he hired me, telling me that they really wanted to secure a college-educated man for the job. I fully understood when I took the job that it was temporary. So when he found Bill Cowan, who had a degree from a university, he let me go as Assistant County Agent, but then Cowen kept me on as his ASCS supervisor.

"So, I was again measuring crop land, making sure farmers adhered to their governmental allotments. If a person planted more than was allowed, some of the crop had to be destroyed. I did that for several years.

"One day I made a woman really mad when I told her we had to destroy part of her crop. It was a shame we had to do it. She had not put her plants in rows; the plants were sparse, scattered here and there. But I had to go by acreage, not individual plants. After we pulled up the excess acreage, she wrote me a letter and cussed me out.

She was a strange woman; everybody said she kept goats in her house. It was a strange-looking house, too—flat on top."

The New Doctor in Town
After closing his office adjacent to the Alimar Theater, Dr. Price saw only a few patients in the cozy, dimly lit parlor of his Pine Street home, an impressive two-story, constructed of stone blocks. Dr. Price had delivered all of Ethel's babies; but because he was continuing to cut back on his practice, it was time to look for a new doctor.

Dr. Clifford Leroy Adams had set up practice right next door to the office where C.G. worked. He was a stocky man with a square jaw and a jovial personality. Before long, his practice was booming. It was not unusual for patients to sit for several hours in one of his waiting rooms labeled WHITE or COLORED. All doctor and dentist offices in the area had segregated waiting rooms then, just as the stores had separate drinking fountains with signs posted accordingly.

Anetha sat on the examination table in Dr. Adams's office one morning, feeling rather poorly; she had an upset stomach. Patsy stood between her sister and her mother, who was seated in a chair with Susanette on her lap.

"What seems to be the problem today?" Dr. Adams asked as he walked in and smiled at Anetha.

"Her stomach is tore up," Ethel answered.

Patsy jerked up Anetha's dress.

"Mama! Her stomach ain't tore up!"

Not long after that, Anetha had to be taken to the doctor again, and this time, it was more serious.

"She had developed a sore place on her stomach and one on her fanny," Ethel said. "At first, we thought they were just bruises, but the one on her stomach became a hard knot and started swelling. Then she got real sick. By the time we got her to the doctor, her stomach looked like it was going to bust. The doctor said it was an abscess that grew inward."

"We didn't have good transportation then," C.G. said, "since I had sold the car. I don't even remember how we got to town that day—probably borrowed Mr. Rye's old truck. Anyway, Dr. Adams got his car, which would go a lot faster than whatever we were driving, and he rushed us to the hospital in Valdosta where Dr. Johnston operated on Anetha—right away—removing the abscesses. (Live Oak didn't have a hospital yet; it didn't get one until 1948).

"After the operation, I rode back to Live Oak with Dr. Adams, and Ethel stayed there at the hospital with Anetha. I went back the next day. And then in a few days when Anetha was better and could come home, I went and got them and brought them home. Delma kept Patsy and Susanette for us."

The surgery left Anetha with a large scar on her abdomen and a smaller one on her butt, but she was alive, thanks to Drs. Adams and Johnston. The whole family would be forever grateful to them for saving Anetha's life;

and the family would be shocked, a few years later, to hear that Dr. Adams had been murdered—shot in his own office by a black woman named Ruby McCollum—his mistress! Eventually a book was written about the murder, but it was banned from sale in the state of Florida.[112]

The surgical scars on Anetha's tummy and one buttock were hidden by her dresses, but this was not the case with the scar she got later, on her knee. Anetha, after getting lots of attention during the hospital stay and during her recovery, had perhaps become a bit spoiled.

"She pitched a little tantrum one day," Ethel said. "She threw her drinking glass, and it broke all to pieces. I made her pick it up, and in the process, she knelt on a shard of that glass. It cut her knee real bad. I should have known better than to make her pick it up—she wasn't but about three years old." When Ethel told this story she winced as if her guilt were a shard that pierced her own flesh.

Clearing the Way for Electricity

"When the construction of Mr. and Mrs. Rye's house was getting underway in late 1943," C.G. said, "Mr. Rye and I went to the REA [Rural Electric Association] office in Live Oak to ask about getting electricity out to our farms. The man there in the office told us 'the REA can't justify the cost of erecting poles and running wires that far out in the country, unless you can convince most of people in your area to sign up for service and pay the required deposits. Plus,' the man said, 'because it's wartime, any new-service customers must *qualify*.' To qualify, our farms had to pass inspection. That is, to get electricity, each farmer would have to earn a certain number of points based on what crops and livestock he produced. The rules were similar to those for getting a deferment from the military.

"So Mr. Rye and I went door to door contacting neighbors, asking them to sign up and pay the deposit. We got nearly everybody in the Ladyland community to commit, and after inspections, all the farmers qualified. But, there was still one more obstacle. Land had to be cleared for the poles and wires.

"All of us got together—Mr. Rye, me, and some of the neighbors—and cleared a strip of land through the woods from Hawley Touchton's place down to B. B. Saunders's place on the Suwannee River. The REA paid us a small amount for our work.

"After the poles were up and the wires strung, Mr. and Mrs. Rye had power. We yet needed to have our house wired."

Old-Fashioned Ideas
"At first, Granddaddy Tip didn't want the light in his and Granny's room turned on," Ethel said. "But after he saw that the rest of the house didn't burn down, he allowed Granny to use the overhead light instead of the oil lamp when they went in their room at night."

Tip Lanier had old-fashioned ideas about more than electricity. He believed, for example, that a woman should never cut her hair. Dosia and Delma never had. He also believed that ladies should never whistle.

"A whistling girl and a crowing hen always come to some bad end," was one of his favorite expressions. Heaven forbid that a lady should smoke or drink.

There's one other saying that he believed, whether or not he made it up: "Do you know the difference between a Yankee and a Damn Yankee? A Yankee comes down to the South for a visit and then goes home. A Damn Yankee comes down for a visit and stays."

Not from Dixie
Louise—the brunette beauty Harold had married—smoked cigarettes and drank beer. Not only that, she was not from Dixie.

Upon his discharge from the Navy, Harold took Louise to Florida to meet his family, thinking he might go into farming with his dad—now that his mother and father owned the homestead instead of his grandfather with whom he had often disagreed as a youngster.

Harold and Louise rented a place in nearby Lake City, and Harold drove back and forth every day, helping his dad on the farm. But old grudges between Tip and Harold resurfaced and disagreements escalated.

Strong-willed Tip Lanier was still the same. Harold was not. He had grown into a man, a man that didn't like to back down.

Delma was caught in the middle. She loved her father and she loved Harold. She wanted so much for it to work out so Harold and Milton could farm together.

There was no denying that Louise was different from the girl Delma might have picked for her son, but then, she

Louise and Sheilah Rye

knew Milton was different from the man her father would have picked for her.

Delma and Milton both liked Louise, and their love for her grew after she gave birth to their grand-daughter, Sheilah.

Tip, however, could not accept Louise, and he and Harold continued to butt heads. The final straw came when Harold overheard his grandfather refer to his beautiful wife Louise, the mother of his daughter, Sheilah, as "a Yankee bitch." Worse still, Louise heard.

Harold and Louise took Sheilah and left. Who could blame them if they never looked back.

A Funeral and a Flood
Dosia had never fully recovered after falling and breaking her leg. Though she still got around, she always needed at

least one crutch. As the years went on, she became more and more feeble and eventually bedridden; and. Delma cared for her mother as she declined, even feeding her near the end.

Dosia was eighty years old when she died on February 16, 1948. She was laid to rest at the Philadelphia Baptist

Church. The funeral was on Patsy's sixth birthday.

That same year, the Suwannee River overflowed its banks, flooding the Ryes' home and other homes for miles around—all except the Howells'. Surprisingly, their house, though even closer to the river than the Ryes', stood on a small island.

Flood of 1948. Milton, after the water started receding from his and Delma's new home.

Gonna Get Rich!

"Around 1950," C.G. said, "I got into the seed-drying business—thought I was gonna get rich! Well, it wasn't just me that thought that. I went in with Joe Hingson, Frank Green, Steiner Kierce, and Wilton Gaston.

"We bought two combines for harvesting seed and planted things like blue lupin, indigo, beggar weed, Bahia grass, oats, rye, and watermelon, just for their seeds. We also bought some land by the warehouses in Live Oak and built a seed plant there, including drying racks and chutes for helping bag the seed. We planned to clean and dry the seeds in the plant, bag them in croker sacks, and sell them.

"For the watermelons, we had two machines built, using car transmissions. After we got everything set up, we could throw watermelons in the machines, and they would chop the melons up and spit everything out except the seeds—just the opposite of what you do when you eat a watermelon.

"We got forty-five cents a pound for Black Diamond watermelon seed and thirty-five cents a pound for other kinds. We bagged them up in fifty-pound croker sacks, but we made it a practice to put fifty-one pounds in each bag.

"A man came in one day and insisted that we reweigh the seeds as he watched. He wanted to make sure he was getting fifty pounds. He wouldn't take our word for it that the bags contained *more* than fifty pounds. Plus, he said he wanted only Black Diamond seed and one other kind. But then he kept hemming and hawing and couldn't decide. We finally told him to forget it—we had work to do; but then he said he would take Black Diamond and two other kinds without us reweighing them, and he did.

"I heard later that the man went and told Mr. Castleberry about buying the seed from us (Castleberry also sold seed in his store) and Castleberry told him, 'Yeah, you messed around and let some farmers out-figure you'— when the man actually got more than he had paid for.

C.G. on his combine, bagging oats

"I soon found out the profits in the seed business weren't worth it, though, so I asked to be released. Joe, Frank, Steiner, and Wilton agreed. For my interest in the business, I got the combine, and over the next few years, I used it to combine lupin, indigo, beggar weeds, and oats."

Zeb Black's Mule

"I was always interested in new things," C.G. said, "so when I heard that Uncle Clarence had a newfangled piece of farm equipment—a corn sheller—I went over to check it out. When I drove up, Melous Johnson was there with Uncle Clarence, trying it out. Melous was throwing one ear of corn after another in the chute, and it was shelling the ears in a hurry. I was pretty impressed.

"After we finished looking at the sheller, Uncle Clarence wanted to show us an old gate he had painted with creosote; somebody had discovered that creosote would preserve wood. We were walking over to take a look at the gate when—

" 'Well, I wish you'd look a yonder,' Uncle Clarence said, pointing out at the field. 'There's Zeb Black's mule coming to visit my Queen.' (Queen was his mule.)

"I looked up and saw the mule walking up with a twelve-foot chain around his neck, and on the other end of the chain was a two-by-four, about six feet long, that the mule was dragging. Suddenly he picked up his pace and galloped over and jumped the fence by the creosoted gate, and when he did, that chain and two-by-four got caught in the fence. That mule whirled his head around as if to see what had happened.

" 'Well, would you look at that!' Uncle Clarence said. 'Anything with that much sense ought to know to stay home!'

"Uncle Clarence didn't like Zeb's mule going over to his place and messing with his Queen; so he decided to teach Zeb's mule a lesson. He got me to put a bridle on the mule while he went and got some Hi-Life. That stuff will make your skin feel like it's freezing. At that time, Hi-Life could be bought at the drugstore. It had a strong sulfur scent. I think it was sulfuric formaldehyde, or maybe it was hydrogen chloride and sulfur, I'm not sure. It was made to keep skipper flies off fresh meat as it was being packed. Skipper flies look like flying ants; they'll lay their eggs in the meat, and when the eggs hatch, the worms will eat the meat. They're nothing but miniature maggots.

"Anyway, Uncle Clarence came back with the Hi-Life and had me hold the mule by the bridle while he poured the stuff on the mule's back. Time he started pouring, that mule started twisting around like crazy. Aunt Daisy and her little granddaughter Nancy had just started shelling corn for the chickens with the new sheller, so I hollered at them to watch out. Aunt Daisy, seeing what was happening, grabbed Nancy up and went inside the barn.

"As soon as I let go of the bridle, that mule headed for the creosoted gate. Then he turned and headed straight at me—biting and pawing—so I headed for the gate—but stopped long enough to pick up the end of a water hose. It was the end that attaches to the spigot. I thought I could use it to keep him away from me; but before I knew it, he had me pinned against the fence and was biting at me while I was evermore slinging that hose at him.

"By that time, Melous Johnson was getting a kick out of my fight with the mule. He was on the ground doubled over laughing and fanning his hat in the air."

Summers on the Farm
The number of cows C.G. had at any one time varied. He no longer had to brand his cattle, as he and others had done in the past. They now had fences that kept their cattle secure. But one summer, C.G.'s young nephew from Miami almost made him reconsider the branding issue.

Every summer, C.G.'s brothers and sisters took or sent their young children to the Howell farm for a summer vacation. It was not uncommon for C.G. and Ethel to have two families visiting at once. Ethel would spread quilts all over the floor to accommodate them. C.G. often joked that if any more company showed up, they would have to "put nails in the walls and hang their guests on the nails."

One year it happened to be Mernest's family of seven and Clara Mae's family of six that were visiting.

Patsy, Anetha, and Susanette, in trying to show their cousins a good time, showed them what fun it was to swing on the twelve-foot wide metal gate that led into the cow lot. The girls knew, of course, not to let the cows out and to latch the gate when the swinging was done. But they failed to share that bit of wisdom with their city cousins.

Patsy, Anetha, and cousin Theron Hingson (Joe and Ruby's son), shelling corn for the chickens

One day, after they swung on the gate, all the older ones left, and nobody was watching when three-year-old Kathy and four-year-old Clarence decided to take another turn on the gate.

"About dusk that evening," C.G. said, "we were all about ready to sit down to eat supper when I looked up and saw my cows roaming all over the yard and some out in the woods. I went out to see what was going on, and that big gate to the cow lot and pasture was standing wide open."

Needless to say, supper was delayed while the cows were rounded up and put back where they belonged and the gate latched.

When C.G. finally came back inside, he wanted to find the culprit.

"Who left that gate open?" he demanded.

Four-year-old Clarence wasted no time in implicating his cousin Kathy.

"Uncle C.G., I tol' her, and I tol' her, and I tol' her to shut the gate—but she *wouldn't*!

Michael Schemer, C.G. and Ethel's nephew, at the cow trough; the gate to the cow lot (fun to swing on!) is in the background.

Another year, Ira and Oleta were visiting with their two sons: Jimmy, who was Patsy's age, and Eddie, who was a year or so younger than Susanette. Eddie was always following his Uncle C.G. around, watching his every move, and that day was no exception. He had climbed up on a sturdy wooden post at the corner of the cow pen and was taking everything in and asking questions as his Uncle C.G.

was penning up a cow that he was planning to fatten up and then butcher.

"Uncle C.G."

"Yeah, son." (C.G. called all little boys *son* or *sonny boy*.)

"How come you're puttin' that cow in that pen?"

"So I can fatten her up so we can soon be eating some good steaks."

Little Eddie sat there on the post for a minute or two, intently watching the cow.

"Uncle C.G.," he finally said.

"Yeah, son."

"She's a gettin' fat-uh and fat-uh!"

C.G.'s sisters, Clara Mae and Laura, shelling peanuts.
Note that electrical wires now run to the Howell's home.

C.G., Ethel, Susanette, Patsy, Anetha, and Tommy

A New House

In the early '50s, C.G. and Ethel had their old house torn down in preparation for building a new house. They wanted the new house erected on the same spot of ground, since that spot had stayed dry during the '48 flood.

"Our new house cost $11,200 to build, C.G. said. "The FHA loaned me $9,230, and somehow I got the down payment together. I borrowed part of that. I got $300 from Joe Hingson. But then I had to borrow $300 from B. B. Saunders to pay Joe back because Joe had ordered a truck and needed his money for that. We got a twenty-year mortgage, and the payments were $680 a year.

"I hired Leo Dunham to build the house. He used the house plan out of a *Farm Journal* that Ethel and I had saved for over seven years. We made a few modifications, like we got rid of the upstairs and added a tiny bath with a shower in the utility room. We also decided against a furnace and went with a fireplace for heat, to save money.

"While the old house was being torn down and the new house was going up, Curtis Johnson (Melous's brother) let us live in his tenant house. We finally moved into our new house in 1952."

View of the Howell's house from the back: C.G.'s new car sits under the carport; Milton Rye's truck is parked in the front yard.

To a passing motorist with an untrained eye, the Howells' backyard might have appeared littered with debris, when in reality it contained several pieces of playground equipment: an overturned barrel and board made a fine seesaw; a wide board on top of a thick block made a dandy jump board; and the three-legged, wrought-iron pot (behind the board in the photo) was perfect for cooking over a fire in the yard. The pot also traveled with the Howells when they went to the Gulf coast, like on Thanksgiving Day, when they gathered with friends—the Curls, Hingsons, Hunters,

Summeralls—for an outdoor fish fry, complete with hush puppies and swamp cabbage.

Off to Miami

The car sitting under the Howells' carport was a 1952 Plymouth that C.G. bought brand new while the house was under construction. The car replaced a wine-colored Jeep he had been driving (Ethel didn't drive yet) since taking over its payments from Thomas Lee Boatright. (C.G. had bought Thomas Lee's Jeep after selling his Model A.)

The first long trip in the new Plymouth was to Miami for a visit with C.G.'s mother, Clara, and C.G.'s brothers and sisters—Ira, Clara Mae, and Laura. (Mernest had joined the military and was now stationed in Biloxi.)

Accompanying them on the trip, but in their own vehicle, was Monroe and Inez Boatright and their two small children, Nancy and Danny.

A highlight of the trip was a day spent at a park in Miami—or Hialeah. Most of the cousins climbed a palm trunk that day for a photo shoot—and even Inez, with Danny in her arms, managed to get one leg over.

Left to right: Jimmy, Patsy, Anetha, Susanette, Garfield, Eddie, Nancy, Inez with Danny, and others visiting a Miami area park.

While on the Nightshift

After C.G. taught Ethel how to drive the Plymouth, she went right out and found herself a job! She wanted to bring in some extra cash to buy a few items they needed—or wanted—for the new house. She had already bought a few things (things she had never had before), like the printed vinyl curtains that now graced the living room windows and the electric heating pad that had replaced her old hot-water bottle.

Her first job was at a Lake City manufacturing plant where chrome parts for cars were made. Neighbors Mertis Avery and Clara Neely (Cary's wife) also worked there, so they rode together and took turns driving. They all worked the nightshift on an assembly line.

One winter night, after their mother went to work, the Howell girls got ready for bed as usual. They plugged in the heating pad their mother had bought and put it in their bed, just as they had done on several other cold nights. The fireplace, the house's sole source of heat, was used only in the daytime, so it got pretty chilly when the temperature dipped below freezing during night.

The three girls still slept together in a full-sized bed, and with six feet trying to make contact with that heating pad, it could get pretty wadded up before morning. That night, it apparently overheated. The girls all said later they remembered having to jerk their feet away from the pad because it felt *really* hot, but it didn't fully awaken them right away. How long the thing smoldered in the bed is anybody's guess. When Patsy finally woke up, there was a layer of smoke hanging from the ceiling. She woke up her sisters and they threw back the covers to see what was going on. When they did, the thing blazed up.

"Daddy! Daddy! Fire!" they all yelled.

C.G. woke up to his daughters' screams. He jumped out of bed, ran to them, and saw the flames. He yanked the electric cord from the wall, and with the cord, dragged most of the blaze to the floor where he smothered the flames with quilts and blankets.

With the fire out, they aired the house out as best they could before going back to bed. The girls spent the rest of the night in the guest bed with no foot warmer.

When Ethel got home from her night job just before daylight, she walked into the house to the smell of smoke and just knew the house was on fire! It scared her nearly to death. What she found, of course, was her husband and daughters fast asleep; a black, hollowed out mattress; a sooty burn on her new hardwood floor; and one of her hand-pieced quilts burned beyond repair. But criticize or complain she did not; she was just happy that her family was okay.

After the heating-pad incident, Ethel quit her nightshift job and got a day job. She and Inez Boatright went to work for an insurance company as census takers. They went door to door in Lake City and Columbia County, asking about people's insurance needs. Based on their interviews, an insurance salesman would know which homeowners to call on and give his sales pitch.

Ethel's most vivid memory of her days with the insurance company was of the day she ran a stop sign— didn't see it—and hit broadside a big luxury car driven by a woman who was quite well known in Lake City. When the policeman came, the other woman was making a big scene about being creamed. The policeman told Ethel he would have to give her a ticket. Then he said, under his breath as he pulled her aside, "What I'd like to do is give you a reward for hitting that redheaded bitch."

After the accident, Ethel wanted to give up driving, but C.G. encouraged her to get back in the car and keep driving, and she did.

In addition to her outside jobs, Ethel also helped C.G. as needed with the farming. Plus, she spent many hours at her Singer sewing machine making her own clothes, her mother's dresses, and clothes for her daughters.

"Don't Tell That One, Melous!"

One night Melous Johnson and his wife, Annie Lou, who taught Patsy, Anetha, and Susanette at Ladyland, were having supper with the Howells. C.G. started his usual joke-telling, and after C.G. told one, Melous said he had one he wanted to see if C.G. would get.

"There was this ole man," Melous started, "that was always coming home drunk."

"Don't tell that one, Melous!" his wife butted in and then in a whisper said, "with the girls here."

"Well, I don't get the joke," Melous said (probably thinking the girls wouldn't either), "but maybe *C.G.* will. Like I said, C.G., the ole man was always coming home drunk, and his wife was always nagging him to quit drinking—telling him, 'You're gonna do something bad one of these days when you get drunk.' Well, one night after a binge of drinking, the man was walking home and saw a dead cow along the road, so he decided to play a trick on his wife. He cut the cow's bag off, stuffed it in the front of his pants, and headed on home. His wife started into him as soon as he got there about him being drunk again. 'Well, I'll punish myself,' the man said to his wife, 'I'll just cut it off,' and standing right next to the kitchen table, he pulled out one of the cow tits, laid it on the table, and with a meat cleaver, gave it a whack. When he did that, his wife up and fainted—keeled over! To make it easier to bend over and tend to her, the ole man pulled that big cow bag out of his pants and threw it on the floor. He saw it had four tits on it, and *he* fainted. But, I don't get the joke, C.G.—do *you?*"

Everybody at the table was snickering or holding back a grin, and Mrs. Johnson, the girls' schoolteacher, was shaking her head in disbelief when her husband's face started turning red.

Tip's Final Days

As Tip aged, he spent most of his time sitting in one of two cane-bottomed rockers on the front porch of Milton and Delma's new house. He had developed dementia, and it progressed rather rapidly. After he started getting hostile with family members, especially Milton, the family decided he would have to be committed to the State Mental Hospital in Chattahoochee.

After staying there awhile, he seemed to improve, so the family took him home. Back in his comfortable rocking chair on the front porch, he constantly repeated himself, and any time some fellow stopped to visit, he would ask him the question: "Aye God, buddy, have you ever been to Germany?"

"No, sir, can't say I have," they'd say.

"Aye God, buddy, people say you gotta cross an ocean to get to Germany, but it ain't so! All I had to do was walk across a ten-foot log behind C.G.'s field and I was there."

If the visitor sat on the porch five minutes, he heard that same question and Tip's response at least a dozen times.

The front porch of the Ryes' house faced the western sun, so it got very hot on that concrete porch during summer afternoons, but Tip never budged from his rocker, except to eat and go to bed when it was time. Not only did he sit there in the sun, he wore long johns, long khaki pants, a long-sleeved khaki shirt, and a navy wool cardigan—winter and summer. If someone suggested on a hot summer day that he might be more comfortable if he removed the sweater, he always had the same retort. "Aye God, buddy, what'll keep out cold will keep out heat."

He also got so he didn't want to bathe, and when Delma insisted on it once a week, he would grumble and curse; but once he was in the tub, he would begin singing, "Way, down upon the Suwannee River, far, far away . . . "

The illness continued to eat away at Tip's mind until eventually he had to be returned to Chattahoochee. He died there on February 22, 1956, at the age of ninety-two. A couple of days later, his funeral was held at Philadelphia Baptist Church, and it was standing room only. He was laid to rest in the cemetery behind the church, beside his faithful wife Dosia.

Patsy couldn't go with the rest of the family to the funeral. She had a beet-red tongue and had to stay in bed (Edith Knight stayed at the house with her); Patsy was quarantined with scarlet fever. Luckily, Patsy soon recovered, and none of the rest of the family caught it.

Risky Business

"Every year, I planted tobacco, corn, peanuts, and usually watermelons," C.G. said. "Tobacco was the most labor-intensive crop, but it also gave the best return.

"Since we always traded work, we never had to hire help. We gathered tobacco one day of the week in Uncle Joe's field, one day in Thomas Lee's,[xiii] one day in Pete's, one day in Mr. Rye's, and one day in mine. That was repeated every week until all the tobacco was cropped, strung on sticks, and hung in the barn. Everybody in each family helped.

"But farming was a risky business because you never knew what the market would be like when it was time to sell your crop or your livestock. The market could make all the difference.

"At first I had fifteen head of cattle. Then I borrowed twenty-two hundred dollars and bought twenty-one head, so I had thirty-six. I would sell a few now and then to make the payment on the note and to pay for the minerals, hay, molasses, and worming materials for the animals."

[xiii] Thomas Lee Boatright had made it home from the war with his body uninjured.

Milton raised cattle too, so he and C.G. often got together to help one another with cattle-related activities. The cows sometimes developed something the farmers called "hollow tail." To cure it, they packed the wound with salt. Surprisingly, the animals remained remarkably still and quiet during the procedure. Not so, with castration. Milton and C.G. castrated their young males because they wanted only the best bull to be the breeder, because castration reduced the animal's aggression, and because they thought the steaks from a steer were more tender than from an uncastrated male. This operation was done without anesthetic, and the sounds coming from the cow lot could be heard a mile away.

Despite C.G.'s efforts to keep his cattle healthy and sell at the right time, his cattle business was about as profitable as his seed-drying business.

"I fed the thirty-six cows I bought for four years," C.G. said, "and they had calves, so after four years, I had sixty-seven head. But when I sold *all* of them, I still owed four hundred dollars on the note at the bank."

As time went on, the Howells (and many other farmers in the area) found it more and more difficult to make a living. In addition to the fluctuating market, there was the weather and such. C.G. would borrow money to make the crops, but the crops wouldn't do well because of lack of rain, disease, or insects, and there wouldn't be enough money from the sale of the crop to pay off the loans.

When Mr. B. B. Saunders approached C.G. about managing his large farm (1,246 acres) along the banks of the Suwannee River, C.G. thought it was a good opportunity; *it might*, he thought, *help him get out of debt.*

Mr. Saunders's farm was south and east of the Howells' place; so to get to work each day, C.G. just had to travel the road around the west side of his farm, cross a cattle gap, and he was there.

"It was in 1955 that Mr. Saunders asked me to manage his farm," C.G. said, "with the understanding that Mr. Red Warren and his family,[113] who lived on the property, would help, and that I could bring in another family as share-croppers. I brought in Odell Curl's family. It was an arrangement where we would all share in the profits.

"The deal with Mr. Saunders turned out to be one of the worst decisions I ever made, especially considering the risky business of farming.

"We planted tobacco; then, it didn't rain, it didn't rain, it didn't rain! I borrowed irrigation pipe and installed it, pumping water from the river, but I had to keep taking the pipes apart and moving them back and forth, trying to cover twelve acres of tobacco. We also had planted his allotted sixty acres of peanuts, but we had no way in the world to water the peanuts."

"Yep," Ethel added, "the peanuts—honest to God—parched in the ground. You could rub the peanuts between your fingers and the husk would fall off."

"Early on," C.G. said, "I had told Mr. Saunders we would dig his peanuts at harvesttime, all sixty acres. Like I mentioned, the government limited the number of acres a farmer could plant. The allotment program was designed to help farmers by preventing a glut of product, which could drive the prices down. Despite the safeguard, prices would still fluctuate; and that year, when the time came to dig the sixty acres of peanuts, peanut prices were *way* down. I knew it would cost more to dig the peanuts than it was worth, so I went to B.B. and suggested we leave them in the ground.

" 'C.G.,' Mr. Saunders said, 'I'll let you have *all*—not half—the income from the peanuts if you'll dig 'em. I didn't get all my allotment last year, and if the peanuts aren't dug and sold this year, my allotment will be cut.' 'So, in other words,' I said, 'you want your peanuts dug, *even* if it's going to cost more to dig and get them ready to sell than any of us will make?' 'That's what I mean,' he said. 'Then they'll be dug,' I told him.

"I came home and hooked up the plow and went down there and plowed them up. We paid his son, Billy, $28.50 per acre to pick them off the vines. When sold, the peanuts didn't bring enough to pay for the picking. Mr. Saunders lost his shirt on that crop, and so did I. Plus I got cussed out by Katherine Curl, Odell's wife, who didn't believe there was no peanut profit for us to share.

"As for Mr. Saunders's tobacco crop that year (he had twelve acres), we added fertilizer at a rate of twenty-six hundred pounds to the acre. But, because it was so dry and we couldn't keep it wet, the fertilizer just didn't do a thing.

"That summer, I think the only day we didn't work was Sunday. I about went under after that year with Mr. Saunders. At the end of the year, I owed nineteen thousand dollars to the bank.

"It bothered me that I couldn't always pay my bills on the date they came due, but I would always go talk to the person I owed and try to work something out, to pay a little or let them know when I thought I could. And I never was one to lay awake at night, worrying about it. I figured God would take care of things like He always had as long as I kept on trying.

"Mr. Saunders should have had a good crop of something the next year with all that fertilizer we put out. But the next year, we didn't get rain either. Of course, by then it didn't matter to Mr. Saunders because he had sold his whole place to some people from up north. They put fancy signs up, calling it the Clark and Hopkins *Ranch*. I did some work for Miss Hopkins, but it didn't amount to a whole lot."

Changing Times
C.G. wondered if Curtis Johnson was making any money catching crickets. Curtis had hooked up with a company

that had set out large brown paper sacks all over his fields. The sacks, scattered in every pasture, could be seen from the road. C.G. asked some questions, but never found out just how profitable the cricket business was—perhaps not very—because the paper sacks soon disappeared, and Curtis was never seen sitting on his porch with his feet propped up. However, Curtis and his wife, Loiselle, did buy a whole set of encyclopedias plus a television set, something nobody else in the community owned. In any event, their wealth did not make them snooty. They still invited the Howell family in when the Howells stopped by, and it was at their home that C.G. got to watch Jackie Gleason for the first time, and the girls got to see Elvis Presley from the waist up on the Ed Sullivan Show. The Johnsons were even kind enough to loan their encyclopedias to the Howell girls for completing school assignments, and they let two of their boys take the Howell girls for at least one horseback ride. Their sons, Larry, Gene, and Truitt, were about the same age as Patsy, Anetha, and Susanette.

At the time that the Johnsons seemed to be doing so well—able to buy an encyclopedia set as well as a television set—C.G. and Ethel didn't feel they could afford to buy one of anything, much less a *set*. Heck, they could not even afford to buy an electric radio; they were still using the large battery-operated one they had bought soon

Patsy, Susanette, and Anetha, in their Easter outfits, stitched by Ethel

after they married, and its battery was dead more than it was not. But when telephones came to the area in the late 1950s, the Howells decided to sign up for one. Their number began with 776 (*SPring 6*), a Luraville extension. Theirs was a party line, which meant their phone calls could be monitored by anybody on the line who wished to listen, and some did. (Just why C.G. and Ethel decided to have a telephone installed when their girls were entering their teen years is anybody's guess.)

"With times so hard," C.G. said, "I started thinking about doing something else; and in the spring of 1959, I heard about some new jobs with the Florida Forestry Service. I applied and got the job of radio dispatcher. As a dispatcher, I would man the lookout tower at the Suwannee County Headquarters off U.S. 90, just west of Live Oak, and operate a two-way radio to dispatch crews to fires in the county. One requirement of the job, though, was that I had to live on-site, to be available at all hours in case of an emergency—a forest fire.

"The house our family would have to live in was still under construction that summer, so until the fall, we stayed on the farm."

In August, the Howell family—all except Patsy, who had graduated in June from high school and gone to work for Prudential Insurance Company in Jacksonville—started packing to move to the forestry headquarters. After everything had been loaded in trucks and trailers of friends and neighbors and the farm house was empty, C.G. started looking around for the keys to lock up the house. It took quite a while because nobody knew where the keys were. Never before had the Howell family ever locked a door.

ᔆ 11   Moving About

In his new job as dispatcher with the Florida Division of Forestry, C.G. alternated between working in the office and climbing the steps to the top of the one-hundred-foot fire tower that gave him a bird's-eye view of the surrounding area.

In addition to the fire tower and office building, the headquarters site had three other structures: a house for the dispatcher, a house for the county ranger, and a garage that C.G. helped construct. All buildings, including the houses, were concrete block, painted two-tone: forest green near the ground and white above. Ethel wasn't crazy about the looks of the outside of her house; but the inside was fine, other than the dazzlingly white tile floors that she knew would be hard to keep that way, considering how much traffic her house always got.

C.G. didn't mind the two-tone exterior or the white floors. What he missed most about the house was the extra bathroom. Admittedly, it could have been worse. Patsy, the one who could spend the most time in front of a bathroom mirror, was permanently settled in Jacksonville. Correction: Patsy was *living* in Jacksonville. She would never be *settled* anywhere. Patsy was always making new friends and finding a better living situation, so her parents soon found that her Jacksonville address changed with the seasons.

At DuPre's

Soon after she got her family settled at the forestry headquarters, Ethel got a job in Live Oak at McCrory's dime store where she had been a faithful shopper for years.

"On my morning and afternoon breaks at McCrory's," Ethel said, "I usually walked down to the Live Oak Drug Store for a Coca-Cola. One day I was there sitting in a booth when Eunice Cameron walked in. She worked across the street at Gibb's, a dry goods store with high prices.

" 'Are you working here in town?' she asked, and I told her I worked at McCrory's.

" 'You might want to talk with Harry DuPre,' she said, probably knowing McCrory's didn't pay too well. 'I hear he's fixing to open a new store; he's buying Garner out.'

"I went to see Harry DuPre, and after we finished talking he wanted to know when I could start work.

"At DuPre's—they sold clothes, shoes, and sewing supplies—I waited on customers, and I also helped Mrs. DuPre (Myrtle Bly) with the alterations. Later on, she turned the alterations entirely over to me."

A Heart Attack

C.G. suffered a heart attack in 1961, at the age of forty-five. It came out of the blue—shocking everybody. C.G. seemed so healthy. But the heart attack reminded members of the family, and C.G. especially, that he had already lived four years longer than his father.

When he was released from the hospital, the doctor gave him strict orders not to climb the fire tower, so C.G.

requested a transfer to Madison County where there was no tower. Meanwhile, his boss, Mr. Ralph Moody, let him perform his job exclusively from the ground.

About the time Anetha graduated from high school that June and headed, like Patsy, for a job at Prudential in Jacksonville, C.G. learned that he got the job at the Madison County headquarters.

Soon after Anetha moved out, C.G. and Ethel began preparing for the necessary move to Madison County. But Susanette didn't want to go. She had only one year remaining at Suwannee High and did not want to transfer to a new school. She thought her life would be over if she had to move to Madison. Milton and Delma said she could stay with them to finish her senior year, so C.G. and Ethel decided to let their baby daughter live. She moved in with the Ryes on the farm, and C.G. and Ethel moved to Madison. For the first time in nearly two decades, C.G. and Ethel were on their own.

A Surprised Thief

Word soon got around in Madison that Ethel was a good seamstress. Before long, women were knocking on her door asking her to make this or that for them and/or their small or teenage children.

"I got tired of that in a hurry," Ethel said. "Some of the stuff they brought me to make—the fabric, the buttons, the trim, lace, rickrack—well, I wasn't proud of the dresses when I finished them. Some were just plain tacky. So, I went looking for a job in town and got one at Cohen's. It was a surplus discount store—lots of seconds with flaws, and scratched and dented merchandise. But you could find some real bargains there.

"While I worked the cash register, I would put my pocketbook up under the counter. One day, somebody grabbed mine when I wasn't looking. But that thief got a surprise. I had about eighteen cents in my wallet. Later, my pocketbook and wallet were found alongside a highway, probably thrown from a car window when the robber saw he didn't get enough money to make it worth the trouble."

Two Weddings and One Grandchild

Patsy loved Jacksonville. Anetha hated it. Soon after C.G. and Ethel got settled in Madison in the fall of 1961, Anetha moved back home. But it was a short stay. She soon married her high school sweetheart, Winston Warner. Oswald Knight (a neighbor of the Howells when they lived on the farm, and the preacher at Winston's church, Marybell Baptist) performed the ceremony in the living room of C.G. and Ethel's Madison County home. After the ceremony, the newlyweds moved to Mayo where Winston went to work in the meat department of a grocery store and Anetha got a job in a physician's office.

The following year, the couple presented C.G. and Ethel with their first grandchild, James Winston Warner Jr. They called him Wint.

A month after Wint was born, C.G. and Ethel's youngest, Susanette, graduated from Suwannee High and headed for Gainesville where she had a steno-grapher's job at the University of Florida.

Then, two months later she announced she wanted to marry Gilbert Baxter, her high school sweetheart, who was then an engineering student at the University. She wanted a church wedding, so Ethel purchased materials for her daughter's white lace wedding gown—pattern, lace, taffeta, zipper, buttons, and thread—at Cohen's, for the sum total of fifteen dollars! But the bride felt like a million in it as she was escorted down the aisle at Westwood Baptist by her father.

Susanette in $15.00 dress

Back to Suwannee County

"On my lunch hour at Cohen's," Ethel said, "I would walk over and shop at Ruby's Fabrics. Ruby, the owner, found out I knew a lot about fabrics and sewing, so one day she asked me about going to work for her. I did, but I didn't work for Ruby very long before C.G. got a chance to move back to his dispatcher job in Suwannee County (the doctor had given him a clean bill of health). We didn't have to think twice about moving back.

"When Ruby found out I would be leaving, she asked me about opening a fabric shop with her in Live Oak. I thought about it but was afraid Live Oak wasn't big enough to support a fabric shop, especially since several other stores, including DuPre's, sold fabrics. Plus, I wasn't sure I wanted the headache of managing a store.

"When Mr. DuPre heard we were planning to move back, he went to see me and said if I would take my old job back, right then, he would pay for my gas to drive back and forth until we moved. I accepted his offer and never regretted it. I thought the world of him and Mrs. DuPre."

Another Grandchild, Then Hurricane Dora

Anetha presented to C.G. and Ethel their first grand-daughter in 1964. She had the daintiest face and strikingly dark eyes. Anetha and Winston named her Carla Denice, but before long, everyone was calling her DeeDee.

In early September of that same year, Hurricane Dora headed for Florida. She moved slowly across the state, and over a seventy-two-hour period around the unlucky thir-teenth day, dumped an estimated eighteen inches of rain on the town of Live Oak.

"It rained and it rained and it rained." Ethel said. "Water filled the streets, and when it looked like DuPre's was going to flood, we started pulling merchandise from the lower shelves and piling the stuff on cabinets and counters. We kept working and the water kept rising. Pretty soon, the water was up on the sidewalk, and then it started running under the doors and into the store. It just kept coming and kept coming, and we kept working faster and faster trying to save the merchandise.

"As the water got higher, the cabinets and counters started to lift up—floating—and because they were unbalanced with all the stuff we had piled on top, they started toppling over. One by one, they toppled, dumping all the new clothes and boxes of new shoes in that dirty water—oily from the street. Watching all that merchandise get soaked in that nasty water was heartbreaking. It was one big mess.

"Seeing that it was hopeless, Mr. DuPre finally told us to go home. So, we gave up and he locked the doors.

"We had to wait until the water went down to begin the cleanup. When we got started, Mr. DuPre told us to take home whatever we wanted and see if we could get it clean. If we could use it, it was ours to keep. I took armloads of Buster Brown clothes home for Anetha's kids. Some came clean. Some didn't. But we salvaged enough that Anetha had clothes for Wint and DeeDee for several years."

Cause for Celebration
For C.G. and Ethel's twenty-fifth wedding anniversary, on September 8, 1965, Susanette baked them a three-tiered anniversary cake. She tried to decorate it just as she had seen her mother do when she decorated a wedding cake for Winona "PeeWee" Hingson when she married Harold Landen. (The Howell girls would forever be trying to emulate their mother in one way or another.)

C.G. and Ethel's anniversary was celebrated quietly that year, just as Ethel preferred. No fuss, no big party, just family gathered together. Ethel never liked fussiness or being the center of attention.

The couple had another reason to celebrate that year,

but they kept it quietly to themselves. They had made the last payment on their twenty-year mortgage; they had paid it off in fourteen. The nineteen thousand dollars they owed when C.G. quit working for B. B. Saunders was now paid in full. For the first time in a long time, they owed no one. The farm and house was all theirs, albeit others were living there now (first the Georges, then the Boatrights), but they knew they would eventually move back there.

C.G. and Ethel

In December of that same year, 1965, Susanette and Gilbert celebrated his graduation from the University, and after spending a few weeks with the Howells, they headed for New Orleans where Gilbert had a job with Shell Oil Company.

About the same time that Gilbert got a new job, C.G. got one too. He was promoted to County Ranger of Suwannee County. In this position, he no longer had to climb the tower and have his ear glued to the radio. Instead, he supervised the Suwannee County forestry staff, including those who worked at towers located throughout the county.

As County Ranger, C.G. was expected to move into the house designated for the ranger. Ethel didn't see the need to move, and said so. But when C.G. told her the ranger's house was not equipped with "that blasted radio speaker" that often woke her up in the middle of the night, it was reason enough to start packing.

As it turned out, the move was a waste of time. The

Howells were hardly settled when Mr. Montgomery, a friendly fellow who lived just across the road from the forestry headquarters and owned a trucking company, persuaded C.G. to leave the Forestry Service and go to work for him.

"It was a good offer," C.G. said, "and I took it because it meant we could move back to our house on the farm. We moved back in the spring of 1966."

Going for a Spin
One weekend that summer, Anetha, Winston, their son Wint, plus Susanette and Gilbert, who had driven over from New Orleans, were visiting at the farm. After a big Sunday dinner, C.G. asked his sons-in-law if they wanted to take a spin with him in his car.

While the guys were gone, Ethel and her girls cleared the table and washed the dishes in the kitchen sink, unaware of the good time the boys were having.

The girls should have known. When they were pre-schoolers, their father had given them a thrill every Sunday morning, without fail, on the ride to church. Where the dirt road meandered through the woods to Philadelphia Baptist, there was a dip in the road that C.G. called a *thrill bump.* As he approached the dip, he would speed up and warn the girls that he was about to hit the thrill bump—as if they had to be reminded; it was the highlight of their day. At the time, there was no such thing as seat belts, so when their father hit the bump, Patsy, Anetha, and Susanette bounced so high their heads nearly hit the car ceiling.

As his girls grew older, though, C.G. was always careful to set a fatherly example when he was behind the wheel of the car.

That Sunday afternoon when the guys returned from their ride, they were all laughing like they'd had a real good time together. Nobody mentioned—that day—just what had happened. But it eventually leaked out.

When C.G. had asked his sons-in-law to "take a spin" with him, they had not interpreted it literally—but they should have.

"After your Daddy got away from the house," Gilbert and Winston told their wives, "he started showing us how to skid the car on the dirt road from one side to the other." In the process, C.G. lost control, and the car ended up in the woods, barely missing a big tree. Luckily nothing was hurt. Nothing except C.G.'s ego.

Milton and Delma Celebrate

On December 16, 1966, Ethel threw her parents a big party in celebration of fifty years of marriage. Everybody in the community showed up, laden with cards and presents, all with a touch of gold.[114]

Delma loved every minute of the day. Milton endured it. He was seventy-two years old and not doing well. The cigarettes he had smoked and the dust he had inhaled in the fields for most of his life had done their damage. He had given up his tobacco addiction—cold turkey—while in his fifties, and he was no longer farming, but the damage to his lungs was already done. He had been diagnosed with emphysema. On several occasions, Brody Harris, who owned an emergency vehicle (along with a funeral home), had rushed oxygen to him.

C.G.'s Big Mistake

"Leaving the Forestry Service when I did turned out to be one of the biggest mistakes I ever made," C.G. said. "On the new job at the trucking company, I asked one too many questions about time sheets (I didn't think some people were being paid properly), and I soon found myself without a job.

"I then got a job selling new cars for Clarence Ratliff, who owned the Ford Motor Company. But I was not there long. Clarence and I had a misunderstanding about my filling up a car with gas and not paying for it the same day. He let me go.

"So, I went over to the Chevrolet dealership and got on there, selling both new and used cars, but that didn't last long either. Just before I lost that job, one of the men there told me I was 'being too damn honest with the customers.'

"When I found out the dispatcher job with the Forestry Service had opened up again, I beat a path to the new county ranger's door and got my old dispatcher job back. Ethel and I then moved back to the dispatcher house with the radio speaker she hated."

Junior Deputy

When C.G. received a package in the mail one day, he couldn't imagine why. He hadn't ordered anything. It wasn't his birthday. And it certainly wasn't Christmas. But he ripped into the package like he was still a boy. And somebody thought he was.

Inside the package was a fuzzy stuffed bear—Smokey Bear—wearing a wide belt, hat, blue jeans, and a sheriff's badge that read: *Prevent Forest Fires.* An enclosed certificate declared: *C. G. Howell is an Official Junior Member of the Smokey Bear Club.*

C.G. learned later that Gilbert and Winston, who had recognized after the joy ride that their father-in-law was still a kid at heart, had sent in his name.

A Bump on the Nose

Anetha, for one, was happy her parents were back at the forestry headquarters. She and Winston had moved back to Suwannee County after living for a while in Lake City. He was now working for Southland Corporation (selling Velda milk), and Anetha was working in Live Oak. She traveled by the forestry headquarters on U.S. 90 every day on her way to and from work at Sears, and that would not change when she went to work for Tax Collector Sara Rawls at the

Courthouse.[115] During the next few years, Ethel and C.G. got to see a lot of Anetha and her children.

Ethel was a good storyteller and would tell the grandchildren stories she had told her daughters, years before—stories like the Three Little Pigs and the Little Red Hen. One day she started telling DeeDee a story she had never told her before; it was one that Patsy, Anetha, Susanette, and grandson Wint had heard and enjoyed time and time again. DeeDee listened intently as her grandmother began:

"There was this little girl," Ethel said (as she took little DeeDee's hand in her own and opened it, palm up), "who lived right here." (Ethel pointed to a spot on DeeDee's palm.) "And, the little girl's mother gave her some money and a bucket and sent her off to the store to buy some kerosene. So, the little girl walked to the store," (Ethel traced a path up DeeDee's fingers and down again, on a circuitous route) "and got the bucket filled with kerosene and paid for it. Then, she started back home." (Again, Ethel traced the path, up one finger and down another, up one finger and down another before stopping in the middle of DeeDee's palm.) "Then the little girl spilled the kerosene right there!" Ethel said (as she poked DeeDee's palm. DeeDee looked up at her grandmother). "See, DeeDee? Right there! Smell it." (DeeDee obligingly put her hand up to smell her palm, and when she did, Ethel bumped it—so that DeeDee bumped her own nose.)

The bump of the nose was the part—the trick—that most children got a kick out of.

DeeDee looked up at her grandmother with a scowl on her face, then took one step back, and hauled off and slapped her grandmother's leg as hard as she knew how.

Milton and Delma Move to Town

After C.G. and Ethel moved away from the farm the second time, Milton and Delma decided it would be a good idea for them to move to Live Oak too, where they would be closer to C.G. and Ethel and to doctors in town.

Milton let it be known that his place, the former Lanier homestead, was for sale. Milton was ready to accept the first offer that came; it was from Leamon Gill, a good friend. But C.G. thought it was too low and persuaded Milton to ask for more.

Milton and Delma looked in Live Oak for a house and found one Delma liked at 520 North Houston Street. It was listed for $6,500 by Earl Mixon, who had been Anetha and Susanette's boss when they worked as teenagers for Van H. Priest's, a dime store in Live Oak. Mixon wanted someone to assume his loan of $4,800 and pay him the difference. In June of 1967, the deal was completed. Milton wrote a check to Mixon for $1,660.76 and took over the mortgage.

C.G., Ethel—and Anetha, who was more than eight months pregnant with her third child—along with several neighbors, including the Corbins, helped the Ryes move.

Their house in town was smaller and had no dining room, so it looked as if Delma would have to part with her treasured china cabinet and buffet—the one Harold had made it possible for her to buy. But Ethel came to the rescue; she cut the legs off both pieces and stacked them so both would both fit in the living room.[116]

Meanwhile, Milton had received a better offer on his farm from Truitt Johnson and his wife Angie (formerly Howard). They were willing to pay $15,000 for the place—the house and 120 acres of land. The offer was accepted. (Later, Truitt also bought Alonzo's forty acres from Alonzo's sons, Buck and Wilbur.)

Delma loved living in Live Oak. Milton never did, and his health continued to fail.

A Birth, a Death, and Another Birth

Anetha's third child was born that summer. She and Winston named him Clay Bradly. Unfortunately, when Anetha checked out of the hospital, she could not take her baby home. A preemie he was not; he weighed nearly ten pounds. The problem was a staph infection that required isolation. Anetha was allowed to be with him only when she nursed him. That required going back and forth for several days. Ethel, of course, was there to help Anetha with the other children, Wint and DeeDee, and with Clay when Anetha could take him home.

A little more than nine months later, Ethel lost her father. Milton passed away on April 22, 1968. All members of the family, including Harold, were there for the funeral—all except Susanette. She was within days of delivering her first child, and her obstetrician advised against travel.

Susanette and Gilbert's daughter Pamela Suzanne was born a few weeks after Milton was laid to rest.

Before Pamela's birth, Ethel had written to her daughter and told her she could be there to help her with the baby— even if she had to travel to New Orleans on the Gulf Wind. Susanette laughed out loud when she read that—picturing her mother flying through the air with the breeze. She didn't know that the Gulf Wind was a passenger train that passed through Live Oak on its way to New Orleans. As it turned out, C.G. and Ethel drove there; he wanted to see the baby too.

Shocked in New Orleans

C.G. and Ethel visited New Orleans several times while Susanette and her family lived there, and on one visit, they took in the French Quarter. There, they enjoyed beignets at Café du Monde, Ethel sat on Jackson Square for an artist to sketch her portrait, and C.G. got a good look at Bourbon Street. He was shocked at some of the sights, but perhaps not as shocked as he was when he tried to cash a check at Schwegmanns grocery. He could not *believe* they would not cash his check! *Could they not tell he was an honest man?* He had never had this happen in the town of Live Oak and he was incensed to say the least.

Patsy Ties the Knot

Patsy was the last of the Howell sisters to tie the knot. She married Harry Pressley in the summer of 1968 on the banks of the St. Johns River in Jacksonville. Anetha served as her Matron of Honor and sole attendant.

C.G. and Ethel went to Jacksonville the day before the wedding for the rehearsal and dinner at the U.S. Naval Officers' Club (Harry was an officer in the U.S. Army Reserve). C.G. had a very good time that night, not that the champagne he drank had anything to do with his being on the dance floor with Harry's Aunt Menia.

"I only had half a glass," he said later, but Patsy reported that he just *thought* he drank a half glass. Every time he looked the other way, the waiter refilled his glass.

Ethel was to spend that night with Patsy at her apartment so she could help Patsy get dressed for the wedding the next morning. Ethel got dressed for bed and was sitting up in bed talking with the bride-to-be as Patsy undressed. Patsy popped off the fake nails she had glued on herself (the few she hadn't lost during the night's festivities) and tossed them on the dresser. She took off her false eyelashes and put them in a dish on the dresser. She took off her hairpiece and laid it on the dresser. Then she took out her contact lens and placed them in a container on the dresser.

"Patsy," Ethel said, eyeing all the items her daughter had laid on the dresser, "after you and Harry get married and he wants to sleep with you, looks like he'll just have to crawl up on your dresser."

Delma's Friend, Ed

Delma had always kept in touch with Ed Randall, the one standing beside her in the photo when she was wearing that watch close to her face (p. 155).

After Milton passed away, she continued to correspond with Ed, and he with her.

Here are a few snippets from letters she kept—

> . . . *your great loss . . . I can fully realize what such a matter can mean to one . . . At my ripe old age, I spend some time reminiscing and recalling the good old days of long ago. I do believe that my sojourn in the Suwannee River area was among the most enjoyable I can recall . . . It is in my sincere hope that you are in the very best of health and that you too have many happy memories of the past . . . had just mailed a Christmas greeting to you when yours reached me. You may be sure that it was more than welcome. . . . in case I should make that long (?) trip up that way, I would like to avail myself of the privilege of a telephone call to your home.*

In 1971, Delma took a trip to California to visit Harold and his family. It was the farthest she had ever been from Suwannee County, and she could not understand that it was not the same time in California as it was in Florida. While out West, she mailed a postcard to her friend Ed, and he was quick to send a reply:

> *My dear Delma,*
>
> *It was real thoughtful of you to send me a card from away out 'yonder.' I have lived in St. Louis and on down the river to New Orleans—then on down to Mexico and Cuba (before Castro). But I have never been West of the Mississippi on land. It must have been a real treat for a nice Suwannee River girl to visit the high land, the mountains . . .*

The Posed Mannequin

Ethel enjoyed working for Mr. and Mrs. DuPre and with colleagues, Polly, Annie Ruth, Wanda, Rusty, and others who helped during summers or during the Christmas rush.

"We were always pulling something on one another," she said. "I never will forget what we did to Rusty one day. Mr. DuPre owned the whole building; the downstairs was the store, and the upstairs was our storage area for out-of-season clothes and extra store fixtures and mannequins. Not far from the top of the stairs was the restroom we all used. Everybody had to knock before opening the door.

"To play a trick on Rusty, some of us got one of the lady mannequins and posed her on the toilet—with no clothes on. Then we closed the door and went back downstairs and went about our work. Sure enough it wasn't long before Rusty had to take a break to use the restroom. After he headed up the stairs and couldn't see us, we ran over near the stairs and listened. He knocked. Nobody answered. We heard the door squeak open—then—'Ohhh! Ohhhh! I'm sorry! I'm so sorry'

"Then we heard the door squeak shut, and here came Rusty, running down the stairs, his face red as a beet. We were all dying laughing, so it didn't take Rusty long to realize what we had done.

"We were always having fun. Another day, a fellow came in and wanted to buy some overalls. I helped him find his size, and he went in the dressing room to try them on. He put them on over his other clothes as you do with overalls and came out and checked the fit in the mirror. He wanted to know if he could keep them on and I said, 'Sure.'

"We both walked over to the counter for me to write up a ticket and take his money. When we got there, he tried to reach his hand down in the overalls to get out his billfold, but with the overalls on, he couldn't get his hand to his back pocket.

" 'Ma'am,' he said to me, 'wonder if you would mind

reaching back there and getting my billfold out of my pants pocket?' So I reached down inside the overalls and found his pocket and pulled out his billfold and handed it to him. He thanked me, paid, and left.

"Well, I wish you could have heard Annie Ruth and Polly and all of them kidding me about putting my hand in that man's pants. But Mr. DuPre heard them kidding me and walked over and said, 'Mrs. Howell, any time you can put your hands in a man's pants and get his money and put it in my cash register, you just go right ahead.' "

"I continued working at DuPre's as long as I could because I really enjoyed the work—and I was about the only one who did alterations. Sometimes people would try to pay me for it or tip me, but of course I wouldn't take it. That was part of my job."

Having never accepted a tip herself, Ethel could never understand why waitresses expected tips. If she was the one they were serving, they could just keep expecting.

Clara Says Goodbye
C.G.'s mother Clara lived in Miami for many years. At some point she and her husband Charles had moved in with Clara Mae and Bob. Then, after Charles passed away, she had moved over to Laura's.

Clara Midgett,
C.G.'s mother

Both Laura and her husband, Etchie, worked outside the home, and as time went on, Laura became concerned about leaving her mother alone because Clara was showing signs of dementia.

Since C.G.'s office at the forestry headquarters was just a few feet from his home, he offered to take his mother. Clara moved there in the late 1960s. Ethel got her mother-in-law settled in the room that had once been Anetha's, and this setup worked fine for a while. But Clara's dementia progressed rapidly, and she soon began to wander, especially during the night; plus there were other problems that old age can bring on. C.G. and Ethel struggled with the situation for quite some time before it got to be more than they could handle: C.G.'s mother needed twenty-four-hour-a-day personal care. They hated to face it, but the State Mental Hospital seemed the only option.

"I never thought you would do this to me," Clara said to her sons, Mernest and C.G., the day they drove her to the Chattahoochee facility.

"It broke my heart," C.G. said later. "I wish now that we would have tried something different, but at the time it seemed the only solution."

Clara died at the Chattahoochee hospital on April 22, 1970. She was buried in the Philadelphia Church cemetery beside the graves of her husband Clarence Howell and young sons Ernest and Cecil.

Patsy and Anetha went home to be with their parents and attend the funeral. Susanette didn't make it. She and Gilbert were in San Francisco where Gilbert was attending a five-month training session. She was eight months pregnant, and her doctor strongly advised against traveling that great a distance.

More Grandchildren

When Susanette and Gilbert's second child was born, Gilbert got to pick the name Jeanne, and Susanette decided on Lyn to go with it.

Patsy had let her siblings get ahead of her in the baby department. But she and Harry soon caught up. Their daughter Lee Candler was born the year after Jeanne; and three and a half years later came Ginger, C.G. and Ethel's seventh, and last, grandchild.

Delma and Alonzo's Visit

Ethel arranged for her mother to visit her brother Alonzo after his wife had passed away and he had moved in with his son Buck and his family. After the visit, he wrote:

Aug 2nd – 73

Dear Sis: I rec'd your letter glad to hear from you and glad that you are back home I hope that you are mutch better now. Sorry about Ethel. I hope she is OK and back home now.

I am feeling a bit stronger now. I am beginning to feel mutch better but I can't gain any weight back. I am sorry you could not stay any longer with us. every body enjoyed you being here and they hope you will come back soon. I hope you enjoyed yourself the short while you were here.

I am sending you a picture that Harriet's father made of you and me at pool I like it very mutch. How is C.G. and the rest of the family getting along?

Sis, let me hear from you as often as you can. I will have to quit now. I am getting as nervous as a cat.

As ever your
Brother Alonzo
611 Oak Hill Road
Catonville Md 21228

Delma and Alonzo when she visited him in Maryland

The Hambone

That Thanksgiving, the family gathered at the Howells' house at the forestry headquarters. Ethel baked a huge ham that day, so big that she had sliced less than half of the meat off the bone, yet filled her yellow platter. The slices were already neatly arranged, and the platter was on the table. As the table was being further prepared, Anetha's husband Winston asked his mother-in-law if she had anything he could feed his bird dog (he planned to go hunting after the noon dinner and wanted his dog in top condition.)

"Yeah, you can feed him the hambone," Ethel said, as she turned and headed to the table with more bowls of food.

After the table was ready, everyone sat down, the blessing was said, and the serving dishes made their way around the table. When the ham platter got back around to Ethel, she saw it was getting low, so she got up to add a few more slices.

When she got to the kitchen counter, there lay the greasy cutting board, *but where was the ham?* Remembering what she had said to Winston, Ethel started laughing. But those sitting at the table waiting for more ham would never let Winston forget the day he fed that meaty hambone to his dog.

The Grandchildren

C.G. and Ethel's grandchildren enjoyed visits with their grandparents, helping their grandmother in the kitchen, playing outside on the log fence at the forestry compound, and climbing the fire tower with their grandfather. From its very top, they could almost see Wint, DeeDee and Clay's house in the distant horizon—and when they timed it right—they could watch the sun set.

Susanette's family lived the farthest away, but then in 1976, they moved closer to the Howells when Gilbert was transferred from New Orleans to Mobile. Anetha, on the other hand, soon moved farther away. After she and

Winston divorced, she got a job in Tallahassee and moved her family there. Only Patsy and Harry stayed put. They were in south Florida with no plans to move.

C.G. and Ethel's Grandchildren (Easter, 1975)
Front row: Pamela, Lee, Ginger, and Jeanne
Back row: Winston, Clay, and DeeDee

Gardening

When C.G. and Ethel first moved to the forestry headquarters, they wondered what they would do about planting a garden, but the dilemma was soon solved. They became friends with each family that lived in the big brick house across the unpaved road from the forestry headquarters, and these neighbors (the Harrells, the Montgomerys, and then the Foys) were happy for the Howells to plant a garden on their property; and friend and neighbor Sandra Tucker and her daughter Kim loved to help them pick the vegetables.

One of the many letters Ethel wrote illustrates what gardening entailed for the Howells. The one that follows was postmarked June 13, 1976.

Monday A.M.

Dear Susanette, Gilbert, Pamela and Jeanne,

Well it may take me two or three days to get this on the road but I'm going to make a start. We have had so much to do and working all hours that I have gotten so I sleep sometimes till 7:00. I did just that this morning. Which means I don't have time to work my pickles, they'll have to wait till tonight. So I'll just get a letter started and hope to get it off soon.

We have done more canning this year than we have for several years. We have done 80 quarts and 36 pints of string beans, 31 quarts of peach pickles, a few jars of jelly and I really don't know how many cucumber pickles and I still have six gallon jars and the crock full in different stages on the counter.

We have not put too much in the freezer yet. The peaches that were too ripe to pickle we sliced and put in cartons, probably about 15 cartons. We have done a few cartons of squash and I have 6 containers of blackberries. I have also put up in the freezer, blackberry juice, peach juice, and mahaw juice to make jelly as we need it. So when you all are coming home we'll make a batch of jelly from each and you can have an assortment.

We have been getting corn and butterbeans and okra for about a week but have not put up any of those yet. This week I expect we'll get some of that done. I have never seen so many string beans as has been gathered from four rows. I expect there has been three hundred quarts or more canned plus all that have been used fresh. They are full of beans now and no one wants them. We have a community canning center here now that is really a help to the people. We canned our beans out there and most of what we have given away have been canned out there. We can prepare our vegetables and take it and our clean jars out there. They blanch the vegetable and sterilize the jars. We pack the jars and clean up our table. Then we can leave them and go back the next day and pick them up after they have been processed and cooled. The charge is 5¢ a qt and 3¢ a pint. Sure wish we'd had that when we had to put everything in jars.

Sat. A.M.

Well I said it might take two or three days but really didn't expect to be on it a week. We have had a busy week tho. Just get your freezer empty before you come home. Bring any freezer cartons and jars you have. I'm sure I'll be able to use them. I expect we'll still have corn and peas when you come home in July.

Girls, if I don't have to give her away I'll have a playmate here for you. A kitten moved in on us and it is really taking over. It is about the most playful cat I've ever seen, goes with us to the garden and tackles our hand when we put it down to pick something. Also climbs all over the back porch and the kitchen windows.

Well, it's 8:00 so I'm going to put this in the mail. I'll just have to wait for you to come to tell you anything more. We can hardly wait to see you all again.

Love, Mama

P. S. Be sure and bring your jackets. When we get over the gardens I can maybe get them done. Also bring the cuff off Pamela's jacket.

Don't think I have told you but I am really enjoying my fry-pan.

ᔥ 12   Retirement Years

Several months before his retirement date in 1978, C.G. started going to the farm every chance he got. He was planting a garden there. He and Ethel were preparing to move back—back to the farm where they had raised their family, back to the Ladyland Community where Ethel had grown up, back to Philadelphia Baptist Church where C.G. had been ordained a deacon twenty years before.

C.G. did not intend to farm again—at least not like he once did—but he had plans for the place. His work with the Forestry Service had made him more aware of the value of pine timber, so before long he had arranged to have half his farm planted in pine seedlings; the remainder was left as a Bahia grass pasture where the cows he bought could graze.

In Her Spare Time
They moved back to the farm that spring. Although Ethel was not yet ready to retire from her job in Live Oak, she was thrilled to be back among old friends, and she soon

made new friends, people who had moved there while she and C.G. had been gone (C.G. had already met them while planting the garden!). Ethel continued working at DuPre's, and while in town each day, she checked on her mother.

Eager to do more quilting in her spare time, Ethel got C.G. to rig up a quilt frame, on chains, in the largest bedroom of the house. The frame could be lowered from the ceiling when she wanted to quilt and raised up out of the way when company came. The chains, of course, ended up getting quite a workout. The Howell house still attracted guests like the outdoor zapper light C.G. bought attracted flying insects. (That thing buzzed every time it electrocuted a bug, so the buzzing was nearly constant.)

Nobody knew at the time (1) how quickly Ethel would reach her goal of making a patchwork quilt—each meticulously hand stitched and quilted—for each of her daughters, (2) that she would then set a goal of making a quilt for each of her grandchildren and reach it,[117] (3) that she would hand stitch each of them a crewel picture, and (4) that she would make baby quilts for all of her great-grandchildren: Wint, Liza, Logan, Kyle, Tanner, Curtis, Rachel, Morghan, and Asher, plus Lane, her great-great-grandson.[118]

Letters from Home

That spring, as C.G. and Ethel were still getting settled on the farm, Susanette called one Sunday (the day she usually called home) and asked if they would mind keeping Pamela and Jeanne for a few days that summer, until Patsy—who had agreed to keep them for a month!—could pick them up. Granted, it was a dumb question; they never minded keeping any of their grandchildren.

The reason, Susanette explained, was that she wanted to go to France. If C.G. and Ethel were shocked that a daughter of theirs would even consider going off and leaving her children and husband for a month (something Ethel would never have dreamed of—much less *done*), they

- 300 -

never expressed it—at least not to Susanette.

In late June, Susanette left Pam and Jeanne in the care of her parents, cried all the way back to Mobile—*what was she doing leaving her children for more than a month!*—and caught her flight to New York and then Paris.

After a quick trek through Paris, Susanette and her college friend, Barbara Standridge, traveled to the coastal resort of Arcachon where they roomed with a French family for four weeks and walked each morning to the local lycée for French classes. They were taking courses for college credit; Susanette was working on a degree in art, with a minor in French, at the University of South Alabama (USA).

Susanette came back from her trip with many fond memories—not the least of which was receiving these three newsy letters from her father, mother, and grandmother:

July 16, 1978

Dear Susanette,

I hesitate to write because you will always say you had to leave the country to get a note from Daddy. But I just wanted to write along with your Mother.

We miss your phone calls but know you are having a wonderful time while over-seas. We love you and hope you the best in your stay. Hope you are with Christians and that you don't become a wine-no. It really won't hurt you if you know when enough is enough. (We trust you.)

Gilbert called us. He is really lonely. We could tell by the way he talked but he is willing for you to be there and enjoy yourself. Us too. But we will also be glad when you get back. But do have a good time as most people don't get chances like that often.

With love,
Daddy

Sunday P.M. 7-16-78

Dear Susanette,

Since Gilbert called me and gave me your address I just had not been able to get down to writing. Then today I got to thinking if you were to hear from me I had to get a letter in the mail.

We have been rather busy since you were here. We had company from Miami that came in on Friday after Patsy and Harry were here. They (Patsy & Harry) only spent one night here. We sure did wish they could stay longer. We hated to see the girls go but I'm sure they have been having fun. Patsy has only called once since they were here. I expect we will call them tomorrow.

Loren and Beth and their children were with us for a week, also Clara Mae. Kathy and her baby were here for most of the week. Clarice & her family and Laura and Etchie were at Mernest's during the same time. Everybody was here on the 4th, <u>Whew</u>. We did have fun but were worn out when it was over.

We have gotten started again on the house. C.G. has just about finished the painting in the utility room, that doesn't mean inside the closets & bathroom. I have started back to painting doors again. We hope to get the floor-covering down in the next day or two and get the freezers moved. Rudolph [Foy] has already taken the cow to the butcher shop and we should be getting the beef in a few days. The white paint on the walls in there really does seem to make the room larger. Of course when we get the two freezers and my sewing cabinet[119] in there it will probably shrink it again.

I have gotten the mirror and the light for the bath room but we don't have them up. I made a mistake on the number of shutters so have to re-order on them. Also I'm going to order the wall cabinet. I have decided I do need it.

There really is not much usable space in the vanity. We tried to get one in Lake City like the vanity but they did not have what we wanted. Then last week we got a sale [catalog] from Sears and they are down to $29.00, so tomorrow off goes another order.

We have made two trips to Jax. to see the La-Z-Boy sleep sofa. We saw an ad in the Times Union that they were on sale. So the first time they had sold out. She got our telephone number and called when they got another shipment. We went Thursday to look at them. I like them as much as I thought I would. To lay down on one is just about like a bed and the spring mechanism has a life time guarantee. She told us a special order would take till about December but that will be ok too. I'm pretty sure we are going to order one.

DeeDee came home with us last Wed. and stayed till Fri. morning. We really enjoyed having her.

Marcell [Gilbert's mother] called me this afternoon after she talked to you. I sure am glad you are having a good time and are with such nice people. Give them our love and tell them I really appreciate them taking care of my <u>BABY</u>. Are you finding it hard to communicate?

We'd like for you to call us collect maybe on your last week the girls will be back here and you can talk to them too. I don't know just when Patsy will bring them back. She talked like they might all come and stay a few days. Of course I think that depends on whether she can go with Harry or not. Sure do hope they can come here for awhile. But don't want to be selfish and wish her not to go with Harry.

I better get this ready for mail.

Love,
Mama

Delma's hands were shaky when she wrote the letter slowly in longhand, but Susanette understood every word and soaked each of them in.

Sunday Night

My Dear Susanette.
A few lines tonight to put in the letter with your Mama's letter She is writing. I read the card and sure was glad to hear from you. I was just looking on the calendar tonight and counting the days you still would be gone. As I understand you are to be gone a month. My it will be such a long time. I guess for one thing you are so far away. but I hope and pray you will get along real good. and that you will receive a great Educational befenit [benefit] from taking this trip over there. And Im sure it will be a great experience for you. Also I feel like you will meet a lot of nice folks. I realy enjoyed the girls the few days they spent with me after you left. was tempted to keep them. but knew they would enjoy being with Patsy and her girls much better as she would be able to take them places to see different things that would please them more. I want to write them a letter and put in with one to Patsy and her girls next week. Susanette Mrs. Renah Robbins[120] was buried yesterday out at Phil[a]delphia Church. that was Jack and Ernest Robins mother. I understand she had been in a nursing home for a good while. down the State some where. she was a good friend and a real nice person to know. honey is the weather very hot over there. it [has] been kinda hot here. but its been raining here some most all day. and it has cooled the air quite a bit. We went to Church today and tonight our Pastor is resigning. so dont know who we will get next. I understand he is retiring. Well honey it is Eleven oclock. so will stop for this time. and I trust to the good lord you get along good. and will

---

have a real nice trip. and we are looking forward to seeing you soon.

I'm having trouble with my left eye again hope it gets better soon. if it dosent will have to go back to the eye specialist again.

so be good and take care. and remember I love you. and hope to hear from you soon and also see you too.

As ever GrandMama Rye

Killing Flies

After Susanette returned from France, her daughters reported that they had enjoyed their visit with Lee and Ginger in South Florida and their stay with their grandparents on the farm—"especially," they said, "killing flies on the porch!"

Knowing that flies could be a problem on the farm, Susanette praised Pam and Jeanne for wielding the flyswatter and thereby helping their grandparents control the indoor fly population. Only later did she learn that their other favorite activity at the farm was holding the door wide-open so more flies could enter and become targets.

Two years after her stay in France, Susanette held her first art exhibition (a requirement at USA for an art degree), and C.G. and Ethel took a trip to Mobile for its opening.

Cooling the Horses

For several summers in a row, Patsy's daughters, Lee and Ginger, and some of their friends from south Florida had spent time at Camp Dovewood, a Christian camp in Suwannee County, near O'Brien, where they went horseback riding every day. Lee and Ginger had fallen in love with the horses there; and now, every time they visited their grandparents, they also wanted to go over to Camp Dovewood and visit the horses.

One year when Lee, Ginger, and Lee's friend, Liz, visited the camp, Mrs. Richards, the owner and director, let them saddle up the horses and ride them over to the Howell farm, a twelve-mile distance. Because it was an extremely hot summer day, Patsy and Ethel met Lee, Liz, and Ginger about halfway the distance; Ethel had packed sandwiches and water for them. Then Ethel and Patsy returned home.

When Lee, Liz, and Ginger arrived at the farm on their horses, they were hot and sweaty—and knew their horses were—so they decided to cool them off. Lee and Liz tied their horses up near the barn and started cooling them with water they got at the outdoor sink that C.G. had rigged up for cleaning fish or washing sand off vegetables.

Ginger, on the other hand, tied her horse up at the back of the house to a four-by-four post that supported the porch roof. There was a garden hose nearby, attached to a spigot, so Ginger gave the handle several turns. As water rushed through the hose, the hose uncoiled, waved in the air, and spooked Ginger's horse. He reared, turned, and galloped off, taking with him the post that supported the roof. Ethel, looking out the kitchen window, saw what was happening and it scared her half to death.

"Oh, my God, Ginger's gonna get hurt!" she yelled.

Patsy ran out to see what was going on and saw the roof sagging, the horse running for dear life, the post still attached to his reins, and Ginger trying to stop the horse.

"In addition to thinking Ginger was going to be hurt," Patsy said later, "I thought I might also have to buy Mrs. Richards a new horse! I thought he would kill himself before that porch post got caught in the Daddy's grapevine arbor.[121] That finally stopped him."

Patsy's daughters enjoyed bringing their friends with them to the farm, but perhaps it was their friends who enjoyed it the most. One of them (I'm not sure which), who had biological grandparents of her own, told Lee after visiting the Howell farm, "You are so lucky to have a *real* Grandma and Grandpa."

Delma's Decline

Delma was becoming very forgetful, just as her father had as he grew older. Ethel checked on her every day, often eating lunch at her mother's house and then checking on her again before she headed home from work at Page's Department Store (Mr. and Mrs. DuPre had sold the store to Rick and Brenda Page.).

As Delma's dementia worsened, Ethel started taking her to the farm to spend nights and weekends. That worked for a while. But, eventually, Delma's house on Houston Street was put on the market, and she and all her belongings moved in with C.G. and Ethel.

Ethel was just beginning to sort through some of her mother's boxes stored in the garage when she wrote:

Tues. P.M – 9-10-85

Dear Susanette, Gilbert & Girls,

Guess I'll give you a real surprise. I have been trying to get around to this all day. It has been so hot I just did not want to do too much but I have fooled around all day. I have a sore hand, put two pretty good cuts on it yesterday with a bad place in a zinc bucket. I was washing it with my bare hand and had not noticed the cut place on the bucket. I'm sure in a day or two it will be ok as I don't usually have much trouble with cuts, etc.

I have been canning a few pears. I have made preserves, Jam and pear butter. I don't think I'm going to put up any more. I have some canned from last year.

We have still not made a start on house repairs. I think every week we'll get started but we don't. For several weeks we had rain nearly every day and it just stays so hot we just can't seem to get in the mood.[xiv] Last week I started some cleaning, doors and trim. I only got about six

---

[xiv] The house was still not air-conditioned.

but they were the bad ones, porch & kitchen & Utility Room. This week I planned to start again but cutting my hand changed my mind.

I still lack a lot going through the boxes of Mama's things. Patsy wanted me to leave it till you all come Thanksgiving. But I wanted to go through the clothes and linens. I am washing up things as I go. All the crochet I am putting away for you all to go through. There is not too much that is good. You know she had not done any for years.

We did finish the sale on the house last Tuesday. Charles bought it and just gave a check in full. We kinda got upset with Revis but since Charles wanted it we were only delayed a few days. I have since heard that Revis and his wife split up again and he may be renting from Charles. I may be telling you something I had already told you on the phone.

Anita called me today and said Wint's trip home is being delayed till November 6.[xv] They are happy that he will be here to see everyone if you all get home for Thanksgiving. We can hardly wait to see every one again.

I told Rick last week that I will be quitting after Christmas, or before if he finds some one that he wants. I do feel I should help through the holidays tho unless he can get some one. He was kinda upset, said he had no idea where he could find some one to do alterations. He made me feel real good, said he could hire some one else but could not re-place me.

I hope to have Jeanne's picture finished in a few days. I'll be mailing it as soon as I get it done. I hope she likes it. As soon as I finish it I will start on Ginger's. Maybe by Christmas I'll get it finished.

Fri. A.M.

Well I really got side tracked. It doesn't take much to get me off writing any more. Joyce and Price [McCullers]

[xv] Wint had married and joined the military.

came over Wed. afternoon to get some grapes and stayed most of the afternoon then she came back Thursday for awhile. If they get anything over here she has to come right back with something for us, so she baked Banana bread and brought over. I asked her about staying some with Mama when I have to work more time for Christmas, only if she will take pay. She refused to take money but said she'd let me sew some for her. I'd rather pay but she just won't have it that way.

Yesterday I went through three more boxes. One was towels & dishtowels and table cloths. I washed and put them away. One box was odds & ends of dishes. Some of them I washed and put out and some I put back in a box for you all to go through. The other box was her china. She had worried about it so much I washed it up. I had ordered some of those china storage things from Sears thinking I'd pack hers in it but changed my mind and packed mine instead. I then put hers in the cabinet. When she gets to worrying about it I tell her to go look in the cabinets. That seems like it is going to help. She wants to see it and think it's being used.

We're sending your deed to the little piece of land. Do you feel like the step child again? Patsy and Anetha got theirs when they were here. I have just been waiting till I could find time to write and send yours. If we had done this when we first started talking about it we could feel like we were giving you all something but land is so cheap now it isn't much.

C.G. is getting started turning some land to plant Rye [grass] for the cows. We had planned to sell several of them but they are dirt cheap now. Don't know if we'll sell or feed a while longer.

Well my time is running out. Today is a work day. I want to get this off today for sure so I have to quit.

Love, Mama

Inside the envelope was a deed for six and two-thirds acres of land; C.G. and Ethel had divided a twenty-acre wooded section into thirds so that each daughter had an equal share.

A New Full-Time Job

Early the next year, Ethel quit her job. She didn't want to, but she felt she had to stay home with her mother. For the next few years, she took care of Delma, day after day, knowing this was what her mother wanted—expected; Delma had cared for Dosia until the day she died. It was all up to Ethel; Harold was not close enough. In his search for greener pastures—even gold—he had moved West.[122]

Delma was eighty. Serving as her sole caretaker took its toll on Ethel, and she concluded that she did not expect or want her daughters to do the same for her.

"I never ever want to be a burden to any of you girls," she began to tell them, "and if I get so I can't take care of myself, then you find a place for me. I want y'all to have a life. I mean it!"

Each time she said this, her daughters assured her they would honor her wishes because they felt the same; they did not want their children to give up their lives for them.

In the late 1980s, Delma fell and broke her hip and was rushed to the hospital in Gainesville. From there, she was transferred to the Suwannee Valley Health Facility, a nursing home, because she was now unable to walk and was too heavy for Ethel to lift. But Ethel visited her mother daily, and when Delma could no longer feed herself, Ethel lifted the spoon for her.

Fiftieth Wedding Anniversary

In 1990 as C.G. and Ethel's fiftieth wedding anniversary approached, their daughters discussed throwing a party for them; but when Ethel got wind of it, she nixed the idea, saying, "I don't want a bunch of gold presents to try to figure out what to do with."

So instead of a party, the Howell sisters decided to take their parents on a road trip to the Rocky Mountains. They would travel together in the Pressleys' van.

Ethel was hesitant. She didn't want to go off and leave her mother. Ethel agreed to go, only after DeeDee (by then married with children and living in Live Oak) promised her Grandma Howell she would visit and feed her Great-Grandma Rye every day while Ethel took a break.

A few weeks before the trip, Patsy sent letters to several of C.G. and Ethel's close friends, asking them to send (to her or Susanette) their best wishes for the anniversary couple, along with photos and stories of good times shared with them.

At the scheduled time, Patsy and Harry drove north from south Florida, picked up C.G., Ethel, and Anetha, and headed for St. Louis where Susanette and Gilbert were living. Over dinner the next night, the Howell sisters took turns reading stories that the anniversary couple had unknowingly received. After each story, C.G. and Ethel had to guess who had sent the story. They never guessed wrong.

With Susanette and Gilbert also on board the van, the family headed for the mountains. In Boulder, Colorado, they stopped to see Ethel's niece Susie, Harold's youngest. (By then, Harold and Louise had three grown children: Sheilah, Harold Jr., and Susie; and each of them was married and had a family.)

Upon arriving in the Rockies, C.G. and Ethel were almost speechless. They had always loved the *land*, but they had never seen anything like *this* land. It was the farthest they had ever been from Suwannee County, and they were fascinated by the different plants that grew in Colorado's rocky soil. The photograph below of the two of them holding hands was taken as they strolled down the side of a mountain, looking at the varieties of leaves and pinecones they picked up.

C. G. and Ethel in the Rocky Mountains, 1990

She Made Her Wishes Known

When Ethel returned from the trip, refreshed, she resumed daily visits with her mother, feeding her at least one meal each day. But as time went on, Delma got to the point that she could no longer swallow food, and because Delma had never made her wishes known regarding end-of-life care, a feeding tube had to be inserted.

On June 19, 1991, Delma passed away. A few days later, she was laid to rest beside her beloved Milton in the Philadelphia Church cemetery. All the family was able to be there together.

During her mother's lengthy decline, Ethel made her own wishes known about end-of-life care. "No tubes." she said, and she and C.G. each signed a "living will" to back up their words.

Within Hollering Distance

DeeDee had always been very close to her PaPa and Grandma Howell and wanted to live closer to them. More than that, she wanted her young children, Liza and Logan, to know them as she did. PaPa and Grandma Howell wanted the same. So everyone started discussing possibilities, and before long, DeeDee and Julian's cottage-style, frame house on Darrow Street in Live Oak was being jacked and loaded up on a flatbed truck. Within hours, the house was set down on the southeast corner of ten acres C.G. had bought from the Drew estate. The spot where the house sat was within hollering distance of the Howells' house, just the way everybody wanted it.

"Liza and Logan were both so cute!" Ethel said. "One day—we couldn't help but laugh when DeeDee told us about it—she was cleaning house, and Liza and Logan were playing in the living room. Logan was crawling around on the floor, when suddenly, Liza grabbed her brother by the back of his shirt and the seat of his pants and flung him over on the couch as she scolded, "Get in there, you son of a bitch!' DeeDee said that's when she knew it was time to have a talk with Julian about what he said to his dogs when he was having difficulty coaxing them into the dog box in his pickup when he was ready to go fox hunting."

Ethel loved telling Liza and Logan stories and teaching them how to cook and clean. C.G. often had a pack of gum in his shirt pocket, so the kids were always climbing on his lap to retrieve a stick, and he was always teasing them by pretending to steal their noses or some other trick. They were usually game for whatever their PaPa handed out, but one day Logan was evidently tired of being teased and put his PaPa on notice.

"I think it was after Logan had started to preschool," C.G. said. "Ethel and I had picked him up when he got out about noon. The kids must have been teasing him that day, or he was just tired. Anyway, as he climbed up in the car, he looked at me and said 'Don't nobody mess with me *this* day.' Then he plopped down in the seat between me and Ethel."

Anetha and Joe

Anetha, after marrying a Mr. Cox and then being single for several years, had married Joe Whitaker from Americus, Georgia. The plan was for her to quit her job with the Circuit Court in Tallahassee and move to Americus where Joe planned to open a new restaurant just out of town (his combination restaurant and gas station in Americus had been quite the spot, thanks to his spicy barbecue and tasty Brunswick stew). But as luck would have it, three months after Joe and Anetha married, he had an accident involving a chain saw, a tree limb, a thirty-two-foot extension ladder, and his right leg.

Joe went home from the hospital with a metal cage around his leg, pins sticking out of it, crutches, pain that might never go away, and the prospect of further surgery. Needless to say, the accident caused Joe to reconsider his plans to build another restaurant.

After Joe sold his business and home in Americus, he and Anetha found a place in Havana, eleven miles north of Tallahassee. The place included a brick home, a brick cottage, a log cabin, a barn and shelter where Joe could cook and store his restaurant equipment, and a large yard that was perfect for Anetha, the only Howell daughter who had inherited a green thumb. The large yard contained plants that flourished in the Big Bend climate; especially beautiful were the camellias that were more like trees than shrubs. There were also palms, pecan trees, and live oaks whose enormous outstretched limbs, laden with resurrection fern, nearly dipped to the ground.

The house itself needed only to be freshened up with a little paint, wallpaper, and perhaps some varnish on the hardwood floors. That was no problem; Anetha knew just whom to ask for help.

The Handymen

Ethel, C.G., and Clay were more than happy to give Anetha and Joe a helping hand. As soon as they arrived at the house in Havana, everyone picked a job and got started. Then Anetha headed out to the yard where weeds needed pulling. She had never been one to work indoors when she could work out.

While in the flower bed near the master bedroom, she noticed a window that she didn't remember! *Where was that particular window on the inside of the house? Was it by her and Joe's bed?* She went in to check. Inside, there was no window there! She told the men what she had discovered, and they went outside to check it out.

"Yep. It's a window all right."

"Can we open it up?" Anetha asked. "It would give us more light in the bedroom."

"Sure," the men all agreed, and Clay left to go get the equipment he would need. C.G. had his equipment. He took up his jigsaw and went to work, cutting into the wallboard exactly where it needed to be cut. He had sawed about five inches when Clay appeared with his skill saw.

"Uh-uh! No, Clay!" C.G. said as he realized what Clay was about to do. "That thing's too big and fast for this Sheetrock. You'll ruin it."

C.G. was all about precision. Clay was all about efficiency.

"Papa," Clay said, "stand back."

"No, Clay, you'll ruin that wall with that thing."

"Papa," Clay said again, "I said '*stand back.*' We're going to do this one my way."

Clay was the only one in the family that knew how to handle C.G. Reluctantly, C.G. backed up and let Clay take over, and later admitted his grandson's work looked just fine. Furthermore, Clay had completed the job in half the time it would have taken C.G. with his jigsaw.

Home Improvements

Over the years, C.G. and Ethel had made several improvements to their home. Whereas they originally had only a single fireplace for heat, they had installed space heaters in practically every room. They had replaced the carport with a two-car garage and enclosed the porch, replacing the screens with awning-type windows (later they changed those out and installed insulated sliding windows).

They had even bought a clothes dryer, something Ethel had vowed she would never own. She preferred hanging clothes on the line because she liked the smell and feel of clothes dried in the wind and sun. She said she would use the dryer only when it rained. But she soon discovered she liked the time it saved, so she forgot she had a clothesline out back.

Their biggest home improvement, though, their family and friends agreed, was when they installed central heat and air—especially air. After that was done, C.G. and Ethel wondered what took them so long.

On the Move Again

The sycamore trees, which C.G. planted when he and Ethel first moved back to the farm, were nearing maturity when Ethel decided the trees were the reason for her chronic bronchitis, so she got C.G. to have all the sycamore trees cut down. Unfortunately, the bronchitis did not go away.

After seeing several doctors in Tallahassee, Ethel was admitted to Tallahassee Memorial Hospital where tests revealed she had colon cancer. She had surgery, and after that, her oncologist recommended chemotherapy.

Ira and Oleta Howell

It made sense for C.G. and Ethel to move to the Tallahassee area, closer to her doctors and treatment facilities (so their daughters thought). After all, Anetha and Susanette were there (Susanette and Gilbert had moved there after they retired). Even Ira and Oleta had moved to Tallahassee. So, C.G. and Ethel agreed to go house hunting, and within a couple of days the perfect home was found in Havana— or so Anetha, Susanette, and C.G. thought! Ethel, on the other hand, did not like it! They kept looking but couldn't find a single house Ethel thought she could live in. After some investigation, though, they learned that Ethel could get chemotherapy at a clinic in Dowling Park, and she agreed to move there (since she would still be within the bounds of the Suwannee River!).

They soon moved into a Wilson Gardens apartment at the Advent Christian Village in Dowling Park. Their daughters thought the move might work out to be permanent. But when C.G. asked their friend and neighbor Virginia Barr about taking care of his cat Fluffy, he said, "while we're gone," so that was a clue that the Dowling Park apartment was temporary.

As it turned out, C.G. enjoyed living at Dowling Park.

There was always someone to talk to, and he could walk out his back door to fish in the Suwannee River. Ethel, on the other hand, hated the place.

"People up here don't talk my language," she said.

Ethel's surgery, or the effects of anesthesia, had affected her short-term memory, and the chemotherapy was compounding her problems. Yet, despite that and feeling sick most of the time, she managed to cook and take care of C.G. Nearly every day she fried up a pan of fish he caught about fifty feet from their back door. But the day Ethel's chemotherapy ended, she was ready to move home.

Dave Lane, who lived near their farm, helped with the move (he beat the Howells' daughters there that morning). Dave ended up doing most of the heavy lifting and provided the trailer; and when C.G. and Ethel arrived at the farm that day, Dave's wife Erie had homemade peanut brittle waiting. Who wouldn't want to live out there—in the woods, Ethel called it—with neighbors like that.

Cousin Peggie

Back at the farm, Ethel enjoyed sitting on the enclosed porch reading or looking out the window at birds building a nest in her crape myrtle, at the goats in the neighbor's fenced lot, and watching for the mail carrier.

One day in the fall of 2001, the mail carrier put in the mailbox a big brown envelope with a Maryland return address. Inside the envelope was a long letter, along with numerous photographs. The letter writer introduced herself as Peggie, the daughter of Buck Lanier (then deceased). Buck was the cousin Ethel and C.G. had tried to "fix up" with their friend Mary Catherine.

Peggie was into genealogy and family history and wanted to know if Ethel could identify people in the pictures and tell her anything about her great-grandparents, Tip and Dosia Lanier, who had died before Peggie was born.

Ethel thought her hands were too shaky to respond to Peggy, so she asked Susanette to write. Peggie had provided an e-mail address, so before long, a friendship had developed between Susanette and Peggie. E-mails were flying back and forth, and in one, Peggie asked what her cousin Ethel thought about her (Peggie's) beloved grandmother Ethel Severn Lanier.

"What should I tell Peggie?" Susanette asked her mother, knowing herself exactly what Ethel thought of her namesake.

"Well, you can just tell her," Ethel said smiling, "that I liked Aunt Ethel just as much as she liked us."

C.G. was sitting there on the porch listening. "Ethel takes her time in sizing people up," he said. "She's not quick to judge, but once she forms an opinion of somebody, that opinion won't likely change, no matter what. I, on the other hand, can usually form an opinion of a person after spending just five minutes talking with them. My opinion won't likely ever change, either, though on occasion, I have been wrong."

In one letter, Peggie related a story her father Buck had told her. It seems that Tip once shipped Alonzo's family a crate containing a brightly colored crowing rooster. Young Buck adopted the rooster, naming him Leon. In describing the rooster, Buck said that Leon was "a fighting cock—a tough-as-nails bird who beat up the neighborhood cats!" Only after the rooster inflicted a deep scratch across Buck's face did his mother decree that the rooster had to go. But instead of cooking it for food—as Tip had probably intended—she had the rooster crated up and shipped back to Florida, from whence it came.

The year after Peggie contacted her cousin Ethel, the Howell "girls," all retired, took a trip to meet Peggie. She, along with her mother, Harriet, showed the Howell sisters a grand time. While in Maryland, Patsy tried the impossible: to get her fill of Maryland crabs.

"Patsy almost turned into a crab herself before we got back," Susanette said to Gilbert, upon their return.

The Howell sisters were always kidding one another (their father had been a good teacher), but they were already planning another sisters' trip—or at least Patsy was.

Patsy, Harriet and Peggie Lanier, Susanette, and Anetha

In September of 2003, Peggie visited her Florida relatives; and while Ethel prepared a feast, C.G. took Peggie to see the Suwannee River, Running Springs, and places of interest she had heard about but never seen.

A Trip South[123]

The following month, Susanette took C.G. and Ethel on a trip south. They spent one day with their good friends, Price and Joyce McCullers, who had settled in Floral City. (The McCullers had lived in Suwannee County for several years; Joyce had helped Ethel with Delma from time to time.)

Next, they stopped to visit C.G.'s sister Laura at an adult daycare in Orlando; she had moved in with her son, Michael, and his family after husband Etchie passed away. In Punta Gorda, they visited Ethel's favorite aunt, Cora Taylor Smith. Her granddaughter Valerie accompanied them to the assisted living facility where Cora was living. [124]

The visits with Laura and Cora were bittersweet; they served to remind everyone present of how time marches on. But, the trip also reminded Ethel and Susanette of how many things remained the same: C.G. struck up conversations with nearly everyone he passed, whether it was in the lobby or the doorway of the motel. One fellow stood holding the door for five minutes while C.G. finished his joke.

Crooked Rows

Each summer when the garden started "coming in," the Howells had more vegetables than they could use, so they always encouraged neighbors to help themselves. Many did. If they didn't, the Howells would pick and wash the corn, beans, peas, okra, squash, tomatoes, or whatever, and deliver the produce to the neighbor's doorstep.

Each summer, the Howell sisters spent a week or more on the farm, helping their parents harvest and freeze the produce, filling two large freezers in the Howells' garage, and taking pint and quart cartons home for their own families. It was not uncommon for them to break, shuck, silk and put up 350 ears of Silver Queen sweet corn in a day—because a delay of just one day in harvesting corn could make all the difference in its taste. They had also— on more than one occasion—suggested to their father (C.G. was, by then, well into his eighties) that he cut back on the size of the garden. "Instead of the half acre," they urged, "why not a twelve-by-twelve-foot plot?"

In early 2004, C.G. came home from a visit with Dr. Andrew Bass and said the good doctor had told him he should continue his regular activities—and that anything he *could* do, he *should* do! That shut his daughters up. He told Ethel to "go ahead and order the seed—maybe just a *few* less, to appease the girls." Ethel ordered the way she always had.

That year, however, when it came time to till the soil, C.G. realized he wasn't physically able to handle his heavy tiller (he had sold his tractor to Roscoe Chauncey). However, he knew he could get someone to help: Jerry Sattler, Bob Talent, Daniel Lyons, Dean Gast, Dave Lane, Wayne Corbin, Tommy Warren, and many other neighbors had helped him on numerous occasions.

As it turned out, his grandson Clay offered to till the soil and lay off the rows for him. C.G. was pleased—until the process actually got underway. Then it was difficult for him to watch. He had to bite his tongue to keep from telling Clay every move to make. C.G. wanted his rows to be straight. He was, after all, *known* for his straight rows.

A few days after Clay laid off the rows, Anetha was visiting at the farm, and several other people were there. Anetha was in the kitchen helping her mother with noon dinner preparations while the others were sitting on the porch talking with C.G. The phone rang and Anetha picked it up. Her son Clay was on the other end. As she talked, C.G. called to her from the porch—

"Who is it? Is it somebody talking about my *crooked rows?*"

"No, Daddy, it's Clay," Anetha said.

"Oh, my, did he hear what I . . ."

"Yeah, he did."

"Tell PaPa," Clay said from the other end of the line, laughing, "next time he can lay off his own rows since I didn't do it to suit him."

When Clay drove out later, his PaPa started back-tracking, trying to apologize. Clay just laughed and ragged him about it.

After all the seeds and potato eyes were in the ground and beginning to sprout, Patsy drove up from south Florida and helped her father plant the tomato seedlings, all seventy-five that Ethel had started off in egg cartons.

Hard Feelings

Shortly after Patsy and C.G. got the tomatoes planted that

spring, she and her sisters prepared for a trip to the Northwest. They were going to visit their Uncle Harold and Aunt Louise. They wanted to take their parents with them, but C.G. and Ethel didn't have the time.

"We've got a garden to tend to," they said. That *was* the truth. But everyone knew there was more to it. They both had hard feelings toward Harold that originally stemmed from the many promises he had made to his mother that he hadn't kept. He would tell Delma he would be there at Christmas, but then something would always come up and he wouldn't show up. Harold, on the other hand, knew the roads ran both ways, and the truth was, they hadn't visited him as much as he had visited them.

Then, there was the money issue. Harold had been *more* than generous when he sent money to his parents for them to build a new house. He had even loaned money to C.G. and Ethel. But later on, when he got in over his head in the construction business, he had asked for help. By then, his father had passed away, so he wrote to his mother, not knowing how meager Delma's funds were. She took out a loan—mortgaged her house so she could send him the money. Harold promised he would make the payments directly to the bank, and he did for a while. Then, his payments stopped without explanation. Delma took over the payments without complaint. But after her hands became so shaky she could no longer write the checks, she asked Ethel to make the payments. Delma was by then dependent on her small social security income (the profit on the farm eaten up by Milton's medical bills). Each month when Ethel had to make the bank payment, it widened the gap that had developed between her and Harold—not to mention that all of the responsibility of taking care of their mother had rested heavily on Ethel's shoulders.

Harold Reminisces

During the visit with Harold in Butte, Montana, Susanette

told her uncle that she wanted to include, in a book of family history she was preparing, the letters he had written to his family while working for the War Department. He said it would be fine. She also gave him a letter that Peggie Lanier had asked her to pass along. After reading the letter, Harold began to reminisce.

"I never will forget a hunting trip with my cousin Buck, Uncle Alonzo, and Granddaddy Tip," he said. Buck was a true Lanier, like his daddy and granddaddy. Granddaddy let Buck use his sixteen-gauge pump shotgun that day. We were out in the woods, and all of a sudden a shot went off *Bam!* Buck had shot from right behind me. Daddy had taught me to hunt, and Daddy would always insist that everybody be on the same line. Nobody with a gun *ever* stayed *behind.* I couldn't believe Buck had shot from behind. But more than that, I couldn't believe Grand-daddy's mild reaction.

" 'You'll learn, buddy. You'll learn,' Granddaddy said to Buck, with no alarm whatsoever in his voice—when I could have had my head blown off! Yeah, Granddaddy was right. Buck would learn, all right. But in the meanwhile, he could kill somebody.

"Granddaddy was always shipping things up to Balti-more—whiskey, cherry and pine bark—and at Thanks-giving, he would always send Alonzo a turkey even if it meant *we* had to eat chicken for Thanksgiving. I got tired of that. So, early one Thanksgiving day, I went out and chopped the head off a turkey so we *had* to eat it. From that day on, I think we ate turkey every Thanksgiving.

Harold also remembered his horse—the one he had traded to C.G. for a typewriter. "Granddaddy Tip bought my colt's mother at auction," Harold said, "and when she gave birth to a beautiful stud colt, Granddaddy Tip gave the colt to me.

"When Granddaddy went to a horse auction, he always took his riding crop, and after he checked a horse's teeth, he would hit the horse with his riding crop. One time he hit a horse and the horse didn't do a thing. 'That horse is blind,' somebody said. 'No, that horse just don't give a shit,' Granddaddy replied. And, Daddy once had a horse he named Tony that was good for nothing! He was addicted to eating his own feces."

Harold did not discuss that day the topic that was probably most on his mind: he had recently learned that he had cancer.

When the Howell sisters returned from their trip, they shared their memories and photographs with their parents, not knowing their uncle would not survive the summer (see Appendix C).

Louise and Harold Rye

Chickens for the Freezer

After Anetha's son Clay graduated from Florida State, he went to work for Goldkist, a chicken processing plant near Live Oak. As an employee he could purchase fresh chicken pieces at discount, sometimes for as little as five cents a pound. So while working there, he kept his grandparents well supplied.

After Clay left Goldkist and went to work for Occidental, the Howells thought they were out of luck when it came to discount chickens. But they were wrong, as the conversation below will demonstrate.

Susanette's phone rang; she picked it up.

"Susanette . . . Do you want some chickens?"

"Chickens? What do you mean, Mama?"

"Chickens to put in your freezer—to eat. We got them from a neighbor—Uh . . . Oh, shoot! I can't remember his name. That's so aggravating."

"Mama, I don't have a freezer, remember? What chicken parts did you get this time?"

"Oh, no. We didn't get chicken *parts*. We got chickens—whole chickens—and they were free. Didn't cost us a penny!"

"Wow! How did you manage that?"

"Well, we were over visiting that neighbor—I still can't think of his name—and he said that he and his wife throw away all except the breasts of their chickens because the breast is the only piece they like. He raises chickens just for the eggs. He's got two big chicken houses—You know your Daddy and I almost got in the chicken business one time. I sure am glad we didn't. That's a lot of work. And stink! My goodness, chicken houses do stink!—Anyway, that man is only interested in layers, so he culls the roosters—kills them—then he just cuts out their breasts because that's the only piece he and his wife will eat! They throw the rest away! Bury it—with all that good dark meat—bury it in a pit he dug in the ground. We told him not to throw any more of that dark meat away, to call us when he cuts the breasts out, and we'll go get the rest. You know, me and your daddy are not that fussy about what piece we eat."

"So, you went and got the chickens minus the breasts—how many did you get?"

"Oh, no. That man—I can't think of his name—said he wouldn't hear of us taking the leftovers. Yesterday he called your daddy and told him he could come and get his extra chickens. Your daddy went over there and brought back forty-five."

"Can you fit forty-five chickens in your freezer? I thought it was nearly full, with all the vegetables and all."

"Oh, they're not in our freezer yet. That's why I was asking you if you wanted some. The chickens are out there running around in the trailer."

"In the—*trailer*? *Running around?*"

"Yeah. Well, actually they ain't doing much runnin', 'cause there's so many in that trailer. We're gonna to feed 'em a few days and fatten 'em up before we butcher 'em."

"But, won't they fly out of the trailer?"

"Oh no, C.G. put some wire fence over the top to keep 'em from flying out. And he's gone to town now to get some chicken feed."

"What did you have to pay for these chickens—these live chickens?"

"Oh that man—I can't think of his name—he didn't charge us a dime. The chickens were free for the taking."

"Mama, I wish one of us could go help you butcher the chickens," Susanette said (lying! She did not wish to help!), "but you know I'm working on that freelance project for Elsevier, and Anetha is still working nearly every day at the sheriff's office, and Patsy—" Her mother cut her off.

"Oh, that's okay, as soon as we fatten 'em up, we'll get it done."

And get it done they did.

As it turned out, C.G. and Ethel could not wait to fatten the chickens up. There were so many crowded in the trailer that the birds started dying from the heat, so C.G. and Ethel started butchering as fast as they could.

Within the week, Ethel called all her daughters to brag that she and C.G. had killed, scalded, feathered, and cut up all forty-some chickens and put them in the freezer.

Other than short-term memory problems, Ethel seemed as healthy as before she had surgery for colon cancer. Her daughters were amazed at her stamina. And many who knew her were not even aware she was experiencing memory loss, since she still seemed to be able to do just about anything she needed or wanted to do.

Ethel's Fried Chicken

As Ethel said, she and C.G. were not particular about what piece of chicken they ate. But C.G. loved the back, and he could get more meat off a chicken than anybody—probably more than a buzzard could if the same piece of chicken were lying out in the open. (The same went for bony fish.)

Ethel's favorite chicken piece was the thigh. "I debone them and cut the meat crosswise the grain," she said. "It fries up faster and more tender that way."

There was no denying that Ethel's fried chicken was the best. Part of her secret might be the fat she used in the pan. She stored all her fat in one pot (an old enamel coffee pot) be it bacon drippings, chicken fat, melted Crisco shortening, or Wesson oil. She was not just being frugal, she knew that food doesn't brown as well in fresh oil. Her other secret for good fried chicken was a thick aluminum frying pan that could be tightly covered so the chicken fried up fast—but got done to the bone.

Early Summer

C.G. had to admit that Clay's crooked rows had not affected the way the plants grew. There would be, as usual, enough to share with friends and neighbors (pictures do not lie)[125] The Howell sisters gathered at the farm in early summer, as usual, to help their parents with the harvest. But when they began to shuck the corn under the shade of the pecan tree, they noticed more flies than usual.

C.G. and Gilbert among corn rows

Chicken $#/+!

Then they noticed a stench coming from a nearby trailer sitting on the other side of the pecan tree. A quick check revealed that the trailer was the one the chickens had occupied, and it contained what those forty-five fowl had left behind. Chicken manure or fertilizer would be the polite word; Patsy used a different one.

"Your Mama wants me to put that on her camellia bushes," C.G. yelled back at Patsy (C.G. had turned eighty-eight that January), "but I was too busy catching up with the garden after we finished butchering the chickens."

Needless to say, the ammonia odor and the flies it was attracting that day made it necessary to roll the stinking trailer away from the corn-shucking area.

Later that week, after all the corn had been processed—nibblets and cream style—for the freezers, Anetha left to go back to her job in Tallahassee, and Susanette prepared to head back to her new home in Gainesville. Patsy planned to stay and help her parents a few more days.

While Susanette was loading up her car, Patsy strapped a dust mask over her nose and mouth and headed out to the stinking trailer, figuring she might as well get that nasty job behind her. She started spreading the manure around her mother's camellia bushes. The "fertilizer" had been wet by rain while in the trailer and was now caked, dry, and dusty.

Susanette hugged her parents goodbye, got in her Nissan, drove over to where Patsy was working, and pushed a button to roll down the window so she could say goodbye to her good sister. *Saying* goodbye to Patsy was all that was necessary; Patsy hated hugs from family members nearly as much as C.G. did.

Sweat was already soaking through the bandanna Patsy had rolled up and put around her head.

"I'll see you later," Susanette yelled.

Patsy threw a shovelful of the fertilizer near the "Jesus Is Lord" sign (a sign like others that dotted the community;

members of Philadelphia Baptist had been encouraged to display the signs in their front yards.)

"With all this chicken shit fertilizer," Patsy yelled back to Susanette, "that sign there might be a billboard when we come back!"

Like her father, Patsy had a way of making others laugh.

Pine Straw Sales

C.G. had continued to grow slash pines for timber sales and was pleasantly surprised when a fellow approached him one day about buying the pine straw that now covered the ground under the trees.

"There's a market for it," the fellow told C.G. "People are using it for mulch in their flower beds, especially up around Atlanta."

"This is unbelievable," C.G. said later while recording in his little black notebook the number of semi-truckloads of pine straw that had been hauled out of his field that week. "Why, I make more money now on pine straw, sitting on my rear end—not lifting a finger except to write some numbers down—than I used to make all year long sweating every day and half the night, trying to make a living at farming."

He had contracted with a company that brought in the hired hands, and C.G. got to watch them work. The men, all Mexicans, raked and baled the straw by hand, working from daylight until dark every day of the week, even Sunday. C.G. was impressed with their work ethic, although he didn't like to see them work on Sunday. That was something he had always tried not to do. On the farm he had succeeded. It was different when he worked with the forestry service; forest fires didn't recognize the difference between the Lord's day and any other.

Philadelphia Baptist

The church was and always had been a big part of C.G. and

Ethel's lives. Each had a strong faith in Jesus Christ, and they were faithful in their attendance. C.G. also felt strongly that everything he had belonged to God and that returning one tenth of it to God—to the church—was the right thing to do, according to Leviticus 27:30.

C.G. also believed strongly in witnessing, according to First John, Chapter 5. Ethel, on the other hand, gave more weight to Matthew, Chapter 6. Her faith was more of a private matter. Ethel had been invited many times, years ago, to join the Women's Missionary Union (WMU). She never did. But she had served her church in other ways, like teaching Vacation Bible School and Training Union classes where she was a great storyteller. When she told of Joseph and the Technicolor Coat, her vivid demonstration of colorful figures moving across a felt board captivated the children's attention.

Teenagers in the church enjoyed having the Howells around; they especially enjoyed C.G.'s youthful attitude and never-aging sense of humor. More than a decade after he retired, they got him on roller skates, though the padding they strapped on him made him look more like a football player than a skilled skater.

As time went on, Ethel preferred to have church friends stop by and visit rather than visiting with them at church. In fact, she had a lot of colds that came on suddenly, early Sunday morning, so she "just couldn't make it to church," but the sniffles or hoarseness disappeared by the time somebody stopped by for a visit that afternoon. Then she would serve them a piece of sour-cream pound cake or slice of coconut or chocolate pie she had made while C.G. was at church. (Ethel never bothered baking just one pie.)

C.G. kept up his church attendance and was always encouraging others to go. Any time a stranger moved into the community, they might as well *expect* a visit from him, inviting them to Philadelphia Baptist. Upon departing, he usually extended his "calling card."

Turned one way, the card read, THE GIFT OF GOD IS ETERNAL **LIFE**. Turned upside down, there was another message altogether. (Try it.)

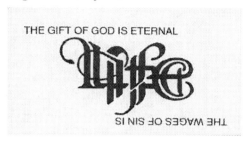

C.G. also carried in his wallet a poem that described how he felt about his church:

The Church

My church should be a friendly church
    with doors that open wide,
    inviting every lonely one
    to fellowship inside.
My church should be a help to those
    who somehow went astray,
    and even now—confused and hurt—
    need help along the way.
My church should be less satisfied
    with thought of selfish gain,
    and lend a helping hand to those
    who falter with the strain.
God grant that when my church shall see
    a boy in need of aid,
    they'll open wide their door to him
    and find themselves well paid.[xvi]

[xvi] Adapted from Trail Echo, Santa Fe Trail Council, Garden City Kansas; the word *church* was changed from *troop*.

Regrets?

Susanette continued to ask questions of her parents to get answers for the family history she was working on, and one day she asked her father if he had any life regrets.

"Oh, I've sometimes wished that I had been able to go to college," he said. "But few people went to college back then, and because of the expense of it, I never gave college any thought. But if I had heard then what I heard later, I might have gone. It was something Gus Smith said to Jimmy North.[126]

"Mr. Smith was a well-to-do farmer that lived near the Pennington farm when I was a boy; and Jimmy North said that Gus Smith said to him one day, 'That C. G. Howell was one boy I would have financed through college.'

"But Gus Smith's comment got to me after it was much too late to pursue it."

The Signs

Next, Susanette asked her father to elaborate on *farming by the signs,* something he had mentioned in a previous conversation (something that sounded like baloney to her).

"Yeah, we've always checked the *Almanac* before planting," C.G. said, "and before marking pigs—even before going fishing. It tells you which days are best."

"Yeah," Ethel added, "we've always liked *The Ladies Birthday Almanac* best."

C.G.'s doubting daughter listened and took notes, but she wasn't buying that stuff about the signs. *Sure, horoscopes were fun to read—but planting crops? Marking pigs? Deciding when to fish? Based on the position of the moon and the stars?* She didn't believe any of that and could not believe her parents did!

Knowing, however, that her father had a fishing trip scheduled for that afternoon and being a bit curious, she picked up the latest *Almanac,* lying on the end table on the porch and read what it said for that date: *Good fishing.*

That afternoon, C.G. came in from his fishing trip with just a *few fish* on a string, the few that wouldn't fit in the *bucketful* he carried in his other hand.

Made to Fish

On occasion, Ethel had gone fishing with C.G., but she preferred sewing or quilting to fishing. So, over the years, he found others who preferred fishing to sewing or quilting. At one time or another, Clarice Boatright and Frankie Foy were his fishing buddies. More recently it was Anderson Curl. But as time went on, Ethel decided C.G. and Anderson were getting too old to go on the river together— just the two of them—and said so.

"Ya'll need," she said, "a younger man in the boat."

Problem was, neither of C.G.'s small boats could accommodate, comfortably and safely, more than two people. So Clay, Wint, and Gilbert started taking turns going fishing with C.G.

When it was Gilbert's turn, they loaded the supplies—a cane pole and a spinning reel and a container of live crickets—into the boat, a twelve-foot aluminum boat with a small battery-powered motor, and headed out, pulling the boat trailer behind the car. They put the boat in the Suwannee River near Royal Springs.

Knowing how much C.G. liked to fish and that he had not been able to fish much lately, Gilbert told C.G. one day to go ahead and fish—that he would operate the motor and guide the boat.

When they got home late that day, Gilbert headed to the outdoor kitchen sink to clean the fish, but C.G. went inside, straight to the couch on the porch, and lay down. *C.G. usually led the way to the sink. What was wrong?*

"Why are you so tired?" Ethel asked as C.G. lay down on the couch. "Because," C.G. replied, "Gilbert made me fish *all day long*! Gilbert wanted to operate the motor and maneuver the boat, so *I* had to fish *the whole day*."

No Time to Breathe

C.G. had hearing aids, purchased at a hefty price; he kept them safe in the box, except for special times, like church services. He had blood pressure medicine, prescribed by Dr. Andrew Bass; he took the pills if he happened to think about it at the prescribed time and was in the kitchen where he kept them. He had oxygen (tanks and a concentrator) to help him breathe if he wasn't so busy talking—or trying to hook a fish—that he couldn't stop long enough to hook himself to the oxygen. That was the case one day when Gilbert went with him to the Ward pond. Aubrey Ward had always kept it well stocked with perch and catfish, and now his widow, Juanita, did. She had told C.G. he could continue to fish there as much as he liked.

Gilbert loaded up their spinning reels and, from Ethel's refrigerator, got the chicken livers—not just any chicken livers, mind you. C.G. had asked Gilbert to pick up the livers on the way through Branford. While Susanette was standing in line to pay for the livers, the man behind her told her how to prepare them so the fish could not snatch them off the hook without getting caught.

"Take one of your old nylon stockings," the fellow said, "and cut you some pieces about two-inches square. Put a little piece of chicken liver in that and tie it up with a small string. Then you snag that nylon on your hook. The fish will smell the liver and go for it—and then you've got him!"

C.G. and Gilbert agreed that the man might have a point, so they got Susanette to secure some livers in some nylon squares cut from a pair of Ethel's knee highs.

When the fishermen returned that day, they showed off their fish, saying "that nylon-stocking-thing was the ticket."

After showing off the fish, C.G. immediately stretched out on the couch. Gilbert went out and cleaned the fish and took them to the kitchen where Susanette and Ethel fried them and prepared side dishes—hush puppies, coleslaw, grits, and ice tea—for supper. When the food was on the table, C.G. was still lying on the couch. He said for everybody to could go ahead and eat, he was just too tired to eat.

"That wasn't like Daddy, tonight," Susanette said to Gilbert on the drive back to Gainesville, "not even wanting to get up and eat."

"Yeah, he got tired while we were fishing. He wouldn't stop fishing long enough to hook up his oxygen. I mentioned it a couple of times, but he wouldn't stop fishing long enough to do it."

Whatnots

Since C.G. didn't stay connected to his flow of oxygen every minute of the day—yet kept on breathing!—Ethel thought he must not need it. So, if the length of tubing, which connected to the oxygen concentrator, got in her path as she walked through the house, she would kick it out of the way. She had *never* liked things lying around that were not needed.

"If it ain't useful," she said, "I don't give it room and board."

Anyone who had known Ethel for any length of time, or had been inside her uncluttered home, knew not to give her knickknacks. If they did, they would probably never see the item on display. She would stick the dust-collector in a closet until she could find somebody else willing to take it and dust it.

As her short-term memory faded, she would forget who gave her what knickknack, so she was apt to offer the gift right back to the giver the next time they visited.

Who Needs a Doctor When They Have Vicks?

Both C.G. and Ethel were proud of their good health and the fact that they did not rely on lots of medicine. They believed in eating well—and going to doctors only if they were sick. Maybe not even then.

Patsy never would forget the phone conversation she

had with her mother (soon after she and C.G. had moved back to the farm after her chemotherapy). Patsy called one Saturday and learned her dad had been sick in bed all week.

"Mama, if he's been sick a week, it sounds like he needs to see a doctor."

"Oh, no. I'm rubbing him down with Vicks," Ethel said.

"I know, Mama, but I think you need to get him to the doctor if he's been sick *all week.*"

"Well," Ethel said, "if he ain't well and he ain't dead by Monday, I guess I'll see that he gets there."

The next week, after a dose of antibiotics prescribed by Dr. Bass, C.G. was back in the saddle.

Getting Affairs in Order

In early 20005, C.G. told Ethel to forget about ordering seeds that year because he wasn't going to plant a garden. He recognized he was not getting any younger, and, with Ethel's memory problems, they needed to start thinking about making a move. After he got Ethel to agree, he asked his daughters to look for a place at Dowling Park.

They found the perfect apartment! Attached to the wall just outside the apartment's door was a framed print of a rural scene that showed a road leading up to a farmhouse, and beside the road was a mailbox with the name *Howells.* This picture behind glass was like a sign from God that this was the right place for their parents.

C.G. and Ethel signed the papers, and their daughters were all set to move them the next week. But before that day came, Ethel had persuaded C.G. that they should stay put on the farm (she forgot she had promised to move!).

When Susanette arrived at the farm that week (she and her sisters were now taking turns helping cook meals), her father said he wanted her to meet this person who said she could help them "as needed."

"Her name is Carol Simpson," C.G. said, and he picked up the phone and dialed Carol's number without looking it up (C.G. didn't need a phone book; all the numbers were in his head).

After meeting Carol, Susanette was sure the arrangement would never work; Ethel's and Carol's personalities were too different. Ethel was quiet. Carol was not. Little did Susanette know.

A Return to the Baptist Children's Home

In June of 2005, when C.G.'s youngest and only surviving sibling passed away, C.G. said he was not up to going to the funeral, so Susanette went and represented him. When she returned, C.G. told her that when he got to feeling better, he wanted to go visit the Children's Home where he and his siblings had lived. It turned out that the whole family wanted to go, so a trip and tour was scheduled.

The Children's Home was no longer a single brick building; it was a sprawling campus, and the staff there spent an afternoon showing the Howell family around.[127]

Ethel, C.G., Susanette, Anetha, and Patsy, July, 2005, Florida Baptist Children's Home campus, Jacksonville

The staff at the current campus told C.G. that the building where he had lived (on Cottage Avenue) no longer stood, but they shared old photos with him and his family.

After leaving the campus, C.G. directed Harry, Patsy's husband, who was driving, through the maze of Jacksonville streets, to the old location. C.G. had always had a good sense of direction, and that day was no different.

Well-Organized

Back at home, C.G. started making phone calls, telling friends how much they meant to him.

He and Ethel already had wills and living wills, and they had even had their lawyer draw up papers giving power of attorney to Susanette (since she lived closest).

The day C.G. turned his paperwork (and checkbooks) over to his daughter, everything was in good order in a tabbed notebook. Subsequently, each time Susanette went to the bank to take care of her parents' financial affairs, she carried the notebook; and she beamed every time someone in the bank saw the tabbed notebook and complimented *her* on being so well-organized.

Sixty-Five Years of Marriage

C.G. had known for several years that he had prostate cancer. His physician had prescribed treatment to slow its progression. But C.G. abruptly halted the monthly injections after learning how much—"outrageous!" he said—the injections were costing his health insurance/Medicare.

In August of 2005, C.G. had to be rushed to a Lake City hospital. There, he was diagnosed with bladder cancer. After surgery, he was transferred to the Good Samaritan Center (at the Advent Christian Village in Dowling Park) where he could get around-the-clock skilled nursing care.

A room in the adjoining Dacier Manor (assisted living) was found for Ethel. To visit C.G., she only had to walk down the corridor; but with several turns, it was a bit tricky, so Dacier's director, Beth Smith, placed a small plaster dog—with a "Welcome" sign in his mouth—outside Ethel's door to helped her find her way back.

By the time their sixty-fifth anniversary rolled around, C.G. had rallied and moved into Dacier with Ethel. It was there, on September 8, 2005, that they celebrated sixty-five years of marriage with their daughters and their new Dacier family. A cake was baked in their honor, and as Dacier residents gathered that day to enjoy cake and ice cream, C.G. bragged about how he and Ethel had stayed together all those years. "When Ethel and I married in 1940," he said, "I told her that I'd handle the big problems and she could handle the small ones. She agreed. And so far all our problems have been small. I also told her that if we couldn't get along, she could go inside and I would go outside. So, in our sixty-five years of marriage, I've spent about sixty-two of them outside!"

C.G. waves to the camera as he and Ethel prepare to eat cake.

Visitors

When friends stopped in to visit the Howells at Dowling Park, C.G. entertained them with jokes, and Ethel showed

Quilt Jeanne made for Ethel; ten blocks represent quilts Ethel made.

off the quilt she kept on a recliner. It was one her granddaughter Jeanne had made for her. It was composed of ten quilted squares that replicated the quilt patterns Ethel had used in quilts she had made for her children and grandchildren.

A favorite visitor to Dacier Manor (and the Good Samaritan Center where C.G. went later), was Clay and Kim's son, three-year-old Asher.[128] Ethel would let him play with her battery-operated furry pink pig that walked and oinked. She had "won" the pig while playing Bingo with other ladies at Dacier. (She won him after the Bingo caller learned that Ethel was drawn to a pink pig salt-and-pepper set, a collectible, that was displayed behind a locked glass door in Dacier's foyer.) Each time Asher said goodbye, Ethel tried to give him the pink pig or the "watchdog" that sat in the hallway by her apartment door.

C.G. and Ethel's grandchildren and great-grandchildren who lived in Suwannee County visited often, and those from out of town drove or flew in to visit: Lee and Ginger from Atlanta, Pam from Miami, and Jeanne and her children, Curtis and Rachel, from Kansas City.

There was a constant stream of old and new friends dropping by—Pete and Alice Boatright were regulars, as was Carol Simpson, who drove C.G. for daily radiation treatments in Lake City.

While sitting one day in the waiting room of the Cancer Center, waiting for C.G. to complete his radiation, Carol wrote:

Carol's Poem to C.G.

As I sit here and watch . . .
    people come and people go.
Cancer seems not to know
    the young nor the old.
I wonder about their lives—
Do they have faith in the Lord
To deliver or rid them; to untangle the cords?
The cords of confusion: Why me? Why you?—
What can we do to show that we care too?

My heart goes out as I listen to them share
Of all of their heartaches, sorrows, and family cares.
Some seem content while others have troubled minds.
And then there are those who choose to stay blind.
Blind to their fate . . . Will they die or be cured?
If only they'd trust Jesus they could be assured.

His love is theirs to reach out and hold
And peace that only He can control.
My prayer for each one that we have met
Is that they know Jesus and be content.
That bitterness would not control them.

As we shared, and some did,
While others chose not to say anything,
Quietness was within.
Each has a story . . . a part of God's plan.
We need only to trust . . . leave it in His hands.

Carol Simpson

While C.G. was away having radiation, Ethel stayed busy with her current project, which was making quilted potholders for anybody who wanted one. And once a week, she enjoyed going to the on-site beauty salon to get Tess to fix her hair.

Ninetieth Birthday

The head nurse at the facility, Linda Ratliff, stopped in often to check on C.G. and Ethel while they were both living at Dacier Manor; and after C.G. had to move back to the Good Samaritan Center where he could get around-the-clock skilled nursing care, Linda made sure he got only the best care. She had known the Howells since she and Susanette were pals in junior high and had spent many a night at the Howell farm.

C.G. had bad days and good.

"When I get better," C.G. said in early January of 2006, "I want to go fishing."

But on January 13 when family and friends came to celebrate his ninetieth birthday, the activity was too much for him. "I know you all mean well," he told them, "but I need quiet, so I can rest."

Fifteen days after his ninetieth birthday, C.G. passed away, with his wife Ethel nearby, along with his grandson Winston and great-granddaughter Morghan.

C.G.'s father had died at the age of forty-one. C.G. had outlived his father by nearly half a century. He had outlived all of his siblings.[129] He had lived a full life. Most of all, C. G. Howell had enjoyed life. And those who knew him had enjoyed him.

Letters to the Editor

After C.G.'s obituary was published in the *Suwannee Democrat,* the following letters were also published:

Suwannee Democrat, Friday, February 20, 2006

Dear Editor:

While checking your Web site, I was saddened to learn of the passing of C. G. Howell.

Some 50-55 years ago, as a young boy, my family worked the old B. B. Saunders farm and Mr. Howell was one of our neighbors.

He was always one of the nicest and kindest persons one could ever know. As the years passed, he would always stop by to check on my mother while she was still living. She would always mention that Mr. Howell had stopped by to check on her and she would say, "He is a very nice man."

With Mr. Howell's passing, Suwannee County has lost one of its finest citizens. He always had time to be a friend and neighbor.

My prayer is, "May his soul always be at peace."

— Robert Warren

Suwannee Democrat, February 22, 2006

Dear Editor:

A recent letter offered that author's tribute upon learning from the Democrat's Web site of the passing of C. G. Howell. From that letter I in turn learned about Howell.

Last year my wife Susan, and I met Mr. and Mrs. Howell at the renovated Royal Spring. We were instantly charmed by this gracious couple. As Mrs. Howell gazed on smiling, Mr. Howell shared a brief history of their life in Suwannee County and, leaning on his cane, revealed that his initials, "C.G." actually stood for CAN'T GO!

What a wonderful man,
John H. Bell

Back on the Farm

Several of C.G.'s nieces and nephews who attended C.G.'s funeral said how nice it would be to get together again at the farm, a place that held so many memories for them.

"Going to farm every summer was the highlight of our year," Clarice said.

So, on July 14, 2007, the Howell sisters hosted a cousins' reunion there. They were flabbergasted at the response to their invitation. Cousin Ruth Howell Miles even flew down from the state of Washington for the event.

The Howell sisters prepared a meal—ham, acre peas, potato salad, fresh tomatoes, and cobbler for dessert—just like they knew their mother would have, had she been able. After dinner, cousins gathered around the dining table and looked at old photographs and shot new ones (unfortunately some had to leave before the one below was shot).

How sad all the cousins were to learn, not three months after that day, that Ruth, the eldest daughter of Mernest and Eloise, had passed away at her home in Washington.

Cousins' Reunion, 2007
Front: Ruth Miles, Garfield Midgett, Michael Schemer with his grandson, Matt, peaking over his shoulder.
Back row: Loren Midgett, Clarice Shatley, Oleta Howell, Arrieane Schemer, and Larry Shatley.

At Surrey Place
Ethel's friends, Merine Hunter and Annie Lou Johnson, were living at Surrey Place in Live Oak. So, when it became necessary for Ethel to move from Dacier Manor, Surrey Place became her home.

She had been diagnosed with Alzheimer's, some time back, and the disease had progressed rapidly. Within a few weeks after C.G.'s death, she forgot that he was gone.

At Surrey Place, Ethel kept trying to find the kitchen so she could "fix supper for C.G." The staff placed a security bracelet on her wrist, lest she wander outside, but she took it off. They moved it to her ankle, but then she began wandering into the rooms of male residents at night looking for C.G.—she just knew *he was in there visiting with somebody and it was time to go to bed!*

Then it was almost as if angels appeared; Carol Simpson, who had helped the Howells before they left the farm and have driven C.G. for daily radiation treatments, offered to "move in with Miss Ethel and care for her at home"—and Vern Haggerty offered to assist Carol.

Too good to be true. But it was.

Back Home
About the first thing Ethel wanted to do when she got home was to check on her peach and pear tree. She was sure it must be about time to can some fruit!

And where had that C.G. gone off to, now? Was he out visiting again?

Ethel with pears

Good Friends and Neighbors

Hardly a day went by that somebody did not stop by to visit Ethel: Elaine Boatright, Wayne Corbin, Russell and Winnie Wadsworth—and neighbors that lived within a mile of the Howell farm. So many of them had done so much over the years, and continued to. Here are just a few examples, in no particular order, to show what good neighbors C.G. and Ethel had (it would take tomes to tell all):

Virginia and Robert Barr fed C.G.'s cat Fluffy for a whole year while C.G. and Ethel were away; and now they shared their dog, Rocky (the dog brought a smile to Ethel's face and made her get out of her chair when nobody thought she was able to).

Dave Lane lent his firm muscles when they were sorely needed, and his wife Erie was always sharing some of her homemade peanut brittle—and those yummy wafer cookies!

Daniel Lyons used his own tractor and equipment for whatever it was that C.G. needed done. His wife Lynette, with Erie's help, created a memory book for, and organized a church celebration in honor of, C.G. and Ethel.

Dean and Nancy Gast spent hours and hours working in the Howells' yard.

Judy and Tommy Warren's granddaughter helped Ethel and C.G. remember what it was like when their own children were small.

Melody and Tony Stanford kept an eagle eye out to make sure nothing went amiss. Though Ethel sometimes complained about "that ugly fence," she *loved* watching the goats and horses behind it.

Bob Talent was there on a moment's notice to help with the new water heater installation. His wife Bernice kept encouraging Ethel to get involved with sewing projects to keep her mind active—even providing the fabric.

Vern and Dick Haggerty sent so many cards they should own Hallmark!

Jerry Sattler cut the garden weeds too many times to count; and his wife Joyce cheered Ethel; in fact, those two women just *clicked.*

Frank Goodson kept the Bahia grass mowed; he was as dependable as the morning sunrise.

Bruce Simpson installed bars and equipment to help make Ethel safe. And Carol, words could not begin to express how appreciative the Howell family was for the loving care she was now providing.

In the Garden

On October 23, 2,007, while a church prayer group was praying for Ethel's peace, Ethel slipped away to join C.G. She passed away in the manner her daughters knew in their hearts she wanted—in the home she loved, on the farm she loved, and in the community she loved—yet not being a burden. Her caretaker, Carol, and her daughters were there, holding her hands.

Mernest and Eloise's son, Clarence, drove down from Tennessee for Ethel's service—when his own sister Ruth had passed away just two days before his Aunt Ethel.

"I couldn't make it to Ruth's funeral in Washington state," Clarence said, "so I wanted to come to Aunt Ethel's."

The choir sang "Shall We Gather at the River" and "Whispering Hope." Russell Wadswoth sang "In the Garden." Loren, Beth, and Garfield Midgett sang, "How Great Thou Art."

Ethel's grandson Clay assisted The Reverend Leroy Dobbs in conducting Ethel's celebration-of-life service. Clay did a remarkable job (on the day before he was to leave on a missionary trip to Honduras!). He told about how his grandmother had taught him how to make pickles and how to prepare fruit and vegetables for freezing and canning. He said it was practically impossible to talk about his grandmother without talking about his grandfather since they were like one.

Carol Simpson, who had made it possible for Ethel to return to her home, described her experience of caring for "this lady who was so kind and beautiful, inside and out."

Winston spoke about his grandmother, as well as his grandfather, who used to take him, Clay, and their sister, DeeDee, fishing.

"Well, actually," Winston said, "I think Grandpa took all of us *together* is his boat just *one* time. After that, I think he decided it was better to take just one of us at a time."

Winston—so much like his PaPa Howell—always joking around—made those who were hurting deeply laugh through their tears.

Ethel's granddaughter Pam told some stories she had heard—like how her Grandma Howell disciplined Patsy, Anetha, and Susanette when they were little girls.

"When two of them started fussing, Grandma would separate them, putting both of them at a window, with one on the porch looking *in*, and the other on the inside looking *out*. She would make them stay there and stare at one another—through the window—until they went from frowning, to making faces at one another, to giggling.

"I still remember," Pam said, "the song Grandma taught us about the kid with all the long names. And I asked Liza the other day if Grandma taught her how to make watermelon teeth. She said, 'Yes, and potato ones too!'

Grandma enjoyed simple things that could bring joy to people.

"I was visiting Grandma on Labor Day, and we were shelling peas on the porch. After a while Grandma looked up and said, 'Have you heard C.G. stomping around out there?' I thought, *Well, Grandma . . . maybe he is.* He is in our hearts and thoughts as Grandma Howell will be. Always."

Afterward

Before leaving Philadelphia Baptist Church's fellowship hall that day, C.G. and Ethel's daughters issued an invitation to friends and relatives to "drop by the Howell house for a visit." Many followed them there, and before long, stories were flowing.

"I never will forget how Uncle C.G. pulled one over on our daughter, Susan, when she was real little," Beth Midgett said. "He got her to sit down on the floor out here on the porch and told her to spread her legs out. He then got a glass of water and two case knives from the kitchen, handed her the knives (they weren't sharp), and then poured a little water on the floor between her legs. 'I'll bet you,' he said to Susan, 'that I can wipe that water up off the floor before you can stick my hand with a knife!' Susan took the bait. But before she knew what had happened, Uncle C.G. had grabbed her feet and pulled her through that water, and wiped every bit of that water up with her little butt!"

"Yes, and I remember . . . .

. . . .

. . . .

. . . .

❧

Family photos follow.

C.G. & Ethel's Daughters and Their Families

**Clockwise from center back:
Patsy, Harry, Ginger, Lee,
and Ryan (Lee's husband)**

**Anetha
and Joe**

Susanette, Jeanne, Pamela, and Gilbert

C.G. & Ethel's Grandchildren/ Great-Grandchildren

C.G. and Ethel's grandchildren
Back row: Winston, Clay, Denice (DeeDee)
Front row: Pamela, Lee, Ginger, and Jeanne

Great-great-grandson: Lane (dark shirt, lower left)
Great-grandchildren, clockwise from upper left:
Kyle, Wint, Logan, Liza, Morghan, Asher, and
Tanner (striped shirt)

Patsy's Daughters and Their Families

Above: Lee and Ryan, with their son, Camden, and their St. Bernard, Bella

Ginger with her Chow Chow, Sasha

Anetha's Children and Their Families

**Winston, Mendy,
and Morghan**

**Clay, Kim,
and Asher**

**Clockwise from front: Denise (DeeDee), Mike,
Liza, Mike Jr., Suzie, and Logan**

Susanette's Daughters and Their Families

Pamela

**Clockwise from back left:
Jeanne, Jeff, Curtis, and Rachel**

Appendix A — **Ethel's Recipes**

Ethel's Sour Cream Pound Cake
1 cup butter or butter-flavored Crisco
3 cups sugar
1 cup sour cream
1 tablespoon vanilla
¼ teaspoon soda
½ teaspoon salt
6 eggs
3 cups sifted cake flour (sift flour, then measure)

Cream Crisco or butter with sugar until well blended and creamy. Add eggs one at a time beating well after each. Sift dry ingredients together and add to batter. When all ingredients are added, beat well until well mixed and fluffy. Bake in large tube pan (or two pans: one bundt, one loaf). Bake at 300-325° an hour or more until done.

* * *

Ethel's Yeast Rolls
2 packages of active dry yeast
¾ cup warm water for yeast
1 large or two small potatoes, boiled (save liquid)
¼ cup sugar
2 teaspoons salt
3 tablespoons shortening
9 to 10 cups all-purpose flour

Peel and boil potato. Remove potato and mash; save water and add enough water to make 2 ⅔ cups warm (not hot) water. Dissolve yeast in ¾ cup warm water from tap. In large mixing bowl, mix together the yeast water, the potato, the 2 ²/₃ cups warm water that includes potato water, and sugar. Then gradually mix in enough flour to make a batter like pancake batter. Let this rise until light and full of bubbles. Next, add remaining ingredients. Dough will be rather stiff. Turn out onto floured surface and knead until smooth. Grease inside of *large* mixing bowl. Place dough in bowl and grease top. Place dough in warm place and let rise till double in size. Knead again. Now you are ready to make your rolls. Cut off pieces of dough and roll in hands to make little ball. Place in greased pans leaving a little space between. Grease tops with melted butter. Let rise again and bake (at 350-375°) until brown.

* * *

Ethel's Pancakes
1 package active dry yeast
½ cup warm water
1 egg
2 tablespoons oil, like Wesson
2 cups unsifted self-rising flour
1 tablespoon sugar
Milk

Dissolve yeast in ½ cup warm water and set aside. In another cup, mix oil and egg together. In mixing bowl, mix flour and sugar together. Then add yeast water, oil and egg, and enough warm milk to make a thin batter. Set aside for 30 minutes. Bubbles will begin to form on top and batter will thicken up. Bake on hot (about 400°) oiled griddle.

Ethel's Crisp Oatmeal Cookies
1 ½ cups brown sugar (packed)*
¾ cup Crisco or butter
6 tablespoons sour milk*
½ teaspoon salt*
¾ teaspoon soda*
1 ½ teaspoon vanilla
1 ½ cups sifted flour*
3 cups quick cooking oats
1 cup chopped pecans

Combine ingredients in order given. Mix thoroughly. Shape into small balls about 1" diameter and place on greased cookie sheet. Press with fork to flatten. Bake at 375º for about 10 minutes or till light brown. With pancake turner carefully transfer to cooling rack

*I sometimes use white sugar, sweet milk, and self-rising flour (in which case I omit the salt and soda).

Appendix B — Tip's Family

Children of Rowan and Emmaline Lanier[xvii]

1. Henrietta Lanier, b. June 29, 1851, Madison, FL; d. Dec 6, 1926; m. James Manuel Brown, June 25, 1875.
2. Florence Josephine (Jo) Lanier, b. Aug 7, 1852, Madison, FL; d. Dec 7, 1943; m. William Henry Ezell, Dec 21, 1871.
3. Porch Miller Lanier, b. Jan 7, 1854, Madison, FL; d. Mar 9, 1917; m. Eliza Cheshire, Feb 14, 1883.
4. Angeline Lanier, b. Feb 3, 1855, Madison, FL; d. Sept 10, 1937; m. Henry Jefferson (or Joseph) Lamb, Dec 24, 1874.
5. Millie Lanier, b. April 5, 1856, Madison, FL; d. Nov 26, 1911; m. George W. Neely, Mar 4, 1877. (Note: George W. Neely had a brother named Lewis whose wife died during childbirth and their baby, Cary Neely, was raised by Tip and Dosia Lanier.)
6. Lewis Crittendon Lanier, b. May 17, 1858, Madison, FL; d. Dec 18, 1941; m. (Martha) Josephine Hingson, Dec 23, 1885. Lewis and his wife had eleven children. One girl married Bob Morrison (who lived for a while near C.G. and Ethel on the former Lyle place). Daughter Ernestine Lanier married Jimmy North and had one child, Betty Jo. Daughter Jane Lanier Ward's children were Aubrey, Henry, and Thelma Ward (Henry's sons were Mattox, Francis, and Baynard).
7. Edward (Ed) Lamar Lanier, b. Mar 10, 1860, Madison, FL; d. Feb 21, 1947; m. Emmaline (Emma) Victoria Hingson, Jan 8, 1885. (Family lore says that Ed's wife, Emma Hingson, was a braggart–but had money. After Ed married her, he started loaning money, and within a year, his brother, Lewis, had married Emma's sister, Josephine!)
8. Asbury Tipton (Tip) Lanier, b. June 15, 1863, Madison, FL; d. Feb 21, 1956; m. Theodosia Dees, Jan 6, 1886.
9. Robert Lee Lanier, b. June 10, 1865, Madison, FL; d. Feb 14, 1937; m. Ella Louise (Lou) Dees, Dec 22, 1885; d. 1935. Lee and Lou had a girl named Dobie, who died when she was just nine. The children who lived to adulthood were Ella, Blanche, Lessie, Dana, Lucy, Eula, and Floyd, the only boy.

[xvii] Compiled from genealogy research supplied by Bill Boatright, Bette Harrison, and Loren Midgett, and from information supplied by Ethel Howell and Bernice Lanier.

Floyd married Sally and had four children: Bernice, Leslie (boy), Wannie Mae (married Weeks), and Norma Jean. Ella married a man named Laky (or Lakey) and had a boy named DuPre and then twins (a girl Elouise that they called Pinky, and a boy named Edward; they called him Linky). Ella died when the twins were just nine days old, so Lou and Lee raised them. Dana almost married John Morgan (a friend of Granddaddy Tip and a teacher at Ladyland), but she ended up marrying Brant Hull. Lucy married Fletcher Boatright (a brother of Doc Boatright) and had a daughter, Dorothy. Eula, their youngest daughter, married Bob Morris; they had four children, Robert, James, Carolyn, and Vivian. Lessie had a daughter, Audrey. Audrey married Grover Fort, who drove a rolling store that stopped at the Howells' home.

10. (Elizabeth) Patia Lanier, b. Nov. 1869; died as an infant.
11. Rowan Monroe Lanier, b. Dec 27, 1870; d. Apr 15, 1897; m. Martha Rebecca Ross, Dec 1, 1894.
12. Minnie Lanier, b. Jan 13, 1872; d. July 22, 1944. (Never married. Had a child at the age of 15: Amanda Lonnie Lanier, b. 1887.)
13. Mary "Mollie" Iola Lanier, b. May 6, 1874; d. Dec 25, 1943; m. Thomas Trammel Hart, June 30, 1898. (Tommy Hart was their grandson. He and Susanette went on a date once, not knowing they were related. He fought in the Vietnam War and was, for years, listed as missing in action. When Patsy, Anetha, and Susanette took their first "sisters' trip" in 2002, they visited the Vietnam War Memorial in Washington DC and found Tommy's name engraved in the granite wall.)
14. Frances (France) Pierce Lanier, b. Apr 15, 1877; d. Sept 23, 1951; m. Mary Mallissa Chauncey, Feb 7, 1901.

Appendix C — **Obituaries**

Suwannee Democrat (2/01/2006)

C. G. Howell

C. G. Howell, 90, of Suwannee County passed away Saturday, January 28, 2006, in the Good Samaritan Center in Dowling Park.

He never met a stranger and was known throughout the county for his willingness to lend a helping hand and crack a joke.

Born in Lafayette County in 1916, Howell moved with his family to Suwannee County at the age of five. Three years later he lost his father, and at the age of 13 when his mother became ill, Howell and his younger siblings lived for a while at Florida Baptist Children's Home in Jacksonville. While he was there, he joined Main Street Baptist Church. Just before turning 15, Howell returned to Suwannee County where he lived with relatives and attended school.

After graduating from Suwannee High School, Howell married Ethel Rye. In the Ladyland community, they purchased land which they farmed for many years. During the early years he worked with the Agricultural Stabilization and Conservation Service (ASCS) while also farming. In the 1960s and 70s, Howell was a radio dispatcher and later a county ranger for the Florida Division of Forestry, serving in both Suwannee and Madison Counties.

He served in the National Guard and was a member of Philadelphia Baptist Church, where he served as a deacon for 45 years. He was also a member of Gideons International.

Survivors include his wife of 66 years, Ethel Howell; three daughters, Patsy Pressley of Coral Springs Anetha Whitaker of Havana and Susanette Baxter of Gainesville; seven grandchildren; nine great-grandchildren; and one great-great-grandson.

Funeral services were conducted at 3 p.m., Monday, Jan. 30, at Philadelphia Baptist Church, Live Oak with the Rev. Leroy Dobbs and the Rev. T. E. Gaskins officiating. Interment followed in the church cemetery.

In lieu of flowers, the family asked for donation to the Florida Baptist Children's Home of Jacksonville, 2300 Bartram Road, Jacksonville, FL 32207, American Cancer Society, or Haven Hospice of the Suwannee Valley, 618 SW Florida Gateway Drive, Lake City, FL 32024.

Daniels Funeral Homes, Inc., of Live Oak was in charge of all arrangements.

Suwannee Democrat (10/26/2007)

Ethel R. Howell

Ethel Rye Howell of Suwannee County died Tuesday at her home in Suwannee County. She was 86.

She was born in Macclenny, Florida. Before she reached school age, her family settled in Suwannee County on the homestead of Ethel's grandparents, Asbury (Tip) and Theodosia (Dosia) Lanier, who had homesteaded one hundred and sixty acres of Florida wilderness in response to the U.S. Homestead Act of 1862. The deed was signed in 1899 by President William McKinley.

On her grandfather's farm, she and her brother Harold enjoyed the annual cane grinding, a daylong event where family and neighbors gathered. The highlight of the day was scraping the rim of the sugar kettle to collect the "polecat" candy that formed as the cane juice turned into rich caramel-colored syrup.

After graduating from Suwannee High School in 1940, she married C. G. Howell, and for nearly two decades, they owned and operated a farm in the Ladyland Community. During the sixties and seventies, Mrs. Howell worked for DuPre's Department Store and Page's Department Store in Live Oak.

She was a member of the Philadelphia Baptist Church.

The Howells celebrated sixty-five years of marriage while living at the Advent Christian Village at Dowling Park.

She is preceded in death by her father and mother, Milton and Delma Rye, by her brother Harold Rye, and by her beloved husband, C. G. Howell.

Mrs. Howell is survived by three daughters and sons-in-law, Patsy and Harry Pressley of Coral Springs, Anetha and Joe Whitaker of Tallahassee, and Susanette (Susie) and Gilbert Baxter of Gainesville, by seven grandchildren, ten great-grandchildren, and one great-great-grandson.

Mrs. Howell enjoyed cooking and sharing her recipes. She also enjoyed quilting, and her goal was to present each of her offspring with a handmade patchwork quilt. In pursuit of this, she pieced and quilted more than twenty treasures.

Visitation will be from 6 to 8 PM Thursday, October 25, at Daniels Funeral Home in Live Oak. Funeral services will be at 3 PM Friday, October 26, at Philadelphia Baptist Church in Suwannee County.

The family requests that expressions of sympathy be made to the Advent Christian Village (www.acvillage.net), P. O. Box 4305, Dowling Park, FL 32064; Alzheimer's Association (www.alz.org), 225 North Michigan Avenue, Floor 17, Chicago, IL 60601; or Haven Hospice (www.havenhospice.org), 4200 NW 90th Blvd., Gainesville, FL 32606.

The Montana Standard (7/30/2004)

Milton Rye, 80

By *The Montana Standard* **Staff**

Milton Harold Rye, loving husband and father figure, finished 80 years of hard, proud work, dying early Thursday morning at his home surrounded by family.

Born Feb. 12, 1924, in Alton, Fla., Milton was the youngest of two children born to Milton Mahone and "Queenie" Delma Rye. He grew up on a tobacco farm in Live Oak, Fla., learning the value of an honest day's work at an early age.

After graduating high school, he went to work with the U.S. Foreign Service and traveled to many parts of the world to construct airports and other major infrastructure. After his work abroad, Milton enlisted in the U.S. Navy, where he served as an airplane mechanic and eventually met his partner for life, Louise Lucille Gaboian, at a dance in Calumet City, Ill. After only six weeks, the two were married on June 3, 1945, and were together through thick and thin until the end. Together they raised three children, son Milton Harold Jr., and daughters Sheilah Arlene and Susan Kathleen.

Drawing upon his previous skills to learn the masonry trade, "Harold," as he was known to family, embarked on a career as a master builder that would last almost 50 years. Many buildings from the Midwest to the West Coast boast his craftsmanship, the qualities of which he instilled in both his son and son-in-law, Michael Vincent, who both are still highly respected in the masonry trade today.

Chicago, San Diego, Vail, Colorado, Arizona, Indiana and Montana are just a few of the places where Milton left his mark. But it was eventually Montana that would become his family's home. The fond memories of Montana he gained after working in Kalispell for one year in the 1950s must have left a deep impression, as he and family relocated to the area from San

Diego in the late 1970s. After spending a short stint in Coeur d'Alene, Idaho, he and Louise relocated to Butte in 1989, where he continued running his own construction business until the time of his death.

Always gently reminding his family members to "take it easy," Milton lived a strong, full life best defined by perseverance, pride and an ability to share his quiet sense of humor through everything he did and endured. In addition to his legacy in the building profession and as a husband, "Geeps" — the nickname given to him by his great-grandchildren — was also a wonderful and beloved grandfather.

Aside from his family and his work, Milton's other interests he enjoyed included mining and prospecting, a pastime in which he dabbled throughout much of his life, always lured by the possibility of striking it rich in gold; fishing; listening to bluegrass, big band and classic country music; and watching CNN and then venting to all who would listen about our country's political woes. And most of all, he always enjoyed a good laugh with the people he knew and loved.

Milton was preceded in death by his parents.

He is survived by his faithful wife of 59 years, Louise and their adoring family; son, Milt Jr. and his wife Nadine Rye of Mount Vernon, Wash.; daughter, Sheilah and her husband Michael Vincent of Butte; daughter, Susan and her husband Chris Newman of Spokane, Washington; grandchildren and their spouses include Matt and Alicia Vincent, Josh and Janelle Vincent, Milt and Michelle Rye, Annie Rye, Mary Rye, Charlie Rye, and Angie Rye, and Chelsea and Scott Newman of Spokane. He will also be missed dearly by his six great-grandchildren Madelyn Vincent, Emily Vincent, McKenzie and Ethan Rye, Maleah Rye and Jaicee Giop. He also is survived by his older sister Ethel and husband C. G. Howell of Florida and nieces Patsy Pressley, Susanette Baxter and Anetha Whitaker.

Cremation has taken place with memorial services to be held Saturday at 11 a.m. at the Gold Hill Lutheran Church at 934 Placer St. In lieu of flowers, please send donations in his name to the American Cancer Society or Gold Hill Lutheran Church.

Appendix D — **Endnotes**

> *Names in italics* — Indicates that the person
> went by that name (e.g., Mary *Annie* Williams
> Madison Howell was called *Annie*).

[1] "I thought Daddy was born in 1881," C.G. said, "and I thought he died on February 29. But the tombstone says he was born in 1882 and died on February 28."

[2] C.G.'s stepgrandmother, Mary *Annie* Williams Madison Howell, married Mr. Williams around 1865, and Henry Madison around 1870, before marrying Jim Howell.

"After my grandfather Howell died," C.G. said, "she married a Brim and had two children: Augustus and Virginia. I heard that, later in her life, she tried to get a government pension based on my grandfather serving in the Spanish-American War. The government told her that James Hiram Howell and James Albert Howell had served, so all she had to do was verify her husband's full name. But she couldn't do it, because she had never thought to ask Jim Howell his full name. She knew that he was buried in the Philadelphia Baptist church cemetery (near his first wife and not far from his son and his grandsons, Ernest and Cecil), but she didn't know the church had records showing his full name as James Hiram Howell, since he had served as one of the first deacons there. When Grandma died in 1935, I don't think she had ever qualified for his pension."

[3] Alexander Monroe (*Mon*) Boatright was born 5/26/1861, died 3/15/1927. His parents were John Wilson Boatright (4/8/1833-8/31/1908) and Eliza Mills (1/21/1836-10/11/1900). (John Wilson Boatright was also one of the first deacons at Philadelphia Baptist, but he was ordained at Macedonia in Madison.) C.G.'s ancestry on the Boatright side of the family has been traced back several generations, and some family members believe his great-great-great-grandfather was Benjamin Boatright, spelled Benjamin Bootritt on a 1768 document stating that King George the Third of Great-Britain granted him a plantation tract of land containing 250 acres of land in South Carolina.

[4] C.G.'s maternal grandmother, Francis *Ella* Hatcher, was born 11/27/1870 in Florida and died 4/14/1902. Ella Hatcher's parents are shown below. John Hatcher (shown in his Confederate forage cap; photo taken 1862-65) was born in Charlton County, Georgia (2/22/1832-6/5/1909); Arabelle Hogans Hatcher, was born 10/6/1838 in Baker County, Florida, and died 8/17/1926 in Suwannee County, Florida.

John Hatcher and Arabelle Hogans Hatcher

[5] Ethel Boatright was born in 1887. She married James *Lawson* Hingson, and she and her husband had three boys and six girls: Oliver, Joe, J.L., Ella, Edna, Claudia, Vita (who lived about eleven years), Lois (who grew up and married Ceril Hart), and an unnamed girl who died at birth. After Lawson Hingson died, Ethel married Brinson Houck, but they had no children together.

[6] John Quincy (*John Q.*) Boatright, born in 1889, married Mamie Johnson, the older sister of Curtis and Melous Johnson (the baby of the family); Mamie also had a sister Verdie, who married Roger L. Lord. John Q. and Mamie had two boys: O'Neal who married Cornelia Marable (Annie Lou Marable Johnson's sister) and Johnnie Quincy who married Mary Drew Brannen.

[7]Joseph (*Joe*) Arch Boatright, born in 1892, married Susan Elizabeth Starling (better known as "Lizzie"). They had thirteen children: Joseph Towns (J.T.) and Susan Myra (both died at an early age), Honorine (married Alex Harris), Thomas Lee (married Marie Turner), Carra (third time, married Lois Jordan), Winifred (second time, married Emory Padgett), Margaret (married Leyron Baker, then Cliff Wilson), Alfred or *Ado* (married Annette Cheshire), Allen Chestley or *Pete*, (married Alice Annin), Billy Ray (married Elizabeth Brown),

Sherwood (never married), Ronald (married Ingrid Kuehne), and Spessard (married Jo Ann Newton).

[8] Clarence Boatright, born in 1895, married Daisy Starling (a sister to Lizzie, who married Clarence's brother, Joe). Clarence and Daisy had seven children: Willie Mae, Monroe, an unnamed girl who lived one day, Lucretia who died at 25 months, Lamera, Clara Inez who died as a baby in January of 1932, and Susan Ella who died at ten months (in 1933).

[9] Ella and Mon Boatright named their second set of twins Andrew J. and Oliver J.; perhaps the "J" stood for John, since Ella's father and Mon's father were both named John.

[10] Della Ross Jones's full name was Lillie Idella Ross. Her father was John O. Ross, and her mother was Roxie Ann Sullivan. Her younger brother was A. Wayne Ross Sr. Wayne's children were: A.W. Ross Jr., who married Mamie Hillhouse; Sydney John (Jack) Ross, who married Evelyn McKnight; James *Howard* Ross, who married Doris Ward (sister to Arthur Ward that married Bernice Crews); and William *Thomas* Ross who married Marie (Mallie Starling's daughter). (Doris Ward and Arthur Ward were children of "Glass-eyed" Will.)

[11] J.G. refers to a man who lived in the community at the time (no relation). His name will not appear again in this book.

[12] "Ross had a slew of boys," C.G. said, "one ran the John Deere place—others were Perry Jim, Allen Wallace (who married Nell Platt), Lavaughn (Tony), Thomas Herbert, and Kenneth Walden. *Lillie* (Mae) married *Elzie* Elston Williams, and they had a girl, Ruth Inez, and two boys, Arthur *Monroe* and *Elzie* Elston Jr.."

[13] Alma F. married Luther Gill (Leamon Gill was their son), and Mary married Charlie *Mack* Holland.

[14] "James (*Jim*) Hiram Howell once owned a farm," C.G. said, "located north/northwest of the farm that Joe Hingson bought. Because of delinquent taxes, the property later fell into the hands of Sheriff Will Lyle. Sheriff Lyle owned several pieces of land, including a section of land south of Tip Lanier's homestead, land Sheriff Lyle later gave to his jailer, Bob Morrison."

[15] Wayne is A.W. Ross Sr.; his son is *A.W.* Ross Jr., who married Mamie Ross, who taught Sunday school at Philadelphia for many years.

[16] Uncle John Q. later sold that house to his brother Clarence.

[17] This small advertisement for Six-Sixty-Six appeared in *The Winter Park Post,* Winter Park, Florida, Saturday, November 10, 1917:

No. Six-Sixty-Six

This is a prescription prepared especially for MALARIA or CHILLS & FEVER. Five or six doses will break any case, and if taken as tonic the Fever will not return. It acts on the liver better than Calomel and does not gripe or sicken. 25¢

---

[18] Marvin Warren was Merine Warren Hunter's father. Merine's mother was Clifford Warren.

[19] Lora Boatright married Bob Herring; they had a son Tommy, whom both Anetha and Susanette dated.

[20] "Seldon Strickland ended up with Daddy's twelve-gauge shotgun at one time," C.G. said, "but Mernest got it back and then gave it to me; it's the one I gave Susanette. Mr. Rye later gave me his twelve-gauge, gas semi-automatic, and he gave his rifle and a 410 pump shotgun to Ethel's brother, Harold."

[21] "Laura Garrett was married to Will Garrett," C.G. said. "They had four children: Annie, Flora Mae, Louise, and Edward. Daddy's other sister, Flora, married Henry Fulford, and they had several children— Frankie was one, but I don't know the others."

[22] Solomon J. Highsmith, a member of Main Street Baptist Church, offered to give an eight-acre tract of land to the Jacksonville Baptist Association to be used to establish an orphanage or home for destitute children. The building, located at 17 Cottage Avenue, was completed in 1926, under the name "The Baptist Children's Home of Jacksonville."

Later, the home became affiliated with the Florida Baptist Children's Homes.

[23] John Henry and Cora Rye's children: Milton Mahone Rye, b. 3/18/1894 at Rocky Sink (a settlement in Suwannee County), FL, d. 4/22/1968; Ruby May Rye, b. 12/10/1895 at Rocky Sink, FL, d. 7/5/1900; John Raleigh Rye, b. 7/29/1898 at Call, FL, d. ?, (m. Bertie Tylar 9/10/1916); Thelma Rye, b. 2/13/1901 at Lancaster, FL, d. 7/13/1901; Jessie L. Rye, b. 12/15/1902, d. 5/30/1903; William Ellis Rye, b. 4/16/1904, d. 2/13/1978; Cora Roberta Rye, b. 4/16/1904 at Thelma, FL, d. 4/19/2004; Erma Rye, b. 8/6/1911 at Rocky Sink, FL; d. 9/5/1919 at Cross City, FL (she had a cleft palate); Oviedo Fred Rye, b. 10/24/1913 at Salt Road, FL, d. ?; Aubrey Newlan Rye, b. 3/11/1916 at Salt Road, FL, d. ?; Edward Lelan Rye, b. 10/5/1919 at Cross City, FL, d. ?.

[24] J. R. Newlan served as Suwannee County Tax Collector, 1895-97.

[25] Milton M. Rye enlisted in the U.S. Army 8/26/1918 in Mayo, FL. His Enlistment Record and Honorable Discharge papers state: When enlisted, he was 24-25 years of age and by occupation a truck driver. He had blue eyes, black hair, fair complexion, and was 5 feet, 8 inches in height. Triple typhoid prophylaxis, Paratyphoid prophylaxis completed 9/3/1918. No A.W.O.L. No absence under G.O. Entitled to travel pay to Mayo, FL.

[26] By the time Milton's brother Aubrey split Tip's wide gold wedding ring, Ethel was married. When Aubrey split the ring, the heat caused a few tiny bubbles to form in one of the rings; Aubrey—knowing that half Tip's band was intended for Delma and half for Ethel (neither had ever had a wedding ring)—hated what had happened to one ring. So, when he gave the two rings to Milton, he also gave him a brand-new gold band. Delma ended up wearing the new band (it closely matched the diamond engagement ring Milton had given her years before), and the damaged ring was tucked away. (Ethel's granddaughter DeeDee now wears the "damaged" ring, and because of its history, she cares not that it has a few imperfections.)

[27] Dosia passed on her Singer sewing machine to Ethel, who passed it on to Anetha's daughter, Denice (DeeDee).

[28] Bertie became Bertie Fletcher when she married, but Nellie married a Brown, so her name never changed.

[29] The Drew Bridge, a railroad bridge, was named in honor of George Franklin Drew, Florida's first Democratic governor after the Civil War.

[30] Maude and Johnny Renfroe wrote the article about the Dees family in Chapter 8.

[31] Author's research: When Dosia Lanier died, her grandsons, Eugene (Buck) and Wilbur, born a few years later, might not have known about the money their grandmother had saved for them. I came across the passbooks while looking through old family papers in 2003. The account of Eugene (Buck) showed an initial deposit on 2/19/1927 of $15 and another on 9/10/1943. The last entry on 1/1/1944 showed a balance of $44.55. Wilbur's account was opened 12/27/1940; deposits of $12, $21, $28.28, and $10 were made. The final entry on 3/18/1944 showed a balance of $71.93. *Was there still money in these accounts?* I wondered. The banks were no longer in business, so I contacted Florida's unclaimed property office in Tallahassee. I learned that there *was* unclaimed money in the name of Eugene Lanier, so, I forwarded the passbooks to Buck's widow Harriet Lanier in Baltimore, along with forms for reclaiming the money. There was no unclaimed money in the name of Wilbur Lanier. Perhaps the bank had been able to get in touch with him when they went out of business (his passbook had a Baltimore address, whereas Eugene's did not). I sent Wilbur's passbook to him anyway, thinking he might want it as a keepsake.

[32] Harold said that after he joined the War Department, he had to take little yellow Atabrine tablets that were supposed to prevent malaria. That drug also turned him yellow; it was a common side effect.

[33] Harold said he could remember one other time his mother got in a hurry. "We had gone to visit Cary Neely's wife's family and were standing in their yard under a big oak tree when a snake fell out of the tree on Mama's head. She did quite a dance that day."

[34] Harold recalled, many years later, that Roadie, for some unknown reason, did not care for his Uncle Alonzo. "That mule," Harold said, "once took a bite out of Uncle Alonzo's ass."

[35] Will H. Lyle was appointed the Suwannee County Sheriff when his predecessor was suspended. Lyle served from 1914 until 1934 when he died.

[36] "I can remember," Harold said, "as many as twenty-five people out picking corn or peas or pears or something at Granddaddy's place."

[37] Bernice Lanier, Lee Lanier's granddaughter, said "I heard that Aunt Dosia divided her sausage with the gypsies to keep the gypsies from putting a spell on her."

[38] Susanette has the radio table now.

[39] "Ethel told me one day when we were walking to school," Oleta said, "that she was 'not going to marry a farmer,' and I told Ethel, 'I'm not going to have a baby until I've been married five years,' but we both ended up doing what we said we wouldn't."

[40] "Edna was very humble," Oleta said, years later when she was reminiscing, "and I was mean as the devil. We had a little playhouse we had built with sticks—it had several rooms—and one day I pooped in one of the rooms. That made Edna so mad! Later on, she got sick—got so she couldn't walk—and had to be carried around. She died in 1925. She was seven and I was four. Maybe she had polio. I don't know. But I remember her real well."

[41] On March 7, 1931, Daisy Ward petitioned the court to appoint her administrator of Edward Ward's estate which consisted of '260 acres of land and personal property not exceeding $500.' An attachment showed: 'One mule sold - $100; Hogs sold - $40, Total - $140. Suwannee County Judge A. C. Johnson granted Daisy Ward the signed Letters of Administration on March 30, 1931, and the Letters of Final Discharge were entered into the public records of Suwannee County, Book Number 2, Page 230, on March 12, 1932.

[42] Ellis was born in 1928; Clyde was born in 1931.

[43] Bernice Lanier recalled the night she danced with Ozzie (Ozie's twin). "Daddy saw me and called me out and made me quit dancing," Bernice said. "Cary Neely came over and said, 'Let's dance! Your daddy won't mess with me!' Cary and I danced about ten rounds and Daddy never said a word."

[44] "Ozie was twenty-one and Mama was thirty-one," Oleta said, "Mama also had a baby boy, but he was born dead."

[45] "After the Rye family lived on the Lyle place," C.G. said, "the Marvin Chauncey family lived there. Later on, Will Lyle gave the property to Bob Morrison, his jailer, when Lyle didn't have money to pay Morrison's wages—or that's what everybody thought. Morrison lived there while he served as deputy sheriff, and the property then became known as the Morrison place."

[46] "You talk about some hard times," C.G. said. "In the 30s, times were tough. From the end of 1929 when the stock market broke until about 1932-33, times were really tight. Nobody had any money 'cause those that had money—the banks—were going broke, so people couldn't get their money. Roosevelt got elected in 1932, and one of the first things he did was close all the banks all over the United States and told them that, until they had federal insurance to insure the people's money, not to open their doors. He made them buy insurance, and you never heard of another one going bust—banks just closing doors saying they didn't have it. Aunt Dosia said she lost—up there at Live Oak—I think it was at [what is now] the Citizens Bank—about $300. Well, $300 back then was worth a lot of money. Oh, I'll tell you right now, when I hear people talking about them 'good old days'—I don't want no more of 'em—I got all of them I wanted."

[47] "Fletcher Boatright was Uncle John Boatright's son." C.G. said. "Uncle John was my great uncle; he was Granddaddy Boatright's brother."

[48] Oleta Howell said she could relate to Ethel's getting aggravated with C.G. for sticking pencils up her curls. "I didn't have any curls for the boys to pull," she said, "but that Anderson Curl would sit behind me and pull my hair."

[49] Woodrow Crews later married a girl named Bernice, and they had a daughter, Wynette Crews. Bernice later married Arthur Ward.

[50] Joe Hingson was a son of Ethel Boatright Hingson Houck (Clara Boatright's sister).

[51] "Charles's daughter Kathleen became the wife of Mr. Hartley, Clerk of the Court in Jacksonville.," C.G. said. "They shared a two-story house on a Jacksonville lake, and at Mr. Hartley's death, his wife Kathleen served out his term—and then some."

[52] "Maybe the Dutch doll quilt had significance to Aunt Dosia," Bernice Lanier said. "Grandma Lou always said she was Dutch. I remember that she had real small feet."

[53] Midwifery was not a licensed profession in Florida then, and was not regulated by the state until 1931, but it was a common practice in the rural south.

[54] "I think Ozie and Ozzie Hurst were Mr. Marvin Warren's nephews—or maybe they were Mrs. Clifford Warren's first cousins," Ethel said. "I'm not sure."

[55] "I've heard some things about what happened the night of Ozie's murder," C.G. said, "though some of it is hearsay.

"Before it all took place, Mailon Hingson came to me in the field one day and asked me if I wanted to help put a whipping on 'the boy.' (He was talking about Ozie.) I didn't. And Mailon wasn't involved in Ozie's murder. (Mailon was Daisy Ward's brother.)

"One of the men that participated in the ambush was supposedly a member of the Wildcat Clan. Some said Will Ward was not in on the shooting itself but was an instigator. The truck used that night belonged to Sam Rye (the son of Billy Rye; Billy's brother was John Rye). It was a dark blue truck, mistaken for black. But Sam wasn't in on the shooting either. After Ozie's murder, Uncle Clarence, Joe Hingson, and I went to see if we could do anything for Daisy. We were in Uncle Clarence's dark truck. Daisy thought she recognized Uncle Clarence's truck as the one that ran them off the road. So, she had one of her kids copy the truck's tag number, and she turned it in to the sheriff. But Sam Rye's truck was the one that was used. Sam told O'Neal Boatright he had loaned his truck that night. O'Neal told his daddy, Uncle John Q., who told Uncle Joe Boatright. Uncle Joe went to the sheriff and suggested that he put Worth Hull, his deputy, on the case. He did, and Uncle Joe told Hull all he knew, and pretty soon the case was solved. The men that did it were put in jail and convicted of murder and sent to prison; one eventually got out on good behavior; the other was put on death row, I think."

[56] The Herring family lived in the Ladyland Community. Lott and his first wife Sadie (Revels) had a boy named Ivydent, then Bob, Cecil, Barney, Louise, Dan, and Lemuel. After Sadie died, Lott married Frieda Goff. She was a lot younger than he was and already had one

child, Tooky Goff. Frieda and Lott had three children of their own: Randy, Lynn and a little girl. Ivydent, Bob and Cecil could play the guitar. Cecil had tuberculosis but recovered. Barney later drove a school bus. Tooky substituted for Barney, and later, for Melous Johnson.

[57] Mary Lunberg later worked at Van H. Priest's dime store. Anetha and Susanette worked with her on Saturdays when they were in high school.

[58] Ethel said O.D. and Fred also had two children, but they must have been born later, since O.D. was younger than Ethel.

[59] Ruby was the daughter of Barney Lanier, who was the son of Porch Lanier, Tip's brother.

[60] When FDR became President, about one-third of Americans lived on farms. FDR's New Deal included a series of farm programs. The Agricultural Adjustment Act (AAA), enacted in 1933, was intended to help farmers by stabilizing the market; but it was controversial because thousands of animals and acres of crops were destroyed. In 1961, the AAA became the ASCS. The program was renamed again in 1994; it is now the Farm Service Agency (FSA), within the USDA.

[61] "After I got that ten dollar loan at the Commercial Bank, it became my bank," C.G. said, in the year 2002. "I continued to do business with them until the bank was sold in the 1960s. The names of the people there changed over the years, but I kept doing business there. Former Governor Hardee was the first president; then there was his son-in-law, Mr. Day, then Mr. Jernigan."

[62] C.G.'s daughters found the poem after his death. The yellowed paper on which it was neatly typed was falling apart, evidence that C.G. had kept the poem in his wallet for years.

[63] Anetha has the pearl-handled fountain pen now.

[64] Mary Catherine Cheshire's mother was the daughter of Ed Lanier, Tip's brother, so she was actually Buck Lanier's cousin.

[65] "Yeah, I 'just happened' to be there," Oleta said, when in her eighties and reminiscing one day, after Ira had died of emphysema and

Russell Courson had come into her life. "I think Ethel had arranged for me to be there that night. I remember we went to Telford Springs over by Luraville for a chicken fry."

[66] "I was paid two dollars for the week," Oleta said, "and I gave the money to Mama every week to buy groceries. Then, I found out Mama was giving the two dollars to old man Overstreet to spend on liquor."

[67] "C.G. and Ira's Aunt Ethel," Oleta said, "told everybody in the neighborhood that 'Ethel and C.G. ought to get married, 'cause they're sleeping in the car together.' One night C.G. and Ethel drove Ira and me home, and then they stopped in the road to smooch. She asked me later if I had seen C.G. turn the lights on in the car and start moving."

[68] Susanette took the watch to Padgett's Jewelers in Quincy in the early 2000s to have it repaired. The repair charge was $212—about what the watch was worth—so the jeweler said. But its value to Susanette went beyond dollars.

[69] "Long after Ethel and C.G. married," Oleta said, "she told me that if she hadn't married C. G. Howell, her daddy would have never let her marry." Both men—C.G. and Milton—always held the other in high regard.

[70] As was customary, the back of Ethel's yearbook was filled with ads to offset costs. Advertisers included Brown Mule Co., Gibbs, Farmer's Hardware, Farmers Milling Co., J. L. McMullen, Perry A. Holmes, County Superintendent, Suwannee Hotel, Sharples, Sid Allen's Dairy, Seminole Café, and Van H. Priest Co.

[71] Leo Land was a well-respected member of Philadelphia Church; C.G. borrowed money from him at least once, probably more.

[72] The bridge over the Suwannee (on Highway 51) was the first suspension bridge in Florida. It was named for Judge Hal W. Adams of the Third Judicial Circuit.

[73] "Old man Overstreet *left*," Oleta said (when asked about this in 2007) "after I gave him a good lick. I was blond and had lots of freckles from working in the sun. I was out sweeping the porch, and he looked down at my legs and said, 'Them shore are some ugly legs.' I

turned around and swung that broom hard—broke the broom handle on his head. He left, and we never heard from him again."

[74] "I don't know why we had to move out of our house," Oleta said, "and live in the tenant house that had no well or pump for water. We then had to haul our water. Daddy had always been a good manager. Mama didn't know how. If only I had been older."

[75] "After Daddy died," Oleta said, "Uncle Will tried to take our land by paying the taxes. I remember the tax man coming all the way out to our house one time to tell Mama about it. That time, she sold a cow to pay the taxes."

[76] The quitclaim deed, dated January 3, 1941, signed by Oleta Howell and Ira J. Howell, states that the agreement was "in consideration of the sum of other valuable considerations and ten dollars in hand . . . ." (Recorded in the Suwannee County Courthouse, Book 32, p. 249.) The quitclaim deed signed by Elsie Mae and Joseph Lyle was similar.

[77] Wess and Alphie O'Neill lived at Wilmarth.

[78] The Warranty Deed, dated, and signed by Daisy Overstreet states that C. G. Howell "hereby assumes and agrees to pay that certain mortgage dated April 17th, 1941, made by Daisy Overstreet and given to the Commercial Bank of Live Oak of Live Oak, Florida, to secure the sum of $525.00." (Recorded May 7, 1941, Book 32, pp. 252-253) The mortgage, of course, did not include the cost of the back taxes and the divorce, which C.G. had already paid.

In the 1970s, C.G. had the good sense to add his wife's name to the deed (That Warranty Deed was recorded at the Suwannee County Courthouse, Book 73, p. 306). And in 1985, C.G. and Ethel deeded a twenty-acre wooded strip of their property to their three daughters, perhaps in hopes that at least one of them or one of their children would build a home there. To date, none has, but the land remains in the family.

[79] "It was the Webb family," Oleta said, "that turned the back room into a kitchen. Later, the old kitchen was torn down, but I don't remember who tore it down. As for that pump, I can remember having to build a fire next to it because it would freeze up when it got real cold."

[80] "Later, when I got pregnant with Eddie," Oleta said, "we had health insurance. Ira worked for A&P for eleven years. Later on, he got a job selling insurance, but he hated that. He had to go out at night to sell. He also worked at a Defense Plant for a while. Then, he got a job with Frito Lay and stayed with them. At some point, I remember we bought a '56 Chevy that was ivory and turquoise. That was a great car."

[81] Later, Clara Mae and Bob had three more children: Clarice, Garfield and Kathy.

[82] In addition to Donald, Mernest and Eloise had four more children: Ruth, Joan, Yvonne, and Clarence. Mernest joined the military in 1949 or 1950 and spent twenty-two years in the U.S. Air Force. He was stationed in Biloxi, Mississippi, about ten years; Germany three years; and Orlando for a short while before being transferred to McClellan Air Force Base in California, from which he retired in 1966. He then returned to Florida and spent his retirement years in Suwannee County.

[83] "When Grandma Lou was growing up," said her granddaughter Bernice Lanier, "I think her family spent some time in Old Town and Cross Creek. Aubrey Fowler, who was in charge of the Production Credit office in Live Oak, was somehow related to the Dees family."

[84] Website: http://ftp.rootsweb.ancestry.com/pub/usgenweb/fl/madison/history/1845votr.txt

[85] Some family members believe that Tip Lanier's family, from Georgia, is related to the famed poet and musician Sidney Lanier, also from Georgia, but no direct link has been established.

[86] This story comes from Bernice Lanier, who said that her mother, Sally, told her about Delma's bout with scarlet fever.

[87] The deed was recorded in Gainesville, Florida. Tip folded the document and tucked it into a drawer. It remained tucked away until late in the twentieth century. It is now framed and hanging in the Susanette's home office in Gainesville, the town where it originated.

[88] It is interesting that the article from the newspaper says "white men." One wonders if there were any black men going to Camp Jackson that Saturday and if so, were they listed elsewhere or omitted.

[89] Delma always told her grandchildren that she knew how to play a few notes on the piano and organ, but she never showed off her musical talents.

[90] Eventually, as Tip got older, he gave up playing the violin at square dances and gave his violin to Cary. When Cary grew into an adult, he married Clara Avery and moved away, taking with him the violin Tip had given him. As the years went on, Cary's family and responsibilities grew, but he found the time to return and visit the family who took him in as a baby after his mother died. One day when Cary and his family were there visiting, Delma asked him if he still played the violin. She hated what she heard: "No, I packed it away and rats ate it up."

[91] Delma's ring contained a small, emerald-cut ruby, flanked by two seed pearls. Later on, Milton gave Delma a diamond ring, so she gave her ruby ring to Ethel. After Ethel lost one of the pearls, she took it to a jeweler. Alas, when she got it back, not only the pearl, but the ruby had been replaced! Ethel was upset, but wore the ring, until she lost the new red stone. She then had it set with a clear one. When Ethel passed the ring on to Susanette, yet another pearl was missing, so, it could be that only the gold setting remains true to the original.

[92] Ethel despised the name Macie and never used it.

[93] Bernice Lanier contributed this story.

[94] Slim Lanier married a woman named Louise. Mamie Lanier married a Cheshire, and she and her husband had three children: Bud who had a speech impediment; Catherine; and Vera, who married a Newbern and then, after he died, she married Mutt Lanier, the youngest son of France Lanier, Tip's brother.

[95] France's son, Chandler, married a woman named Bonnie and they lived in Jacksonville. France's daughter Abby married Horace Williams and had two boys, Jimmy and Raymond; daughter Erma married Curtis Gamble; Verdie married a Richardson; and Edna, the baby, married a man from Texas.

[96] Eliza Cheshire's brother was Ed Cheshire. His granddaughter is Annette Boatright, wife of Alfred Boatright. Annette's father's name is Gelon Smithton.

[97] Porch Lanier with his wife Eliza Cheshire Lanier had had three sons, Lucian, Arthur, and Barney; and five daughters, Bertie, Dora, Eva, Rosa, and Mary. Son Lucian died when he was twenty-one; son Arthur married Laura Cason and had a daughter, Bernice (Crews) Ward, one of Ethel's good friends, whose husband Arthur worked with C.G. to clear new ground and grow watermelons in the 1950s; son Barney (back row, with the ink mark above his head) had four children: Barney, Jr. (b. 11/2/1918), Ruby (b. 10/25/1914; she married Joe Hingson), Nellie May (b. 10/9/1912; d. in infancy), and Annie Merle (b. 10/29/1910; d. 11/15/1932). Porch and Eliza's daughter Rosa married Frank Houck; daughter Mary married Phil Goff; and their other three daughters married men named John: Bertie married John Brannen (he was Bette Harrison's grandfather); Dora married John Mills; and Eva married Little Johnny Grant. According to Ruby Hingson, her grandfather, Porch, would often say, "The devil owed me a debt and he paid me off in Johns." Ruby said, "Nobody thought he disliked his sons-in-law, though; it was just something he said."

[98] Bernice Lanier said the Bonds woman had a little blue-eyed girl.

[99] Later on, the old kitchen became Milton's corn crib.

[100] When Delma moved to town, she couldn't fit all of her living room suite into her house on Houston Street, so she gave one chair to Anetha. Unfortunately, it was eaten up by rats while being stored. When Delma moved in with Ethel, Susanette got the rest of the set. Knowing her Grandmother could use the cash, she paid her $150 for the set (sofa and chair) and U-Hauled the pieces to St. Louis where she had them recovered in blue chintz. It was then passed on to Jeanne. The couch finally broke beyond repair, but Jeanne still has one chair.

[101] Susanette has some of Delma's blue willow serving pieces; Anetha has the green cookie jar and the pink glassware; Patsy has most of the crock-like serving bowls that belonged to Dosia.

[102] Anetha has the kitchen table that Milton built for Delma.

[103] Anetha has the trunk; Susanette refinished the bureau and gave it to daughter Pam.

[104] Over two decades later, when Milton's health was failing and he and Delma were forced to sell the house along with Tip & Dosia's homestead and move to town, Harold's letters moved with them, still tucked in the top drawer of the buffet. After Milton died and Delma moved in with her daughter, Harold's letters moved with her. Even after Delma died, and Ethel had little contact with her brother, she held on to his letters.

[105] After Patsy, Anetha, and Susanette were grown and married, they were visiting their mother and wanted her to sit and talk. She kept getting up, staying busy. "She just kept going and going," Patsy said, "like the Energizer bunny. We asked Mama—we told her—we begged her—to sit down and talk with us and rest for a while. She would not! So, I got the idea of doing to Mama what she had done to me. The three of us ganged up on her, sat her in a chair, and tied her to the chair. Then she *could* sit and talk! Mama got a big kick out of it."

[106] Gambrels, sticks for suspending slaughtered animals, can be made of iron or wood. The gambrels used on the Lanier place, where C.G. slaughtered hogs, were hand hewn. For a vivid description of hog-killing day, read *A Childhood: The Biography of a Place*, by Harry Crews.

[107] If people grew their own vegetables, the *mass-produced* vegetables could be purchased more cheaply by the War Department for troops. One national poster campaign said, "Our food is fighting." Another read, "Plant more in '44." Approximately twenty million Americans planted Victory Gardens, and these gardens produced up to forty percent of all vegetable product consumed in the nation.

[108] The Agriculture Adjustment Act, part of President Roosevelt's New Deal, restricted crop production by paying farmers to reduce crop area. Its purpose was to reduce crop surplus and thus effectively raise the value of crops, giving farmers relative stability. The farmers were paid subsidies by the federal government for leaving some of their land idle. The Act created a new agency, the Agricultural Adjustment Administration (AAA), to oversee the distribution of the subsidies. By the time the AAA began its operations, the agricultural season was already under way, so the agency oversaw a large-scale destruction of existing crops and livestock in an attempt to reduce surpluses; an estimated six million pigs and 220,000 sows were slaughtered in the

AAA's effort to raise prices. Many U.S. citizens could not believe their government was encouraging the destruction of crops and livestock when many were starving during the Great Depression; and, in 1936, the Supreme Court declared the AAA unconstitutional. Congress then created the Soil Conservation and Domestic Allotment Act of 1936 which lasted until the second AAA was created in1938. This second AAA was funded from general taxation, and therefore acceptable to the Supreme Court. The AAA also oversaw the measuring of cropland to be sure farmers adhered to their allotments. (Adapted from the website: http://www.answers.com/topic/agricultural-adjustment-administration)

[109] "After the government did away with the soil bank," C.G. said, "we were allowed to sell allotments, so I sold the tobacco allotment to Joan Newman and the peanut allotment to Leo Thomas."

[110] Bob Miller served as Clerk of the Court in Live Oak, 1933–37.

[111] Louise's parents were first generation Americans. They were Armenian, and Louise was born in Constantinople. She had a brother, Al, and three sisters, Virginia, Sadie and Elgin. Mr. and Mrs. Petrosoft, Louise's stepfather and her mother, visited the Rye's home in the late 1940s or early 1950s.

[112] *Ruby McCollum: Woman in the Suwannee County Jail,* by William Bradford Huey is a must-read for anyone interested in 1940s Suwannee County history. A copy is available at the Gainesville Matheson Museum. Or, check with a rare book dealer, e.g., *www.abebooks.com*.

[113] Red Warren's wife was Lorine. Their son, Lewis, was a polite young man who was blond, and very, very tall compared to C.G.—or to Mr. Saunders, whose width was catching up to his height.

[114] Delma and Milton received many best wishes on their fiftieth wedding anniversary—some spoken, others printed on greeting cards— but one was just a small scrap of paper that Lillie George handed to Delma. On the paper, Lillie had written in longhand, "This is the way I feel about you and Milton. I couldn't express it half so well." It was signed "Lillie," and following her signature were these typed words: "Friendship: Oh, the comfort, the inexpressible comfort of feeling safe with a person, having neither to weigh thoughts nor measure words, but pouring them all right out, just as they are, chaff and grain together,

certain that faithful hand will take and sift them, keep what is worth keeping, and with a breath of kindness, blow the rest away." Delma tucked Lillie's note away and kept it, always.

[115] Anetha was unaware, during the years she worked in the office of the Tax Collector, that her great-great grandfather J. R. Newlan had once been the Suwannee County Tax Collector (1895 to 1897).

[116] Susanette has Delma's cut-off buffet and china cabinet.

[117] Ethel used different quilt patterns for each of her offspring: Double Wedding Ring (Patsy); Dresden Plate (Anetha); Wheel of Fortune (Susanette); Texas Star (Winston); Pinwheels (DeeDee); Grandmother's Flower Garden (Clay); Bride's Bouquet (Pamela); Grandmother's Fan (Jeanne); Burgoyne Surrounded (Lee); Hearts and Gizzards (Ginger).

[118] C.G. and Ethel's great-grandchildren: Winston III (Wint), 1981; Liza, 1986; Logan, 1988; Kyle, 1990; Tanner, 1993; Curtis, 1996; Rachel, 1998; Lane, 2001; Morghan, 2002; Asher, 2003; Camden, 2006. Camden never got to chew on the corners of a quilt pieced and stitched by his great-grandmother, but she got to hold him in her arms and in her heart. He was born while she was living in Dacier Manor (assisted living) at the Advent Christian Village; Lee brought him there to see his Great-Grandma Howell when he was just a few months old.

[119] The sewing cabinet Ethel referred to in her letter was the one C.G. built for her when they lived at the forestry headquarters. It had four large drawers and a table for her slant-needle Singer sewing machine. The table was on rollers so that it and the machine could be pulled out for sewing or pushed back behind closed doors when not in use.

[120] Renah Robins's husband, John, predeceased her. He was murdered in their home near Peacock Slough. Renah was, at the time, staying at a house they owned in Live Oak. John was found, dead in bed, by his sister, Lillie George. He was seventy-eight, and she thought he had died in his sleep. But his car was missing, and sheriff deputies discovered tracks leading to the Suwannee River. There, a Ford Falcon was found submerged in the water. After the Ford was identified, four juveniles, ages 14-17 were charged with his murder. They had smothered him

with a pillow case, after which they had stolen his watch, his 1975 Datsun, and eleven dollars.

[121] A new neighbor, Mr. Cassidy, who had traveled widely, got C.G. interested in growing grapes. He had planted two varieties—one white, one red—that could be made into wine. C.G. had tried Mr. Cassidy's wine, but Ethel decided the grapes made better jelly than wine.

[122] Delma visited Harold and Louise while he lived in California. C.G. and Ethel went too. But they never visited him at any of his homes in the Northwest, nor did Delma. By the time he settled there, Delma was not able to travel that distance.

[123] A couple of years before their trip South, C.G. and Ethel took a trip "North." Anetha and Susanette were headed for South Carolina to visit friends and invited their parents to go along. There, C.G. and Ethel stayed with Ray and Clyde Chastain, friends who had lived with them for several weeks when their home on the banks of the Suwannee River was inaccessible because of flooding.

[124] For years, Cora's daughter, Dot, had lived across the street from her mother in Punta Gorda; but after Dot and her husband divorced, she and her ex-husband's brother, Bill, got together. They moved up to Columbia County and often drove over to visit C.G. and Ethel. (Dot reminded Ethel of her Aunt Cora, so Ethel enjoyed Dot's company; and Bill liked to fish, so he and C.G. hit it off.) One day when they were visiting with C.G. and Ethel at Dowling Park, while Ethel was receiving chemotherapy, Dot handed her a hundred dollar bill and told her to use it toward the extra expenses she knew they were having with all the doctor bills. Ethel protested but Dot insisted. A couple of years later, Dot asked Ethel if she could hire her to make a quilt for her grandson. Ethel told her, "No." Then she went to the back bedroom and came back with a quilt she had just finished. She asked Dot if she liked that one. Dot did. So Ethel gave it to her. When Dot's mother, Cora, passed away at the nursing home in Punta Gorda, the Howell family went down for the memorial service at the home of Valerie, Dot's daughter; but Dot was unable to attend; she had been admitted into the Alzheimer's unit at a nursing home in Lake City. Ethel visited her there several times before Dot passed away—three or four years after her mother, Cora, had passed.

[125] In the photo of C.G. and Gilbert among the corn rows, C.G. has a bandage on his face, having had skin surgery the week before. "So I will be handsome for my granddaughter's wedding," he said. Ginger was planning a fall wedding at a Georgia winery.

[126] Jimmy North was married to Delma Rye's first cousin, Ernestine; they had a daughter, Betty Jo.

[127] Before leaving the Florida Baptist Children's Home campus that day, C.G. took his checkbook from his shirt pocket and made a sizeable donation in hopes that it would help the Children's Home to help more children as it had once helped him. (A subsequent Florida Baptist Children's Home newsletter featured C.G. as one of oldest surviving former residents.

[128] Asher was born on Delma's birthday.

[129] Mernest Donald Howell d. 4/28/1991; Clara Mae Howell Midgett d. 11/15/1998; Ira James Howell d. 2/14/2002; Laura Belle Howell Schemer d. 6/5/2005.

About the Author and the Book

As an editor for a health-science publishing house for more than a decade, Susie Baxter recruited physicians to write books for the clinical market and in 1997 was named Times Mirror's Medical Editor of the Year. Until now, however, she had never written a book herself.

Upon her retirement, she began writing about her rural childhood—of growing up on a tobacco farm in north Florida. The pages soon piled up, and one thing led to another, until eventually, *this* book was born.

C.G. and Ethel: A Family History focuses, not on Baxter's childhood, but on the lives of C.G., her father, the son of a sharecropper, orphaned at a young age; and Ethel, her mother, who grew up in the log cabin her grandfather built in the 1800s on land he had homesteaded in the Florida wilderness.

This self-published[1] collection of stories was written for family and friends, for those who have known C.G. and Ethel, or for those who wish they had. Proceeds from any sales will go to the Advent Christian Village at Dowling Park, Florida.

When not writing or playing golf, Baxter serves as a freelance editor for her former employer. She also conducts memoir-writing workshops for the Alachua County Library System in Gainesville, Florida. She often begins the workshop with a quote by Alex Haley:

Whenever a person dies, a small library burns.

Baxter believes that *everyone* has a story to tell. In fact, her business card reads: "Memoir . . . Write yours, now!"

---

[1] The manuscript was typed in Microsoft Word; images were inserted into the text as TIF files; and the document was then converted to a PDF file for the printer.